END-TIME SURVIVOR

A practical handbook for overcomers in the last days

Neil Turner

Copyright ©2013 by Neil Turner. First published in December 2013.
All rights reserved. No part of this publication may be reproduced or transmitted in any form or by any means, electronic or mechanical, including photocopying, recording, or any information storage or retrieval systems.

The right of Neil Turner to be identified as the author of this work has been asserted by him in accordance with the Copyright, Designs and Patents Act 1988

With the exception of Chapter 3 Part 2, or unless otherwise stated, Scripture is taken from the NEW AMERICAN STANDARD BIBLE®,
© Copyright 1960, 1962, 1963, 1968, 1971, 1972, 1973, 1975, 1977, 1995 by The Lockman Foundation. Used by permission.
www.Lockman.org

The Book of Revelation in Chapter 3 part 2 is adapted from the 1769 King James Version

Front Cover: End-Time Survivor. Abigail Joy Bowen ©2013

ISBN 978-1-908387-88-2

This book is also available as an eBook

ISBN 978-1-908387-89-9 (ePUB)
ISBN 978-1-908387-90-5 (Kindle)

Book and eBook designed and typeset
by Oxford eBooks Ltd.
www.oxford-ebooks.com

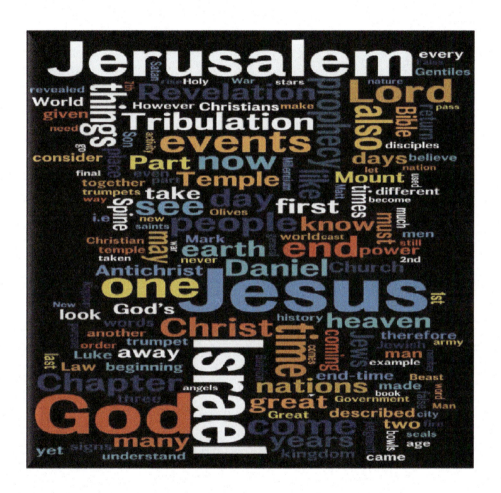

Be faithful until death and I will give you the crown of life

Revelation 2.10

Contents

Acknowledgments 15
About the author 16
Key 17
Preface 19
Health Warning! 31

Chapter 1 — The Spine of Biblical Prophecy 33
Part 1 – Jerusalem: Passover AD29 33
Part 2 – Jesus' great end-time prophecy - the 4 Laws 41

Chapter 2 — Spine of Biblical Prophecy - an analysis . . . 57
Part 1 – Jesus' Near-Term prophecy concerning the destruction of the Temple AD70 58
Part 2 – The disciples' questions to Jesus 71
Part 3 – Jesus' End-Time prophecy and His Return 73

Chapter 3 — The Revelation of Jesus Christ 87
Part 1 – Patmos 96AD 87
Part 2 – The Book of Revelation 92

Chapter 4   Revelation – an analysis 135
Part 1 – Introduction 135
Part 2 – Seals, Trumpets and Bowls 139
Part 3 – Babylon 153

Chapter 5   The Big Picture: an overall end-time chronology 155
Part 1 – Introduction 155
Part 2 – the Bigger Picture: from everlasting to everlasting 156
Part 3 – The Spine and Revelation combined 160
Part 4 – End-Time Politics: The Kingdoms of Daniel 2 and 7 166

Chapter 6   The Gathering Storm : pre-requisites for the end 181
Part 1 – Introduction 181
Part 2 – Preparing the Stage – 12 Pillars 183
Part 3 – The Beginning of Sorrows 197
Part 4 - Summary 209

Chapter 7   Israel – chosen people, promised land 211
Part 1 – Introduction 211
Part 2 – The God of Israel 214
Part 3 – The Land of Israel 218
Part 4 – Israel and the Church 233
Part 5 – Conclusion 240

Chapter 8   The Temple rebuilt 243

Part 1 – Introduction 243

Part 2 – The Tabernacle – Moses 245

Part 3 – The First Temple – Solomon 248

Part 4 – The Second Temple - Herod 250

Part 5 – The Third Temple 251

Chapter 9   The Antichrist – man of sin 261

Part 1 – Introduction 261

Part 2 – Names of Antichrist 263

Part 3 – Types and Forerunners of Antichrist 265

Part 4 – The Nature and Activity of Antichrist 269

Part 5 – The False Prophet 274

Chapter 10   'War on the Saints': The Great Tribulation 277

Part 1 – Introduction 277

Part 2 – The purpose of the Tribulation 278

Part 3 – The Four Stages of the Tribulation 284

Chapter 11   The Return of Jesus Christ – Thy Kingdom come · 301

Part 1 – The Incomparable Christ · 301
Part 2 – Rationale · 303
Part 3 – Armageddon: Zechariah & Ezekiel's preview · 304
Part 4 – The Return of Christ: one event yet many · 309

Chapter 12   Judgment – days of reckoning · 319

Part 1 – Introduction · 319
Part 2 – The Nature of the Judge · 320
Part 3 – Three Groups of People · 324
Part 4 – Three types of Judgment · 325
Part 5 – Spiritual Geography · 328

Chapter 13   End-Time Survivor – get ready, get set, go · 339

Part 1 – Introduction · 339
Part 2 – Jesus' End-Time Parables & Instructions · 345
Part 3 – The Kingdom Prayer · 352
Part 4 – Dealing with practicalities · 353
Part 5 – Martyrdom · 355
Part 6 – Conclusion · 356

Chapter 14   The Millennium and after · · · · · · 359

    Part 1 – Introduction · 359

    Part 2 – Restoration of the Land · 362

    Part 3 – Restoration of the City · 368

    Part 4 – Restoration of worship · 372

    Part 5 – Restoration of the People · 379

    Part 6 – Final Judgment · 384

    Part 7 – All things new - New heavens and new earth · · · · · · · · 386

The Sinner's Prayer – an open invitation · 389

Bibliography · 393

Picture References and Credits · 394

List of Tables

The 4 Laws of the Spine 41

'Times of the Gentiles' – Part 1: Beginning of Gentile Dominion over Jerusalem 66

The disciples' questions 72

Various Sieges / Battles of Jerusalem 75

The Spine: basic sequence of end-time prophetic events 79

The letters to the churches 96

Outline of Revelation 138

The 5 Laws of Revelation 141

Chronological Key: arrangement of Seals, Trumpets and Bowls 142

Biblical Dispensations - a notional framework 157

Prophetic Chronology - the Spine and Seals / Trumpets / Bowls combined 162

'Times of the Gentiles' - Part 2: End of Gentile dominion over Jerusalem 167

Daniel 2 and 7 compared: the beginning & end of gentile dominion over Jerusalem 180

False Christs 200

Frequency of Individual Wars 202

Casualties of War 203

Number of earthquakes Magnitude 6 and above by decade 206

Most significant famines	207
Pestilence and disease	208
Scriptural references – the land belongs to Israel	226
The 3rd Temple – a project overview	258
Major Persecutions through history	282
Modern-day Persecution	282
The seven years of Tribulation in Daniel	288
Schedule of Christ's Return	311
Names of God	321
Eternal Judgment	333
Seven End-Time parables and instructions	346
End-Time – Specific responses	351
10 Clauses of the Lord's Prayer	353
Millennial Produce of the Land	367
New Names of Millennial Jerusalem	370
Mosaic Law v 4th Temple ritual	377

Acknowledgments

Many have influenced my view of the end-times, chief amongst whom have been Dr Derek Prince, David Wilkerson, and EW Bullinger. I have also been greatly enlightened by the teaching of David Pawson, whose selfless dedication to preaching controversial topics has provided both inspiration and affirmation. David gets into those difficult and thorny issues which are too-often ignored by other teachers and always makes me think. The Rev Keith Mason has been my mentor, friend and counsel for many years. Thank you all.

Having written End-Time Survivor as a first-time author, I needed a guide to help me through the complexities of publication. Andy Severn of Oxford eBooks came very highly recommended and has not disappointed. His expert knowledge of the process, encouragement, attention to detail and innovative suggestions have been essential in placing this book in your hands.

I'd also like to thank and recognise the immensely talented Abigail Joy Bowen who designed the front cover and other powerfully evocative images you will find throughout the book. Please take time to reflect on them, as her pictures speak every bit as clearly as the words. You will need courage and boldness to endure the days ahead, and Abigail's front cover portrait of the lion emerging from the flames with a triumphal roar evokes the spirit of the overcomer, the true end-time survivor.

All glory to God.

About the author

Neil Turner is a management educator who has trained over 14,000 professionals in project management techniques. He has a passion for history and field archaeology, and has studied Bible prophecy for over 30 years. He became a Christian aged 13 in 1973, in the aftermath of the UK Festival of Light. In his early twenties, he received a word from the prophetess Jean Darnall that he '*would bring many to the Lord, and be a great strength to his brothers and sisters*'. His goal is to make, train and equip disciples who will stand in the last days.

His background gives him a unique and original perspective in the field of eschatology, the study of end-time prophecy. He has led a small fellowship, and is a Bible teacher. He has worked in the UK, Europe, the Far East, South Africa, India, Australia and the USA. He has a wife and two children and lives in rural England.

Key

As the reader progresses, you will find certain keys alongside the text. These are provided to highlight key thoughts or actions.

Black boxes highlight general principles or "laws" for interpreting the Bible.

Blue boxes highlight specific prophetic signs we should watch for.

Red boxes indicate the secret things of God, mysteries currently hidden from our sight, which will be revealed by Him at the appropriate time. We can (and should) prayerfully speculate, but may have to hold our ideas lightly and evolve them in the light of events.

Suggested Bible verses to memorise

Actions – practical responses for personal preparation

Preface

Thus says the Lord, the Holy One of Israel, and his Maker:

"Ask Me about the things to come concerning My sons,

and you shall commit to Me the work of My hands"

Isaiah 45.11

Future Perfect

It's a perfect day. We're here; we made it through and are descending a gentle, grassy slope as we approach the City of the Great King. A wide mountain valley reaches up to the newly divided Mount Olivet on our left towards the west. We aren't alone and thousands of saints continue northwards with us, joyfully singing songs of Zion. We cross a beautiful river of cool, fresh water which brings abundant life to what men used to call the Dead Sea, away down to the east. In the distance we can see Zion, its beautiful white limestone walls bright on the far side of the valley, the sides of the north. Towering over the city is the Sanctuary, where we are going to worship the Lord. It is exactly as was prophesied by Zechariah and Ezekiel, who we soon hope to meet. This is the Millennium and we have a thousand wonderful years to praise our God, enjoy His presence and prepare ourselves for an eternal future.

I'm speculating, clearly, but it might surprise you to learn that almost everything described above can be found in your Bible. This wonderful day lies ahead and will surely come. But first, we must concern ourselves with the here and now.

Present Tense

When was the last time you told yourself that the world had become a fundamentally better place? I would suggest that most believe the opposite is true. Take a moment and you will see that the situation around us is rapidly deteriorating. It feels less safe, less stable and age-old traditional values we take for granted are being eroded. Conflict, economic turmoil, famine, disease and natural disasters are almost daily in the news. Social disorder and family breakdown drive increasing lawlessness and the authorities seem helpless and confused. When will it end? Will it get worse? Why is it happening?

Bible-believing Christians in the nations of the west are witnessing the demise of established denominations, as error and despondency creep in. They have long awaited the return of Jesus Christ, but when will He come? Could it be any moment and what will happen in the meantime? True believers are dismayed by the departure of the established Church from scriptural doctrine, whilst governments are steadily criminalising the Christian faith. Many who work in teaching, the public sector, or large corporations are being hounded-out by militants of political correctness. Whereas society used to be founded on Judaeo-Christian principles, it is now clear that something is changing. Even the sanctity of marriage between man and woman is being challenged. Where will these things lead and what should we be doing about them?

God-fearing Jews too are looking for the return of their Messiah, for deliverance from a world where anti-Semitism[1] and Jew-hatred is the norm. The tiny country of Israel, with nearly eight million inhabitants but no bigger than New Jersey or Wales, is vilified by the majority of the media and boycotted by many in business and academia. It is exposed to double standards, but few care. It is pressured by the UN and many governments to divide both its land and capital city to make way for a Palestinian State. Its close neighbours seek its destruction through terrorism and jihad. Are Israel's critics justified in their accusations? Why has Israel been singled out for this treatment?

When you pick up a letter it is prudent to check whose name is on the envelope.[2] This book is addressed primarily to Christians who want to understand current events and their relationship to God's prophetic plan. As we investigate,  we will see that the future of the Church and Israel are inextricably linked from beginning to end. We are related and interdependent and it is time that Christians understood their responsibility towards Israel.

---

1. Strictly speaking, anti-Semitism would apply to all the descendents of Shem. For the purposes of this book we will use the term in its more generally accepted sense, as the discrimination against or hatred of the Jewish people
2. When reading the various books of the Bible we should always consider who is being addressed. In Paul's epistle to the Romans, for example, he is addressing Christians in Rome. If I open my neighbour's mail by mistake, I will be confused if I try to apply it to myself. Always check the address on the letter, and context of the passage.

The Purpose of Prophecy

In *End-Time Survivor* we are going to turn to the Bible for answers to some tough questions. However, in many churches, believers are told not to become preoccupied with prophecy. Yet if God did not want us to study prophecy, why did He give us so much of it? Prophecy is one of the central themes of scripture.

Jesus divided His Bible, the 'Old Testament', into the Torah (The Law), the Prophets and the Psalms. The New Testament has added the Gospels, Acts of the Apostles, epistles (letters) and the Book of Revelation. The Book of Revelation (that we will later consider in depth) is almost entirely prophetic. Much of Jesus' ministry was prophetic. Moses was a prophet, and in Deuteronomy 18.15-18 he makes a promise:

> *The LORD your God will raise up for you **a prophet like me from among you**, from your countrymen, you shall listen to him. This is according to all that you asked of the LORD your God in Horeb on the day of the assembly, saying, 'Let me not hear again the voice of the LORD my God, let me not see this great fire anymore, or I will die.' The LORD said to me, 'They have spoken well. I will raise up **a prophet from among their countrymen like you**, and I will put My words in his mouth, and he shall speak to them all that I command him'*

This prophet like Moses is Jesus.

It has been calculated that the Old Testament lists some 1,239 prophecies, the New Testament 578, described in 8,352[3] verses. There are approximately 31,000 verses in the Bible and when we consider the major prophets, minor prophets and prophets of the Church age, we must conclude that prophecy is beyond doubt a major theme of scripture, one verse in four, and therefore must be taken seriously.

Of these prophecies some have assessed that to date, around 80% have been fulfilled. Many relate to God's dealings with Israel and a significant number foretell the first incarnation of Jesus Christ. Authors such as Josh MacDowell have done excellent work in proving this beyond reasonable doubt, showing for example that there are 332 specific predictions in the Old Testament[4] relating to Christ's human incarnation. In this book, we will look in detail at those prophecies that relate to His so-called Second Coming. You will be amazed at how much the Bible has to say

---
3. J.Baron-Payne, *Encyclopaedia of Biblical Prophecy*
4. J.McDowell, *Evidence that Demands a Verdict*

to this generation.

So what is the purpose of prophecy? I suggest there are five key reasons for predictive[5] Scriptural prophecy, and every one of them is highly practical:

- to prove God's word – He said it, He will do it

- to demonstrate God's faithfulness – He does exactly what He says He will

- to warn both His people and those who do not follow Him – He is entirely fair and lets us know the consequences of our actions well ahead of His judgements. Nobody will be able to say 'I did not know' or 'I was not warned'

- to allow His people to prepare for what is to come – He gives us time to get ready. Forewarned is forearmed

- to strengthen our faith – as we see His words coming to pass we will learn that He can be trusted, is in full control of events and we will not fear

When my children are going into a new situation, I feel it is my responsibility as their father, to warn and prepare them as far as I can about what to expect. Your heavenly Father is no different. He has provided us with prophecy, not to be in any way mysterious, but because He loves us enough to ensure that we are properly and effectively prepared. Not only does our Father forewarn us, but His grace provides for us. Grace is your sufficiency, everything, more than enough for your needs. As with prophecy, it is entirely practical and useful.

Consider for a moment that there was no prophecy. We would not know what to expect. We could not prepare. Events would either take us by complete surprise, or merely go unnoticed.

Amos 3.6-7 states:

> *If a trumpet is blown in a city will not the people tremble? If a calamity occurs in a city has not the Lord done it? Surely the **Lord God does nothing unless He reveals His secret counsel to His servants the prophets***

If we want to know what is to come, we must study what the prophets have to say.

---

[5]. Not all prophecy is predictive. Some is to 'forthtell' God's word, and does not relate to future activities but provides advice or instruction for the present. The above list concerns predictive prophecy

Isaiah 45.11 states:

> *Thus says the Lord, the Holy One of Israel, and his Maker:* **ask Me about the things to come concerning My sons** *and you shall commit to Me the work of My hands*

He commands us to ask Him what is going to happen. Have you ever taken time to ask Him? If not, then you are disobeying a direct commandment. Start now. Ask. Seek.

In Mark 13.33, Jesus states:

> *Take heed,* **keep on the alert;** *for you do not know when the appointed time will come*

He commands us to keep on the alert or watch, i.e. to give strict attention to notice what is happening around us. These three verses thus provide us with our mandate: Study; Ask; Watch; Pray. We will consider what it means to watch, and how to do it.

Jesus warned the Pharisees and Sadducees:

> *Do you know how to discern the appearance of the sky, but cannot discern the signs of the times?*
>
> Matthew 16.3

The first thing we learn from this verse is that there are specific signs that define the times in which we live. Secondly, these signs cannot be interpreted by those whose hearts are hard with an external form of religion.

Jesus also advised His disciples regarding end-time prophecy:

> *of that day and hour no one knows, not even the angels of heaven, nor the Son, but the Father alone*
>
> Matthew 24.36

When His disciples asked Jesus if he was going to restore Israel's kingdom, He responded:

> *It is not for you to know times or epochs which the Father has fixed by His own authority*
>
> Acts 1.7

And also

> *But when these things begin to take place, straighten up and lift up your heads, because your redemption is drawing near*
>
> Luke 21.28

Paul, when writing to the Thessalonians stated:

> *Now as to the times and the epochs, brethren, you have no need of anything to be written to you*
>
> 1 Thess 5.1

There is a fine balance therefore between what has been revealed and what is hidden. It is also clear that certain things could be hidden at a particular time but would later, at the appropriate moment, be revealed.

We cannot therefore be specific about the day or hour of Jesus' return and we are certainly not in the business of predicting dates, but we will know the immediate season or general timing when that time comes. We ignore Biblical prophecy at our peril.

As we make our journey through the prophecies defining end-time events, we will use a number of laws to help us to interpret scripture. We will start by looking at the Law of First Mentions: the first time a word, expression or topic is mentioned in the Bible generally gives us important clues as to its meaning and interpretation.[6]

We will apply this law to the first Bible prophecy given in Gen 3.15, where God is speaking to Satan and says:

> *I will put enmity between you and the woman, and between your seed and her seed. He shall bruise you on the head, and you shall bruise him on the heel*

Herein lies the essence and purpose of the Lord's prophetic plan and how God in His omniscience chooses to reveal His perspective of events to man. We learn how following man's fall from grace and the entry of sin into the world, the Lord put enmity between Satan and the Seed of Eve. This Seed would bruise Satan's head, and Satan would bruise the Seed's heel. (We might ask how a woman can have a

---

6. An example of this is the number #6, first mentioned in Genesis 1.31, where man was created on the 6th day. The number 6 therefore tends to be associated with man, and will be 'perfected' in the 'man of lawlessness', the Antichrist whose number is 666. Nebuchadnezzar's statue in the book of Daniel was 6 cubits high, representing the best that man could achieve.

seed. Surely, this is the man's contribution? But of course we know that Jesus was born of a virgin and God was His Father, thus the virgin birth is foretold here[7]). These brief words from Genesis encapsulate much of the Bible: Satan's war on God's chosen people (Jew and Christian) and God's dealings with Satan. This reveals the major purpose of Biblical prophecy i.e. how the Lord God brings salvation to fallen people through His Seed, Jesus, and how He will ultimately deal with Satan.

This also starts to address the fundamental and age–old question why am I here? Mankind is central to God's plan for redemption and reconciling of matters heavenly and earthly through His Son Jesus Christ. There can be no spectators, no bystanders. We are all involved in one way or another.

We should also understand that prophecy doesn't always take a straight line. The Jews in 1st Century Judaea were looking for a King who would deliver them from Roman oppression and re-establish the Kingdom of David. It must have surprised them when their long-awaited King arrived in Jerusalem seated on an ass. But He came first as Saviour. When He returns He will come on a white war horse as King, Judge and Deliverer. This is the 'depth of field'[8] principle of prophecy and is often shown in prophetic statements where a large passage of time may separate two seemingly consecutive events.

Moving forward in history to the present day, what about now? How does the Bible relate to the 21st Century? What about the Economic Crash? The Boxing Day or Japanese Tsunamis? or 9/11? The Middle East crisis, whether it be Israel, Iran or the Arab Spring? We'll explore these events in the light of Bible prophecy and you can make your own mind up as to whether the Bible has something to say to us, right here, right now.

We don't have the answer to all our questions though. The Bible is clear on this:

---

7. This is an example of how prophecy can be veiled at a particular time, but is then later revealed in God's own time. The same is true now, in that certain truths are currently hidden to be revealed later. These are known as 'mysteries'.
8. When viewing a distant mountain top our eye can deceive us into thinking that mountains between us and that far peak are part of the same group and in close proximity to each other. As we get closer we see that they may be separated by many miles, where foreground and background become clearer. So too with prophetic timescales: distance often foreshortens perspective.

The secret things belong to the Lord our God, but the things revealed belong to us and to our sons forever, that we may observe all the words of this law

Deut 29.29

Only God is all knowing, but He chooses in His wisdom to keep some things hidden from us. One of these, not even known by His Son, is the exact time of Jesus' return to earth. However, there is much He has chosen to reveal if we care to look carefully.

Deep Foundations

Any house requires a solid foundation, so we will start with the words of Jesus a few days before His crucifixion. Here He shared with His disciples the whole panorama of end-time prophecy and the timing and key events of His return. To this base we will then add insights from the Book of Revelation. This will give us a working chronology which we will then supplement with other scriptural sources. Be patient as you read. We have a lot to understand and will build our picture gradually.

We will then proceed to relate these signs to world events, both historical and anticipated. We'll need to develop some new skills, particularly those of the trained observer. It is possible to look but not see. Try spending a day with an expert on wildlife, geology or astronomy. You'll be amazed at how the untrained eye misses things that are plain to see, but with practice and dedication your seeing will improve. I hope this book can help you in that training. Don't rely on the media, the government, academia, or even your church necessarily to warn you. It's up to you. Like any skill, you can develop it with prayerful practice. Hebrews 5.14 states (my words in bold):

> *But solid food is for the **mature**, who because of **practice** have their senses **trained** to discern good and evil*

My prayer is that you be found ready, that you are prepared for trouble and become an end-time survivor, and that your faith doesn't fail in these testing times. My hope is that the book will help you to prepare for what is to come. *Jesus said he who has **endured to the end** shall be saved*. You may be martyred, but you will be safe. Surely, this is a contradiction? No, actually.

To explain this paradox we must look at Luke 21, where Jesus warns the inhabitants of Jerusalem:

> *But you will be betrayed even by parents and brothers and relatives and friends, and they will **put some of you to death**, and you will be hated by all because of My name. **Yet not a hair of your head will perish***

Did you notice? *They will put some of you to death* but *not a hair of your head shall be lost.* This is a different perspective for some of us and requires an end-time, selfless, cross-centred, eternal perspective. Christians living today in China, Saudi Arabia, Pakistan and Nigeria understand this perfectly. It is soon coming to the west too. The principle is repeated in Revelation:

> *They overcame him (Satan) because of the blood of the Lamb and because of the word of their testimony, and they did not love their life even when faced with death*

End-time overcomers will be those who maintain the testimony of Jesus and *love not their lives unto death.*

As believers we are also required to invest in the Kingdom of God and there will be plenty of opportunity in the days ahead. We'll consider what can be done, how and why.

One of my responsibilities as a management trainer is to sift through many sources of information, so that I can synthesise them into useful, practical knowledge that may be applied by my customers. I have taken the same approach in this book. I am an experienced project manager and have trained many thousands of professionals. I understand the principles of scheduling, and have attempted to bring the same logical discipline to the field of prophecy. I believe that we need a disciplined approach to building a reliable schedule. We cannot take leaps of imagination in defining the end-time schedule and must clearly differentiate between that which is certain and that which is uncertain. I have tried to respect this principle. I am sad to say that much of the currently available literature on the end-times demonstrates a lax attitude to prophetic scheduling and will inevitably result in disappointment and confusion.

I hope that you will be inspired to search your Bible and build your own picture. I certainly don't have all the answers on this subject, but for what it is worth, the book shows my own views, developed over 30 years or so. During that time I've read my Bible through and through, listened to many excellent Bible teachers and had my views shaped and changed. At the back of the book you'll find some of these sources listed. I have tried to attribute the work of others where appropriate and apologise in advance if I have been in any way remiss. You may wish to follow them up yourself. The fact that I have listed a source does not mean that I agree 100% with the author – I usually don't. However, each was an invaluable help in writing my book.

It is beyond doubt that Israel, Jerusalem and the Jewish people are central to God's end-time plan. I believe that God wants Israel to possess the whole land that He promised to them. Individuals, governments and the media love to apply standards to her that they do not apply elsewhere. For example, those who hate Israel like to boycott her, but conveniently forget that much of their mobile phone or computer technology was developed by Israeli innovators. This prejudice also applies to Christian denominations who accuse her. Neither Israel nor the Church is perfect – far from. We weren't chosen because of any quality we possess, but because of God's love and mercy. I discovered about 20 years ago that my Bible made much more sense when I stopped spiritualising the word Israel: when it says Israel it means Israel, and not the Church. God has given me a love for Israel, its land and people and I make no apology for wishing to identify with her.

Finally, I'll admit to you that this book is not a perfect work. It is however my best effort, the way I see things and how I am advising those I hold most dear. It is the book I wished I could have picked off a shelf and read but couldn't find, and that, together with an urgent sense of purpose from God, is why I wrote it. It has been over 20 years in the making and I hope it is a help to you. The dictionary defines a survivor as one who is still alive after an event in which others have perished. I pray that you not only survive, but overcome.

Ultimately, you must decide what you believe and how you will prepare. It is your duty to be a Beroean[9] and test these words against your Bible. May the Lord bless you and reveal His plans to you as you earnestly seek Him.

Neil Turner

June, 2013

---

9. Acts 17.11

Health Warning!

We will learn much from the prophet Daniel on our journey. Here is your first lesson: as Daniel began to understand end-time prophecy he became overwhelmed....

> *So I was left alone and saw this great vision; yet **no strength was left in me, for my natural color turned to a deathly pallor, and I retained no strength**. But I heard the sound of his words; and as soon as I heard the sound of his words, I fell into a deep sleep on my face, with my face to the ground.*
>
> *Then behold, a hand touched me and **set me trembling on my hands and knees**. He said to me, 'O Daniel, man of high esteem, understand the words that I am about to tell you and stand upright, for I have now been sent to you'. And when he had spoken this word to me, I stood up trembling.*
>
> *Now I have come to give you an understanding of what will happen to your people in the latter days, for the vision pertains to the days yet future.*
>
> *When he had spoken to me according to these words, I turned my face toward the ground and **became speechless**. And behold, one who resembled a human being was touching my lips; then I opened my mouth and spoke and said to him who was standing before me, 'O my lord, as a result of the vision **anguish has come upon me, and I have retained no strength**. For how can such a servant of my lord talk with such as my lord? As for me, **there remains just now no strength in me, nor has any breath been left in me**'.*
>
> *Then this one with human appearance touched me again and strengthened me. He said, 'O man of high esteem, do not be afraid. Peace be with you; take courage and be courageous!'.*
>
> Daniel 10. various verses.

If Daniel was so affected by what he saw, we may be also. John certainly had the same experience as Daniel when he received the Revelation on Patmos. It is therefore vital that you enter this study prayerfully. At times in the preparation of the book I have found myself swinging between despair and elation, overwhelmed by the events described.

Do not be afraid. Peace be to you. Be strong and of good courage.

Be a Daniel.

The disciples were about to receive the ultimate Masterclass – let's join them back in 1st Century Judaea and listen in to what they were told...

Chapter 1   The Spine of Biblical Prophecy

Jerusalem, Jerusalem, who kills the prophets and stones those who are sent to her! How often I wanted to gather your children together, the way a hen gathers her chicks under her wings, and you were unwilling. Behold, your house is being left to you desolate! For I say to you, from now on you will not see Me until you say, 'Blessed is He who comes in the name of the Lord!'

Matthew 23.37-39

Figure 1. Worshippers at the Western retaining wall of Herod's Temple.

Part 1 – Jerusalem: Passover AD29

First century Judaea conjures up powerful images in the mind: an illustration from a children's Bible, a poster on the Sunday school wall, or the drama of Hollywood. But what was the reality? In Chapter 1 we will separate fiction from fact, and set the scene of the most detailed and lengthy prophecy Jesus was to share with His followers. We will consider the politics of the situation, the season, religious background,

Chapter One

together with the geography and layout of Jerusalem. Suitably equipped, we may then journey back in place and time to witness the events. Put your 21st century mindset aside for a few moments, and try to see the situation from the perspective of those who were there...

Who's who?

Judaea was a Roman province, but surprisingly not overly oppressed by its Imperial master.

Pontius Pilate, Rome's Prefect[1] over Judaea, was backed by the military but this was rarely deployed during the time of Christ. The Gospels provide us with a number of glimpses into Roman influence: a

Emperor	Ruled
Augustus	27BC-AD14
Tiberius	AD14-37

census in Bethlehem under Augustus Caesar; a faithful Centurion; a Roman coin; Pilate's governance (headquartered in Caesarea) and the inevitable collection of taxes. Contemporary historians such as Josephus, who we will hear more from later, record little open conflict between Rome and Jerusalem in the early first century, but do reveal the simmering Jewish resentment at their subjugation. Pilate, a bad tempered man, was the latest of a series of inadequate Roman Prefects who lacked both the diplomacy and ability to oversee this peculiar but Chosen people. He had made the 80 mile and 2,500' ascent from Caesarea on the coast to oversee Passover from his Jerusalem residence and was presumably hoping for a quiet time.

Herod the Great, so-called for his magnificent building projects, had died in the year of Christ's birth, 4BC. He was half-Jewish, half Arab and was distrusted by the Jews as an outsider. The construction of a stunningly beautiful new Temple was his attempt to win favour with the Jews. Jerusalem's Antonia Fortress too, built by him on the North West wall of the Temple, was named after Mark Anthony. Caesarea also had been named to appease Rome. We will look again in Chapter 9 at the character of Herod the Great.

Into Herod's shoes stepped his son, **Herod Antipas**, Tetrarch,[2] who would rule

---

1. A Roman Prefect had authority from Rome for the administration of a Province, including the dispensation of Roman justice and collection of taxation. In effect, he was 'Rome' and spoke on its behalf
2. A Tetrarch was the relatively junior ruler of a divided Kingdom. On Herod the Great's death, his kingdom had been split between three of his sons. Antipas ruled the major part, Judaea, Samaria and Idumaea

until AD40. This was the Herod that had beheaded Jesus' cousin John the Baptist and the man that Jesus described as 'that fox' – cunning, predatory and amoral. When brought before Antipas during His trial, Jesus remained silent and would not recognise him. The ambitious and crafty Antipas had frequently lobbied Tiberius Caesar, requesting that he be made fully king of the region, but without success. The founding of the town of Tiberias on the Sea of Galilee was his attempt to buy his Emperor's favour and was used as Antipas' Galilean seat of government. Despite ministering in the vicinity, Jesus never went there, and this was characteristic of His ministry, choosing to largely (but not completely) ignore the elite political classes, but embrace the meek and lowly, ordinary people.

As the ruling family, the Herods were very much hand in glove with Rome. Their dynasty was based on many years of highly adept political manoeuvring to ensure continued Roman patronage, and exploit it to the full. Like his father, Antipas was a ruthless and murderous schemer, paying public lip-service to the religion of Israel. The Jews had one God, the Romans, many. The Jews were tolerated, if rather condescendingly and suspiciously by Rome. However, the Pax Romana (Roman Peace) had allowed Judaea the stability to prosper, and Herod the Great had taken advantage of this to develop the magnificent structures of Jerusalem. Antipas' father was therefore responsible for constructing much of the physical stage on which the final stage of Christ's visit to Jerusalem would be enacted.

As with the Herods, so too with the Priesthood: whilst it was necessary to prove that priests were descended from the line of Aaron and Tribe of Levi, it was also clear that the Herods influenced who became High Priest. These religious and political aristocrats were dominated at this time by Annas, the father- in -law of **Joseph Caiaphas**, the High Priest. The family was unpopular in Judaea, seen as using their privileged position to line their own pockets with taxes. This elite of rulers and priests lived in palatial Roman-style mansions on the other side of the Tyropaeon Valley to the West of the Temple.

When and where

Accurate historical dates for the Passover are not straightforward to establish due to the time elapsed and differing calendars used then and now. However, the Gospel accounts are clear that Jesus had come to Jerusalem some four days earlier, when

Chapter One

He had cleansed the temple and rebuked the moneychangers. He had since then made His triumphal entry and wept over the city. As He wept, He had prophesied:

If you had known in this day, even you, the things which make for peace! But now they have been hidden from your eyes. For the days will come upon you when your enemies will throw up a barricade against you, and surround you and hem you in on every side, and they will level you to the ground and your children within you, and they will not leave in you one stone upon another, because you did not recognize the time of your visitation.

Luke 19.42-44

Now, on or around the 13th day of Nisan (or Tuesday 2nd April) and the day before the crucifixion, He had entered the Temple again, probably from the village of Bethany to the east of the city. This time he would prophesy Jerusalem's future, foretell His own return and describe the events leading to the end of the age. The sunrise on that Judaean Spring day would have been around 6am and the Sun would have set that evening about 7pm.[3] We are not given a weather report, but temperatures based on Israel's current climate could be up in the 70's or down in the 40's at this time of year.

Who's here?

Jerusalem was a city of similar splendour and magnificence to Rome and was packed with pilgrims and their families who had gone up for Passover. The courts of the Temple would be teeming with people. Many Jews, from both Israel and surrounding nations such as Crete or Babylonia had made the journey. Some scholars say it might be possible for the population of Jerusalem to triple in size during the feast, maybe from a potential 70,000 to well over 200,000 people. If we imagine a modern holiday resort in high summer, combined with a major sporting event, we may be somewhere near to appreciating the bustle and energy in the city. Jews were required under the Law to ascend[4] once a year and make a sacrifice for their sins through the shedding of blood. If they could afford it, a family would sacrifice a lamb, so it is likely that many thousands of animals were purchased in

---

3. This is a good approximation although it should be noted that there are difficulties reconciling the ancient Hebrew calendar with our modern dates. We should also note that a Jewish day runs, not from midnight to midnight, but from sunset to sunset.
4. Jews 'went up' to Jerusalem, as it was in the mountains of Judaea. The phrase remains today, with Jews who return to live in Israel making 'aliyah', or 'going up', or making ascent.

the Royal Portico to the south of the temple complex. Imagine for a moment that you were there: what would you see, hear, smell, or feel? Crowds, the chatter of many voices in different languages; excitement; reverence; prayer and dust. The strong scent of blood, incense and smoke from burnt offerings wafts on the breeze, accompanied by the plaintive bleating of lambs. Around and above you are the hills of Jerusalem, to which many would lift up their eyes. This was the temple on that day before Passover AD29 and into its midst came the Lamb of God, who was soon to take the sin of the world upon Himself.

Jesus' disciples were approaching the end of their three-year fast-track spiritual masterclass. These ordinary men had witnessed miracle after miracle and their rudimentary theology had been turned upside down. Herod was about to be confronted by the true King of the Jews. Pilate was to ask *what is truth?* and be faced with the One who is 'The' Truth. The High Priest and his cronies would come face to face with their God-incarnate, but would not recognise Him. The Jewish people had been offered the Kingdom of God and on the following day were to reject it and face two thousand years of persecution and a silent heaven.

The Gospel Account

On this day, 24 hours before His crucifixion, Jesus chose to share a significant amount of information about events to come that would affect Israel, Jerusalem and the lives of His followers in the near and distant future. This is the starting point for our prophetic journey and is known as the Spine of Biblical Prophecy. You may have read Matthew 24, Mark 13 and Luke 21 and noticed that they look similar. On superficial examination these passages do appear to give us individual perspectives by three authors of a single end-time prophecy by Jesus from the Mount of Olives. However, a more careful analysis of the relevant passages reveals that Jesus actually gave two distinctly separate prophecies:

- **The First Prophecy** was given from within the temple and is described in Luke 21. The previous chapter sets the scene for us, that *on one of the days while He was teaching the people **in** the temple...* To confirm His location we are further told in the 21st Chapter of Luke that *He looked up and saw the rich putting their gifts into the treasury.* Jesus was therefore still in the temple when He gave the prophecy recorded in Luke 21, as the whole conversation with His disciples follows without any break from Jesus' description of the widow's mite. Ancient Jewish sources describe thirteen trumpet-shaped collection boxes called *shofarot* or *shofar* (trumpet) chests. These were located in the Court of Women.⁵ Built of metal, they funnelled monetary offerings into wooden chests for later collection. The noise made by the coin would reveal how much was given, rather like the tinkling rattle of coins dropping onto a church collection plate.⁶ The widow's mite, a small copper coin, a little smaller than the nail on your little finger, and known as a *prutah*, evidently made so little noise that Jesus was able to discern her gift was small, yet profoundly generous. In order for Him to see and hear this act, He must therefore have been present in the Court of Women, and very close by to where these *shofarot* were located. As the widow's mite and first prophecy were part of one conversation, it is reasonable to surmise that the first prophecy was given in the Court of Women, where any Jewish adult had access.

Figure 2 Judaean Prutah from the time of Herod Archelaus. The lowest denomination coin in circulation at the time of Christ.

- **The Second Prophecy** is a later discourse given by Jesus on the Mount of Olives as described in Matthew 24 and Mark 13. Matthew 24.1 tells us that *Jesus came out from the temple and was going away... (v3) He was sitting on the Mount of Olives, the disciples came to Him privately.* Mark 13.1 also confirms that *He was going out of the temple... (v3) He was sitting on the Mount of Olives opposite the temple; Peter and James and John and Andrew were questioning Him privately...* It is clear therefore that Jesus was later on the Mount of Olives.

New Testament Greek uses two words for temple:

- **Hieron** is a more general term which describes the general temple area of Jerusalem, comprising the whole of the complex, including all buildings, balconies, porticos, and the courts of the men of Israel, women and priests.

---

5. The Court of Women was not restricted to women only, but was the furthest point a woman could access in the temple. Gentiles were forbidden entry here on pain of death, so Jesus' 1st prophecy must have been given to Jews only and excluded Gentiles.
6. See 'The Quest' by Leen Ritmeyer for a detailed understanding of the layout of the Temple

This is normally shown as temple with a small 't'.

- ***Naos*** is a specific term for the Sanctuary, or Holy Place including the Holy of Holies. This is normally shown as Temple with a capital 'T'. It could be accessed only by the Priests, and only the High Priest had access to the Holy of Holies on the Day of Atonement.

Figure 3. Herod's temple looking west (HolyLand Hotel Model). The Court of Women, the location of the first prophecy, is the open area in front of and below the Sanctuary. The shofarim were located in the porticoes around its sides.

Up to this point, Herod's temple had taken some 46 years[7] to build, and recent archaeological finds suggest that construction was still ongoing at the time of Christ. It was the centrepiece of Judaism and a building that Flavius Josephus described as a structure more noteworthy than any under the Sun. Some 52M high, 52M long, 52M wide, the Naos was faced-off in white limestone blocks, with plates of solid gold covering its external walls.

---

7. John 2.20

Chapter One

Figure 4. View from Mount of Olives looking south-west towards the Temple Mount. This position was Jesus' probable perspective for the second prophecy.

Earlier we considered the chaotic scene within the temple. Let us now move up to the tranquil and airy slopes of the Mount of Olives for the setting of Jesus' second prophetic discourse. The temple had been part of His life since infancy and with this short half-mile journey He was leaving it for the last time. How long it must have seemed to Him, but might have taken perhaps twenty minutes to walk out of the temple through the crowds, down into the Kidron valley and up the far slope to reach His destination on the western side of Olivet. Matthew 24.1-3 tells us that the disciples came to Him, so it seems that Jesus had walked from the temple alone and was (a little later) joined by them.

Mark 13.3 describes their location as over against the temple (*hieron*). This phrase implies that the group sat opposite and at the nearest point at which one might sit to face the temple, neither looking up at it, nor down upon it. The summit of the mountain is a lofty 2,683', but Jesus would have been around 2,440' and around half a mile from the Holy of Holies, assuming a similar elevation to the Temple itself. The picture above shows the probable aspect that Jesus would have seen (albeit taken in the 19th Century). Was it significant that the slopes of the mountain were strewn with the graves of Jews who had been buried there and that within two days[8] Jesus would have been crucified? The tombs of Haggai, Malachi and Zechariah are said to be there, and these would bear silent witness to the greatest prophet of them all. It would make a quiet but sombre backdrop for Jesus' final advice to this small group of His closest disciples.

The disciples had voiced their awe as to the magnificence of the temple and its surrounds and remarked so to Jesus. His reply would astonish and shock them.

Part 2 – Jesus' great end-time prophecy - the 4 Laws

Laid out below are the relevant accounts from Matthew, Mark and Luke from that day. Because elements of the first prophecy (Luke 21) are repeated in the second (Matthew 24 and Mark 13) the passages have been aligned in parallel to show identical themes and events.

The key themes have been summarised in the right-hand column, and will be discussed further in Chapter 2.

In arranging the passages below, a number of Laws have been applied. These are intended to ensure consistent and accurate presentation of the prophecy.

The 4 laws of the Spine

The 4 Laws of the Spine

Spine Law 1 'identical events'	Where there is a clear, definite and irrefutable similarity between passages in both content and phrasing, events have been aligned and assumed to describe the same activities
Spine Law 2 'Matthew & Mark together'	Matthew and Mark relate the same prophetic discourse from the Mount of Olives. The events described are identical and have been aligned accordingly
Spine Law 3 'Luke first'	If the passage does not fit with Law 1, then as the prophecy in Luke was uttered first, passages/events from Luke are given priority and pre-eminence in the schedule
Spine Law 4 'Luke's parenthesis'	Jesus uses the phrase 'before all these things' in Luke 21.12. The events up to 21.24 are therefore brought forward and shown on their own

---

8. Remember that the Jewish days run sunset to sunset.

Chapter One

Matt 24-25 on Mount of Olives	Mark 13 on Mount of Olives	Luke 21 in the temple courts	Key Themes See Ch2
2nd Prophecy	2nd Prophecy	1st Prophecy	
¹Jesus came out from the temple and was going away when His disciples came up to point out the temple buildings to Him.	As He was going out of the temple, one of His disciples ¹said to Him, "Teacher, behold what wonderful stones and what wonderful buildings!"	⁵And while some were talking about the temple, that it was adorned with beautiful stones and votive gifts, He said,	**NEAR-TERM PROPHECY** **Destruction of the Temple AD70** (See Ch 2 Part 1)
²And He said to them, "Do you not see all these things? Truly I say to you, not one stone here will be left upon another, which will not be torn down."	²And Jesus said to him, "Do you see these great buildings? Not one stone will be left upon another which will not be torn down."	⁶"*As for* these things which you are looking at, the days will come in which there will not be left one stone upon another which will not be torn down."	
³As He was sitting on the Mount of Olives, the disciples came to Him privately, saying,	³As He was sitting on the Mount of Olives opposite the temple, Peter and James and John and Andrew were questioning Him privately,	⁷They questioned Him, saying,	**The disciples' five questions about the future** (See Ch 2 Part 2)
"Tell us, • when will these things happen, • and what *will be* the sign of Your coming, • and of the end of the age?"	⁴"Tell us, • when will these things be, • and what *will be* the sign when all these things are going to be fulfilled?"	"Teacher, • when therefore will these things happen? • And what *will be* the sign when these things are about to take place?"	
⁴And Jesus answered and said to them,	⁵And Jesus began to say to them,	⁸And He said,	**END-TIME PROPHECY** See Ch 2 Part 3
"See to it that no one misleads you. ⁵For many will come in My name, saying, 'I am the Christ,' and will mislead many.	"See to it that no one misleads you. ⁶Many will come in My name, saying, 'I am *He*!' and will mislead many.	"See to it that you are not misled; for many will come in My name, saying, 'I am *He*,' and, 'The time is near.' Do not go after them.	**False Christs / Deception #1**
⁶You will be hearing of wars and rumors of wars. See that you are not frightened, for *those things* must take place, but *that* is not yet the end.	⁷When you hear of wars and rumors of wars, do not be frightened; *those things* must take place; but *that is* not yet the end.	⁹When you hear of wars and disturbances, do not be terrified; for these things must take place first, but the end does not *follow* immediately."	**Wars**
⁷For nation will rise against nation, and kingdom against kingdom,	⁸For nation will rise up against nation, and kingdom against kingdom;	¹⁰Then He continued by saying to them, "Nation will rise against nation and kingdom against kingdom,	**Ethnic conflict**
and in various places there will be famines and earthquakes.	there will be earthquakes in various places; there will *also* be famines.	¹¹and there will be great earthquakes, and in various places plagues and famines;	**Famine / earthquake / disease**

Matt 24-25 on Mount of Olives	Mark 13 on Mount of Olives	Luke 21 in the temple courts	Key Themes See Ch2
2nd Prophecy		1st Prophecy	
⁸But all these things are *merely* the beginning of birth pangs.	These things are merely the beginning of birth pangs.		**(the beginning of labour pains)**
		and there will be terrors	**the "phobetron": massive fear and terror** ('Fearful sights' or Greek 'Phobetron' is a state of terror encountered by the imagination of people who are sick)
		and great signs from heaven.	**Great signs from heaven** ('Great signs from heaven' are certainly one-off end-time events, thus the context must lie in the future.)
		PARENTHESIS (¹²"But before all these things, they will lay their hands on you and will persecute you, delivering you to the synagogues and prisons, bringing you before kings and governors for My name's sake. (This section is shown as a parenthesis, as Jesus states 'before all these things' i.e. before the events of vv8-11. He is in effect going 'back' to AD70 to describe these events)	**Jesus returns to the AD70 prophecy** (See Ch 2 Part 1)

Chapter One

Matt 24-25 on Mount of Olives	Mark 13 on Mount of Olives	Luke 21 in the temple courts	Key Themes See Ch2
2nd Prophecy		1st Prophecy	
		¹³It will lead to an opportunity for your testimony. ¹⁴So make up your minds not to prepare beforehand to defend yourselves; ¹⁵for I will give you utterance and wisdom which none of your opponents will be able to resist or refute.	
		¹⁶But you will be betrayed even by parents and brothers and relatives and friends, and they will put *some* of you to death, ¹⁷and you will be hated by all because of My name. ¹⁸Yet not a hair of your head will perish. ¹⁹By your endurance you will gain your lives.	
		²⁰"But when you see Jerusalem surrounded by armies, then recognize that her desolation is near. ²¹Then those who are in Judea must flee to the mountains, and those who are in the midst of the city must leave, and those who are in the country must not enter the city;	
		²²because these are days of vengeance, so that all things which are written will be fulfilled.	
		²³Woe to those who are pregnant and to those who are nursing babies in those days; for there will be great distress upon the land and wrath to this people;	
		²⁴and they will fall by the edge of the sword, and will be led captive into all the nations; and Jerusalem will be trampled underfoot by the Gentiles until the times of the Gentiles are fulfilled). PARENTHESIS ENDS	

Matt 24-25 on Mount of Olives	Mark 13 on Mount of Olives	Luke 21 in the temple courts	Key Themes See Ch2
2nd Prophecy		**1st Prophecy**	
⁹"Then they will deliver you to tribulation, and will kill you, and you will be hated by all nations because of My name. ¹⁰At that time many will fall away and will betray one another and hate one another.	⁹"But be on your guard; for they will deliver you to the courts, and you will be flogged in the synagogues, and you will stand before governors and kings for My sake, as a testimony to them.		**END-TIME PROPHECY** **Tribulation / persecution. Hated by ALL nations. Offence Betrayal Persecution**
¹¹Many false prophets will arise and will mislead many. ¹²Because lawlessness is increased, most people's love will grow cold. ¹³But the one who endures to the end, he will be saved.			**False prophets / Deception #2** **Lawlessness / Christians' love "grows cold"**
¹⁴This gospel of the kingdom shall be preached in the whole world as a testimony to all the nations, and then the end will come.	¹⁰The gospel must first be preached to all the nations. ¹¹When they arrest you and hand you over, do not worry beforehand about what you are to say, but say whatever is given you in that hour; for it is not you who speak, but it is the Holy Spirit.		**Gospel goes world-wide**
	¹²Brother will betray brother to death, and a father his child; and children will rise up against parents and have them put to death.		**Family betrayal**
	¹³You will be hated by all because of My name, but the one who endures to the end, he will be saved.		**Universal hatred of Christian and Jew**

CHAPTER ONE

Chapter One

Matt 24-25 on Mount of Olives	Mark 13 on Mount of Olives	Luke 21 in the temple courts	Key Themes See Ch2
2nd Prophecy		1st Prophecy	
¹⁵"Therefore when you see the abomination of desolation which was spoken of through Daniel the prophet, standing in the holy place (let the reader understand), ¹⁶then those who are in Judea must flee to the mountains. ¹⁷Whoever is on the housetop must not go down to get the things out that are in his house. ¹⁸Whoever is in the field must not turn back to get his cloak. ¹⁹But woe to those who are pregnant and to those who are nursing babies in those days! ²⁰But pray that your flight will not be in the winter, or on a Sabbath.	¹⁴"But when you see the abomination of desolation standing where it should not be (let the reader understand), then those who are in Judea must flee to the mountains. ¹⁵The one who is on the housetop must not go down, or go in to get anything out of his house; ¹⁶and the one who is in the field must not turn back to get his coat. ¹⁷But woe to those who are pregnant and to those who are nursing babies in those days! ¹⁸But pray that it may not happen in the winter.		**Abomination of Desolation** (See Ch 9 part 2. The 'when' and 'then' statements are in relation to the Abomination of Desolation and the Great Tribulation. It is a one-off, unique, end-time event. It is different to the prophesied events of AD70 described in Luke 21.20-24.)
²¹For then there will be a great tribulation, such as has not occurred since the beginning of the world until now, nor ever will. ²²Unless those days had been cut short, no life would have been saved; but for the sake of the elect those days will be cut short.	¹⁹For those days will be a *time* of tribulation such as has not occurred since the beginning of the creation which God created until now, and never will. ²⁰Unless the Lord had shortened *those* days, no life would have been saved; but for the sake of the elect, whom He chose, He shortened the days.		**The Great Tribulation**
²³Then if anyone says to you, 'Behold, here is the Christ,' or 'There He is,' do not believe *him*. ²⁴For false Christs and false prophets will arise and will show great signs and wonders, so as to mislead, if possible, even the elect.	²¹And then if anyone says to you, 'Behold, here is the Christ'; or, 'Behold, *He* is there'; do not believe *him*; ²²for false Christs and false prophets will arise, and will show signs and wonders, in order to lead astray, if possible, the elect.		**False Christs / Deception #3** **(with supernatural power)**

Matt 24-25 on Mount of Olives	Mark 13 on Mount of Olives	Luke 21 in the temple courts	Key Themes See Ch2
2nd Prophecy		**1st Prophecy**	
²⁵Behold, I have told you in advance. ²⁶So if they say to you, 'Behold, He is in the wilderness,' do not go out, *or*, 'Behold, He is in the inner rooms,' do not believe *them*. ²⁷For just as the lightning comes from the east and flashes even to the west, so will the coming of the Son of Man be. ²⁸Wherever the corpse is, there the vultures will gather.	²³But take heed; behold, I have told you everything in advance.		
²⁹"But immediately after the tribulation of those days the sun will be darkened, and the moon will not give its light, and the stars will fall from the sky, and	²⁴"But in those days, after that tribulation, the sun will be darkened and the moon will not give its light, ²⁵and the stars will be falling from heaven, and	²⁵"There will be signs in sun and moon and stars,	**Great signs in Sun, Moon and stars.**
		and on the earth dismay among nations, in perplexity at the roaring of the sea and the waves, ²⁶men fainting from fear and the expectation of the things which are coming upon the world;	**National distress. Seas and waves roaring.**
the powers of the heavens will be shaken.	the powers that are in the heavens will be shaken.	for the powers of the heavens will be shaken.	**Powers of heavens shaken.**
³⁰And then the sign of the Son of Man will appear in the sky, and then all the tribes of the earth will mourn, and they will see the Son of Man coming on the clouds of the sky with power and great glory.	²⁶Then they will see the Son of Man coming in clouds with great power and glory.	²⁷Then they will see the Son of Man coming in a cloud with power and great glory. ²⁸But when these things begin to take place, straighten up and lift up your heads, because your redemption is drawing near."	(see Ch 12) **Sign of the Son of Man.** **The earth mourns.** **Jesus returns**
³¹And He will send forth His angels with a great trumpet and they will gather together His elect from the four winds, from one end of the sky to the other.	²⁷And then He will send forth the angels, and will gather together His elect from the four winds, from the farthest end of the earth to the farthest end of heaven.		**Angels sent with great trumpet sound.** **The elect gathered.**

Chapter One

Matt 24-25 on Mount of Olives	Mark 13 on Mount of Olives	Luke 21 in the temple courts	Key Themes See Ch2
2nd Prophecy		1st Prophecy	
³²"Now learn the parable from the fig tree: when its branch has already become tender and puts forth its leaves, you know that summer is near; ³³so, you too, when you see all these things, recognize that He is near, *right* at the door. ³⁴Truly I say to you, this generation will not pass away until all these things take place. ³⁵Heaven and earth will pass away, but My words will not pass away.	²⁸"Now learn the parable from the fig tree: when its branch has already become tender and puts forth its leaves, you know that summer is near. ²⁹Even so, you too, when you see these things happening, recognize that He is near, *right* at the door. ³⁰Truly I say to you, this generation will not pass away until all these things take place. ³¹Heaven and earth will pass away, but My words will not pass away.	²⁹Then He told them a parable: "Behold the fig tree and all the trees; ³⁰as soon as they put forth *leaves*, you see it and know for yourselves that summer is now near. ³¹So you also, when you see these things happening, recognize that the kingdom of God is near. ³²Truly I say to you, this generation will not pass away until all things take place. ³³Heaven and earth will pass away, but My words will not pass away.	**Parable of the Fig Tree**
		³⁴"Be on guard, so that your hearts will not be weighted down with dissipation and drunkenness and the worries of life, and that day will not come on you suddenly like a trap; ³⁵for it will come upon all those who dwell on the face of all the earth. ³⁶But keep on the alert at all times, praying that you may have strength to escape all these things that are about to take place, and to stand before the Son of Man."	**Guard your heart**
³⁶"But of that day and hour no one knows, not even the angels of heaven, nor the Son, but the Father alone. ³⁷For the coming of the Son of Man will be just like the days of Noah. ³⁸For as in those days before the flood they were eating and drinking, marrying and giving in marriage, until the day that Noah entered the ark, ³⁹and they did not understand until the flood came and took them all away; so will the coming of the Son of Man be.	³²But of that day or hour no one knows, not even the angels in heaven, nor the Son, but the Father *alone*.		**Days of Noah** (See Chapter 13)

Matt 24-25 on Mount of Olives	Mark 13 on Mount of Olives	Luke 21 in the temple courts	Key Themes See Ch2
2nd Prophecy		**1st Prophecy**	
⁴⁰Then there will be two men in the field; one will be taken and one will be left. ⁴¹Two women *will* be grinding at the mill; one will be taken and one will be left.			
⁴²"Therefore be on the alert, for you do not know which day your Lord is coming. ⁴³But be sure of this, that if the head of the house had known at what time of the night the thief was coming, he would have been on the alert and would not have allowed his house to be broken into.	³³"Take heed, keep on the alert; for you do not know when the *appointed* time will come.		**Parable of the Thief in the Night** (See Chapter 13)
⁴⁴For this reason you also must be ready; for the Son of Man is coming at an hour when you do not think He *will*.			
⁴⁵"Who then is the faithful and sensible slave whom his master put in charge of his household to give them their food at the proper time? ⁴⁶Blessed is that slave whom his master finds so doing when he comes. ⁴⁷Truly I say to you that he will put him in charge of all his possessions. ⁴⁸But if that evil slave says in his heart, 'My master is not coming for a long time,' ⁴⁹and begins to beat his fellow slaves and eat and drink with drunkards; ⁵⁰the master of that slave will come on a day when he does not expect *him* and at an hour which he does not know, ⁵¹and will cut him in pieces and assign him a place with the hypocrites; in that place there will be weeping and gnashing of teeth.			**Parable of the Faithful and Wise Servant** (See Chapter 13)

Chapter One

Matt 24-25 on Mount of Olives	Mark 13 on Mount of Olives	Luke 21 in the temple courts	Key Themes See Ch2
2nd Prophecy		1st Prophecy	
25 ¹"Then the kingdom of heaven will be comparable to ten virgins, who took their lamps and went out to meet the bridegroom. ²Five of them were foolish, and five were prudent. ³For when the foolish took their lamps, they took no oil with them, ⁴but the prudent took oil in flasks along with their lamps. ⁵Now while the bridegroom was delaying, they all got drowsy and began to sleep. ⁶But at midnight there was a shout, 'Behold, the bridegroom! Come out to meet him.' ⁷Then all those virgins rose and trimmed their lamps. ⁸The foolish said to the prudent, 'Give us some of your oil, for our lamps are going out.' ⁹But the prudent answered, 'No, there will not be enough for us and you too; go instead to the dealers and buy some for yourselves.' ¹⁰And while they were going away to make the purchase, the bridegroom came, and those who were ready went in with him to the wedding feast; and the door was shut. ¹¹Later the other virgins also came, saying, 'Lord, lord, open up for us.' ¹²But he answered, 'Truly I say to you, I do not know you.' ¹³Be on the alert then, for you do not know the day nor the hour.			**Parable of the Ten Virgins** (See Chapter 13)
¹⁴"For it is just like a man about to go on a journey, who called his own slaves and entrusted his possessions to them. ¹⁵To one he gave five talents, to another, two, and to another, one, each according to his own ability; and he went on his journey.			**Parable of the Talents** (See Chapter 13)

Matt 24-25 on Mount of Olives	Mark 13 on Mount of Olives	Luke 21 in the temple courts	Key Themes See Ch2
2nd Prophecy		1st Prophecy	
¹⁶Immediately the one who had received the five talents went and traded with them, and gained five more talents. ¹⁷In the same manner the one who had received the two talents gained two more. ¹⁸But he who received the one talent went away, and dug a hole in the ground and hid his master's money. ¹⁹"Now after a long time the master of those slaves *came and *settled accounts with them. ²⁰The one who had received the five talents came up and brought five more talents, saying, 'Master, you entrusted five talents to me. See, I have gained five more talents.' ²¹His master said to him, 'Well done, good and faithful slave. You were faithful with a few things, I will put you in charge of many things; enter into the joy of your master.' ²²"Also the one who had received the two talents came up and said, 'Master, you entrusted two talents to me. See, I have gained two more talents.' ²³His master said to him, 'Well done, good and faithful slave. You were faithful with a few things, I will put you in charge of many things; enter into the joy of your master.'			

Chapter One

Matt 24-25 on Mount of Olives	Mark 13 on Mount of Olives	Luke 21 in the temple courts	**Key Themes** See Ch2
2nd Prophecy		1st Prophecy	
²⁴"And the one also who had received the one talent came up and said, 'Master, I knew you to be a hard man, reaping where you did not sow and gathering where you scattered no seed. ²⁵And I was afraid, and went away and hid your talent in the ground. See, you have what is yours.' ²⁶"But his master answered and said to him, 'You wicked, lazy slave, you knew that I reap where I did not sow and gather where I scattered no seed. ²⁷Then you ought to have put my money in the bank, and on my arrival I would have received my money back with interest. ²⁸Therefore take away the talent from him, and give it to the one who has the ten talents.' ²⁹"For to everyone who has, more shall be given, and he will have an abundance; but from the one who does not have, even what he does have shall be taken away. ³⁰Throw out the worthless slave into the outer darkness; in that place there will be weeping and gnashing of teeth.			

Matt 24-25 on Mount of Olives	Mark 13 on Mount of Olives	Luke 21 in the temple courts	Key Themes See Ch2
2nd Prophecy		**1st Prophecy**	
³¹"But when the Son of Man comes in His glory, and all the angels with Him, then He will sit on His glorious throne. ³²All the nations will be gathered before Him; and He will separate them from one another, as the shepherd separates the sheep from the goats; ³³and He will put the sheep on His right, and the goats on the left. ³⁴"Then the King will say to those on His right, 'Come, you who are blessed of My Father, inherit the kingdom prepared for you from the foundation of the world. ³⁵For I was hungry, and you gave Me something to eat; I was thirsty, and you gave Me something to drink; I was a stranger, and you invited Me in; ³⁶naked, and you clothed Me; I was sick, and you visited Me; I was in prison, and you came to Me.' ³⁷Then the righteous will answer Him, 'Lord, when did we see You hungry, and feed You, or thirsty, and give You something to drink? ³⁸And when did we see You a stranger, and invite You in, or naked, and clothe You? ³⁹When did we see You sick, or in prison, and come to You?' ⁴⁰The King will answer and say to them, 'Truly I say to you, to the extent that you did it to one of these brothers of Mine, even the least of them, you did it to Me.'			**Sheep and goat nations** (See Chapter 13)

Chapter One

Matt 24-25 on Mount of Olives	Mark 13 on Mount of Olives	Luke 21 in the temple courts	**Key Themes** See Ch2
2nd Prophecy		1st Prophecy	
⁴¹"Then He will also say to those on His left, 'Depart from Me, accursed ones, into the eternal fire which has been prepared for the devil and his angels; ⁴²for I was hungry, and you gave Me nothing to eat; I was thirsty, and you gave Me nothing to drink; ⁴³I was a stranger, and you did not invite Me in; naked, and you did not clothe Me; sick, and in prison, and you did not visit Me.' ⁴⁴Then they themselves also will answer, 'Lord, when did we see You hungry, or thirsty, or a stranger, or naked, or sick, or in prison, and did not take care of You?' 45Then He will answer them, 'Truly I say to you, to the extent that you did not do it to one of the least of these, you did not do it to Me.' 46These will go away into eternal punishment, but the righteous into eternal life."			
	³⁴It *is* like a man away on a journey, who upon leaving his house and putting his slaves in charge, *assigning* to each one his task, also commanded the doorkeeper to stay on the alert. ³⁵Therefore, be on the alert—for you do not know when the master of the house is coming, whether in the evening, at midnight, or when the rooster crows, or in the morning— ³⁶in case he should come suddenly and find you asleep. ³⁷What I say to you I say to all, 'Be on the alert!'"		The Far Country (See Chapter 13)

Before we move on, spend a few moments reflecting on the Word Cloud for the above passages. Words that appear more often are bigger...

Figure 5. Jesus' final prophecies - Word cloud

CHAPTER ONE

Chapter 2 — Spine of Biblical Prophecy - an analysis

Daughters of Jerusalem, stop weeping for Me, but weep for yourselves and for your children

Luke 23.28

Figure 6. The Siege and Destruction of Jerusalem by the Romans under the Command of Titus.

The parallel passages shown in Chapter 1 may be conveniently broken into three sections for further analysis:

- Part 1 – Jesus' near-term prophecy concerning the destruction of the Temple AD70

- Part 2 – An analysis of the disciples' questions

- Part 3 – Jesus' end-time prophecy and His return

Chapter Two

Part 1 – Jesus' Near-Term prophecy concerning the destruction of the Temple AD70

In Luke 21.12-24 Jesus describes the following events:

- Jerusalem would be surrounded by armies
- those in Judaea should flee
- great distress and wrath would come upon the people
- people would fall by the sword
- people would be led away captive into all nations
- Jerusalem would be trampled by the Gentiles until the times of the Gentiles were fulfilled

Almost exactly 40 years after Jesus spoke these words, around the 13th Nisan (April) AD70, Jerusalem was besieged by the 5th, 10th, 12th and 15th Legions of the Roman Army. They were led by Titus, son of the Emperor Vespasian. For political purposes, Vespasian, who had become Emperor in AD69, needed a swift and dramatic victory to be able to present himself to Rome as a hero. The Jews would pay the price for his ambition.

Figure 7. VESPASIAN. 69-79 AD. Æ Sestertius. Minted to celebrate Rome's victory over Judaea

You might ask why Rome had to punish Judaea. For this, we need to turn to Flavius Josephus. Josephus had been a general in the Judean rebel force, but had been captured by Vespasian before he became Emperor. He 'prophesied' that Vespasian would one day be Caesar, and was rewarded by being granted citizenship and favour. His account of the Jewish wars is a fascinating read and our guide here.

Some four years prior to Titus' assault, in May 66AD, a dispute had broken out between Jews and Greeks over access to a synagogue in Caesarea. The Roman Governor of Judaea, Gessius Florus, had been paid by the Jews to side with them, but took their eight talents of silver and did nothing. Gessius then sought to provoke the Jews to rebel so that he could punish them, and took seventeen talents of gold from the Temple treasury. After the ensuing unrest, he turned his troops loose into one of Jerusalem's markets with instructions to kill everyone, resulting in the death of 3,600 men, women and children. The people of Jerusalem were then forced to 'welcome' two cohorts of Roman soldiers to demonstrate their submissiveness to Rome. The crowd signalled their displeasure and further bloodshed resulted.

Not only were the Jews in rebellion against Rome, but also riven by factions between themselves: one for peace with Rome and one for war. The Jews were further offended by the requirement that regular sacrifice should be made in the Temple on behalf of the Emperor. Consequently, at this time, a Roman cohort of some 600 men was garrisoned in the palace that had once belonged to Herod the Great and this was effectively placed under siege by the Jewish rebels. The garrison agreed to lay down their arms and depart, on condition that their safe retreat would be honoured. However, as they left the Jews attacked and slaughtered them.

Roman retaliation was now inevitable and in November 66AD the Roman Governor of Syria, Cestius Gallus, arrived from Antioch in Judaea with a sizeable force. The Jews counter-attacked, killing over 500 Romans. The Romans offered pardon to the rebels, but, with growing confidence on the rebels' part, this was ignored. Cestius now moved onto Jerusalem, establishing his camp on Mount Scopus, which overlooks the city from the North and East. He besieged Jerusalem, quelled the rebellion and burnt the gates of the Temple. At this juncture, on the very point of total victory, he withdrew. Historians query why this happened. Was he bribed? Did he think he had achieved his objectives?

Either way, the siege was lifted and the force departed westward to the coast. Certainly, the hand of God was at work here to fulfil Jesus' prophecy.

To understand this we need to turn to Jesus' advice that when his followers saw Jerusalem surrounded by armies, that those in Judaea should flee. The historian of the early Church, Eusebius (AD 263 – 339) tells us that this was when Judaea's Christians made their escape, taking refuge in the city of Pella to the east of the Jordan River.

Cestius' withdrawal to the coast was harried by Jewish rebels through the small and high-sided valleys. As they retreated through Gibeon and Bethoran they were

Chapter Two

attacked incessantly and eventually routed, with the loss of over 5,000 infantry, nearly 500 cavalry and siege engines.

After Cestius' humiliating defeat, Nero commanded the experienced Vespasian, a 56 year old veteran of the British conquest, to deal with the Judaean rebellion. Vespasian arrived in the Galilee in 67AD via Syria, having taken command of the 5th and 10th Legions. His son Titus would arrive via Egypt bringing the 15th Legion with him. And so the retribution began.

I recommend the reader to check out the full account of this conflict in Josephus's account; however it can be appreciated why Rome was now motivated to deal with Judaea in general and Jerusalem in particular. If one Roman province had rebelled and was seen to get away with it, so might others. Not only had Rome to act, but also be seen to act decisively.

Figure 8. Destruction of the Jewish Temple. Nicolas Poussin 1594-1665

It took Rome three years to subjugate Samaria and Judaea, during which time the tyrant Nero had committed suicide and Vespasian had become Caesar. By 70AD, Titus' army numbered around 80,000 men including locally recruited auxiliaries who had a fierce hatred for the Jews. To put this in context, the force was around twice the size of Aulus Plautius' army that had invaded Britain at Claudius' command in 43AD.

Titus's legionaries fought their way into the city, breaking through walls and barricades, into tunnels and barricaded rooms. As the net drew tighter within the City, the people grew hungry and famine developed. Armed gangs of Jews roamed the streets in search of food, and even cannibalism took place.

Both Josephus and Tacitus estimated the ensuing slaughter of the inhabitants of Jerusalem at somewhere between 600,000 to one million people. The city was bursting with men, women and children at the time of the siege, who had gone up to celebrate Passover. Remember also that Titus was under political pressure for a fast and decisive victory for Vespasian, so enacted the siege very rapidly, trapping this mass of people (residents and pilgrims and their families) within the city walls. The numbers may possibly be exaggerated, but certainly serve to give us a sense of the level of violence and bloodshed.

A few minutes before his crucifixion Jesus had prophesied:

> *Daughters of Jerusalem, stop weeping for Me, but weep for yourselves and for your children. For behold, the days are coming when they will say, 'Blessed are the barren, and the wombs that never bore, and the breasts that never nursed.' Then they will begin to say to the mountains, 'Fall on us,' and to the hills, 'Cover us.'*
>
> Luke 23.28-30

Josephus describes the roar of flames, the groaning of victims, and the city as a 'burning pile'. He claimed he could hear the war cries of the legions and the howling of the rebels from his vantage point.

Chapter Two

Figure 9. The Destruction of the Temple of Jerusalem.

Jewish resistance came to an end around the end of September AD70. The Holy City had become a charnel house, with the numbers of dead exceeding the battlefields of Waterloo or Gettysburg. Leading up to the siege, the Romans had systematically crucified those Jews they had captured, so the city and surrounding roads were littered with crosses from which hung decomposing corpses. The dead lay everywhere and the stench of blood, burning and putrefaction filled the air.

At Titus' decree, the Temple complex and city were now levelled. Every stone of the Holy of Holies, Holy Place, courts and porticoes was removed and 'cast down', as Jesus had prophesied.[1] The Legions systematically demolished the rest of

---

1. This did not include the Temple Mount platform. This had been constructed by Herod the Great to enlarge an area on which his grander Temple could be constructed. The platform still exists today and 50M of the Southern section of its South Western ('Wailing') Wall is visible. Tourists to Jerusalem may also access the Western Wall Tunnel to view the massive limestone ashlars or (retaining blocks) that Herod used to buttress the foundation walls of the Temple, some weighing over 200 tons.

Jerusalem, with the exception of a few buildings that might be of use. One of these was Herod's Citadel, where the 10th Legion made their base. It can be seen today.

The razing of Jerusalem was a significant engineering task, which must have taken considerable effort. The material from this destruction litters Jerusalem today and archaeologists, treading very carefully in this most politically sensitive area, make regular finds of temple material and artefacts.[2]

Forty Years

As we progress through our prophetic journey, we will see that numbers have spiritual significance in scripture. The fact  that Titus' siege took place almost exactly 40 years after Jesus' AD29 prophecy is interesting. In the Bible the number 40 is normally associated with a period of probation, trial or judgment.[3] That Jerusalem's judgment should come in AD70, 40 years after Jesus prophecy, was no coincidence. This was judgment. We should bear this in mind as we progress through our prophetic journey. Numbers provide us with powerful keys for interpretation.

Figure 10. Broken pavement at the SW corner of the Temple Mount. Here the Roman soldiers threw down massive building blocks of the Temple's Royal Portico to shatter the pavement of the street below.

The Captivity

Those who the Legions didn't kill they enslaved. Many tens of thousands of slaves

---

2. The Temple Mount Sifting project is one such example. Construction of a mosque under the so-called Stables of Solomon removed vast quantities of foundation material from the south of the Mount and this was dumped in the Kidron valley. Dr Gabriel Barkai, a renowned Israeli archaeologist, retrieved this material to a secure site, where it is now processed by volunteers. Visitors may participate in the rescue of material.
3. For example Jesus spent 40 days in the wilderness to be tested by Satan; the Children of Israel wandered for 40 years in the wilderness as a punishment; and Noah was 40 days and nights in the Ark.

Chapter Two

were transported away from Jerusalem to meet the needs of the Empire. It was reported that the price of slaves fell dramatically at that time due to the glut on the market. Since the time of the Babylonian Captivity in the 6th Century BC, Jews were already widely dispersed across the Mediterranean. The Roman expulsion of the Jewish slaves now swelled the numbers of the 'Diaspora'.[4]

Figure 11. Titus's Arch in Rome shows the 'triumph' that followed the destruction of Jerusalem.

Despite this some Jews still remained in Judaea and Galilee, and there has been a continual and unbroken Jewish presence there right up to the founding of Israel in 1948.[5] Plunder from the Temple, together with 20,000 Jewish slaves, was used by Vespasian to fund the construction of his showpiece, the mighty Coliseum, which would later provide a stage for the martyrdom of Rome's Christians.

'The Times of the Gentiles'

We should now consider the phrase times of the Gentiles used by Jesus. That there

---

4. A Greek word meaning *scattering* or *dispersion*, typically of a people.
5. Many ignore or downplay this fact, seeking to delegitimise Jewish claims on the land of Israel in general and Jerusalem in particular.

is more than one time is evident from the plural use of times. But how many times are there and what is their significance?

It is clear from the context that Jesus connected the times of the Gentiles only to Jerusalem i.e. the phrase should therefore only be understood in relation to that city. He also stated that Jerusalem would be (future tense) trampled by or trodden down by these Gentiles.

Some 600 years before Christ's incarnation, Nebuchadnezzar had marched on Jerusalem and besieged the city. He took the King and 10,000 of her inhabitants, captive. The exiles were put to work in Babylon, some as personal servants to the King. During this time Nebuchadnezzar had a dream (see Daniel 2). It fell to Daniel to provide the interpretation, and with God's help Daniel was able to describe five separate and successive Kingdoms that would come to pass. It is possible that he also revealed a sixth in Daniel 3.44 (which we will look at in Chapter 5). The table below shows our understanding of the identity of those Kingdoms.

Before we progress we should note that the Old Testament is not meant to provide a general encyclopaedia of world history, but a view of history only in as much as it relates to God's people, Israel. Other nations or kingdoms are therefore only referred to only in so far as they relate to God's chosen people. The first of these Kingdoms referred to by Daniel was Babylon. The others are reckoned as they came into successive possession of Jerusalem.[6]

The table below records how Jerusalem has been occupied and ruled over by successive Kingdoms or Empires:

---

6. The dates show when each Kingdom came into possession of Jerusalem, not necessarily when that Kingdom started. Some dates need to be treated with caution, particularly those relating to the early Islamic occupation, as few reliable historical sources exist.

CHAPTER TWO

'Times of the Gentiles' – Part 1: Beginning of Gentile Dominion over Jerusalem

Temple Mount / 'Holy Place' under Jewish rule	Temple Mount / 'Holy Place' under Gentile rule	duration of rule over jerusalem	Key figures affecting status of Jerusalem	Prophetic perspective of Kingdoms from Nebuchadnezzar's Vision (Dan. 2)	Comments	Certainty in identifying nationality in prophecy
Kingdom of David / Solomon		1000 – 586BC	David Solomon			Certain
	Babylon	586 – 550BC	Nebuchadnezzar	**1st Kingdom** – Head of Gold	1260 years from Babylon to end of Roman possession of Jerusalem	Certain
	Medo-Persia	550 – 323BC	Cyrus the Great Artaxerxes Darius	**2nd Kingdom** – Breast and arms of Silver		Certain
	Greece / Ptolemaic	323 – Sept 31BC	Alexander the Great, Ptolemy Antiochus Epiphanes	**3rd Kingdom** – Belly and thighs of Brass	Government of Jerusalem passed in succession from one Kingdom to the next, from Babylon, to Medo-Persia, to Greece, to Rome	Certain
	Rome / Byzantine	31BC - 637AD (Note the 666 years of Roman rule over Jerusalem commencing at Roman victory at Actium 31BC)	Pompey, Caesar Augustus, Herod(s), (Jesus Christ), Constantine	**4th Kingdom** – Legs of Iron		Highly probable
	Islamic Caliphate	637AD – present	Omar, Mohammed			
	Umayyad (Crusader)	750AD 1099 – 1187 (The nominal Christian rule over Jerusalem during the Crusader Kingdoms is not revealed by Dan 2. The Church, as God's 'surprise packet', was not revealed until Jesus' Ministry 600 yrs later. As Gentiles therefore, the Crusaders were still 'trampling' Jerusalem underfoot.)	King Richard I Saladin	**5th Kingdom** – Feet of Iron & Clay part 1	1260 years from Islamic reign over Jerusalem to Herzl's proclamation	Speculative
	Ottoman / Turkish	1517 - 1917				
1897 – Herzl's pronouncement – the Israel clock begins to tick						
	British Mandate / Islamic Waqf	1917 – 1948	Balfour, Churchill, Bevin	**6th Kingdom** – Feet of Iron & Clay part 2		Speculative
	Jordan	1948 - 1967			Jerusalem divided by the Jordanian army	Speculative
State of Israel	Islamic Waqf	1967 - present			Jerusalem re-united after Israel's victory in the 6 Day War. Israel now a sovereign nation but Temple Mount still under Islamic Waqf i.e. 'trampled' by Genties.	Certain

'Times of the Gentiles – Part 2: End of Gentile Dominion over Jerusalem' is found in Chapter 5

CHAPTER TWO

How confident can we be that the feet of iron and clay correspond to the Islamic nations? It is certainly an historical reality that Roman dominion over Jerusalem was succeeded by Islam. My view is that we can attach a high degree of probability to this assumption.

Little is known from reliable primary historical sources from this period, but around 691AD the Caliph Abd el-Malik built the Dome of the Rock. It was originally constructed to protect the sacred foundation stone, but now dedicated to the  Islamic deity on the site of the Temple Mount. It is the third most holy site of Islam. The Shrine remains in situ today and the Waqf (Muslim Religious Authority) retains control over the Temple Mount. This authority had carried over from Ottoman times and was recognised by the British Mandatory government, who concurred in the status quo that the Temple Mount belonged to the Moslems. Jews are still prohibited from any religious activity there, for example prayer,[7] or blowing the Shofar as part of Rosh Hashanah and Yom Kippur. When Israel was victorious in the Six Day War in 1967, it captured the Temple Mount and the Israeli flag was lifted on top of the Dome for just two hours, but then removed. Moshe Dayan, Defence Minister at the time, decided that the Waqf should retain control of this hotly contested site. Consequently, Jerusalem is still 'trampled down' by Gentiles and thus the 'times of the Gentiles' remain today. The Dome of the Rock is the physical symbol of this 'treading down' and whilst it stands those 'times' cannot be considered to have been fulfilled. It is clear that we should watch any developments on the Temple Mount closely.

---

7. Any religious Jews today who visit the Temple Mount are followed around and observed to ensure that their lips are not moving in silent prayer. If detected, they are forcibly removed and may be prosecuted. The advice from Israel's Chief Rabbinate is not to visit, to avoid the possibility of standing on and defiling the place where the Holy of Holies once stood. This has resulted in surprisingly few Jews visiting the Mount (approximately 8,000 in 2012). However, the position seems to be softening amongst other less orthodox Rabbis, and this shift is resulting in a gradual increase in visits. Moshe Feiglin is one of a small number of Members of the Knesset who are also trying to encourage Jews to visit and claim back their heritage.

Chapter Two

Figure 12. The Dome of the Rock

In the succession of Kingdoms and Empires shown above, Israel's autonomy over her own affairs was subject to foreign powers. In effect Israel required permission for any action from her occupier, whether they be Roman, Arabic or British. Today, Israel is a free sovereign state, yet Jerusalem remains trampled by Gentile Islamic authority over its most holy place. Furthermore, there is a limit to what Israel can and cannot do today, particularly with reference to Jerusalem. At the time of writing, the United Nations General Assembly for example, has passed some 224 Resolutions concerning Israel and the UN Security Council over 130 resolutions.[8] We will return to the treading down of the Holy Place later.

Jerusalem has never at any time in history been the capital city of any country other than the nation State of Israel. It is also true that under the dominion of every other nation Jerusalem has generally languished into disrepair and decay. Under Jewish rule, she has always been cherished, restored and has prospered.

Jerusalem was (and still is) special to the Lord Jesus Christ. He said of it:

---

8. It is interesting to watch how the UN, US government, and European Union react when the Israeli government builds homes in its capital city. This is a clear sign as to Jerusalem's pivotal role in future events.

CHAPTER TWO

Jerusalem, Jerusalem, who kills the prophets and stones those who are sent to her! How often I wanted to gather your children together, the way a hen gathers her chicks under her wings, and you were unwilling. Behold, your house is being left to you desolate! For I say to you, from now on you will not see Me until you say, 'Blessed is He who comes in the name of the Lord!

Matthew 23.37

So why did the God of Israel allow Gentile dominion over Jerusalem and its house, to become desolate? The answer is that Jerusalem's destruction was self-imposed. When Israel came under the Law at Sinai, the children of Israel came into a Covenant relationship with Jehovah. The Lord agreed that they would be His children, and that He would bless them and provide for them if they followed His Laws. The people of Israel agreed to take upon themselves blessings for obedience and curses for disobeying His commandments. Their continual, persistent and wilful disobedience resulted in the triggering of the curse that they themselves had spoken.

We need to look at the blessings and curses in Leviticus 26.18. Here the Lord is speaking to the children of Israel and states:

If also after these things **you do not obey Me**, *then I will punish you* **seven times more** *for your sins*

Are these seven times a reference to successive Gentile kingdoms that would tread Jerusalem down? It is a possibility. The way the above table has been divided possibly shows six nations or Empires trading down Jerusalem:

- Babylon
- Medo-Persia
- Greece
- Rome
- Ottoman / Islamic
- British / Islamic

This leaves room for a seventh phase of punishment in the future to do with the Antichrist. We can only speculate about this, and will examine this more closely in

69

Chapter 9.

We will come back to Leviticus 26 in Chapter 8, when we consider Israel's right to the land.

Two sets of 1260 Years

We often find numerical symmetry in the Bible. In the table, we can see an interesting example. We note that there are 1260 years from the commencement of Babylonian rule over Jerusalem to the end of the Roman rule. If we then move forward in history another 1260 years we come to 1897. Any Christian Zionist will recognise the importance of this date.

In August 1897 the 1st Zionist Conference took place in Basle, Switzerland. Theodore Herzl presided over it and wrote in his diary 'At Basle, I founded the Jewish State. If I said this out loud today, I would be greeted by universal laughter. Perhaps in 5 years and certainly in 50, everyone will know it'. Fifty years from 1897 takes us to 1947, the date that the British Mandate over Palestine ended. This was a significant year for the fledgling State of Israel, and the 'times of the Gentiles'.

Our two sets of 1260 contain further interest:

> 1260 x 2 = 2520. 2520 is also the product of 7 x 360. There were 360 days in the Lunar or Zodiacal year as calculated in ancient Middle-Eastern history. Hold that thought.

The Bible normally considers the word 'times' as a number of years (e.g. Daniel 4:25, 7:25, 9:24-27 and 12:7). Lev 26.18 (above) also speaks of seven times of punishment. Is it possible though that these 'times' are years of 360 days, or periods of 360 years? I am uncertain but do find it of interest. Make your own mind up.

A further reason for the judgment on Jerusalem is that the Jews pronounced a curse on themselves at Jesus' trial:

> *Pilate said to them, 'Then what shall I do with Jesus who is called Christ?' They all said, 'Crucify Him!' And he said, 'Why, what evil has He done?' But they kept shouting all the more, saying, 'Crucify Him!' When Pilate saw that he was accomplishing nothing, but rather that*

a riot was starting, he took water and washed his hands in front of the crowd, saying, 'I am innocent of this Man's blood; see to that yourselves.'

And all the people said, **'His blood shall be on us and on our children!'**
Matthew 27.22-25

Words have power, then as now, and this self-imposed curse has resonated down the history of the Jewish people.

In summary then, we see how Jesus' prophecies concerning both the destruction of the Temple and the captivity and dispersion of the Jewish people, were specifically, literally and accurately fulfilled. This was not figurative language. In His 'near term' prophecy He had provided His followers with advice about what to do when they saw the Roman armies surrounding Jerusalem. They acted upon this and escaped. How much more should we study and seek to understand His words regarding the longer term prophetic warning describing the affairs of the end of the age?

This is precisely what His disciples did when they asked Jesus their questions.

Part 2 – The disciples' questions to Jesus

On hearing Jesus' prophecy concerning the destruction of the Temple, the disciples ask Him a number of questions. They sense things are coming to a climax with Jesus' ministry but seem unclear about what is going to happen.

In order to fully understand Jesus' response, we must properly consider:

- who asked the question ?
- when was the question asked ?
- where was it asked ?
- what was the question about ?

Chapter Two

The disciples' questions

	The Public Prophecy Luke 21	The Private Prophecy Matt 24 / Mark 13
Who asked?	'some' of the disciples (v5)	Peter, James, John & Andrew (Mark 13.3)
When asked?	earlier in the day	later in the day
Where asked?	in the Court of Women	on the Mount of Olives
Question #1	'when therefore will these things happen?'	'when will these things happen?' (It is possible this could be a separate sixth question, relating to the things Jesus had said earlier in the Temple i.e. 'when will the (end-time events) be?')
Question #2	'what *will* be the sign when these things are about to take place?'	
Question #3		'what *will* be the sign of Your coming?'
Question #4		'(what will be the sign) of the end of the age?'
Question #5		'what will be the sign when all these things are going to be fulfilled?'

Let us consider each of these questions....

Questions 1 & 2 asked in the temple focus on the phrase 'these things'. This is a clear and definite reference to Jesus' comments about the destruction of the Temple in AD70, and He answers them in detail in Luke 21.12-24. These questions were asked by 'some' of the disciples (Luke 21.5) i.e. a larger and more general group, but it is likely that Peter, James, John and Andrew, as part of the twelve, were present. They would also have had time to ponder the statement Jesus' had made two days earlier that:

> *the days will come upon you when your enemies will throw up a barricade against you, and surround you and hem you in on every side, and they will level you to the ground and your children within you, and they will not leave in you one stone upon another, because you did not recognize the time of your visitation.*
>
> Luke 19.43-44

These four disciples would have understood that not only was Jesus teaching them about the destruction of the Temple, but also about the events prior to His return. Consequently their questions (3, 4 & 5) asked later on the Mount of Olives were looking for more detailed information specifically about Jesus' return and the events at the end of the age. The questions on the Mount of Olives in Matthew and Mark therefore focus here. Looking at them again with this in mind:

- 'when will *these things* happen?' – 'these things' could refer to the sacking of Jerusalem, but could now also equally refer to the context of Jesus' return.
- 'what will be the sign of *your coming*?'
- 'what will be the sign of the *end of the age*?'
- 'what will be the sign when *all these things are going to be fulfilled*?'

Jesus now responds in private (and in greater detail) to these more enlightened and focused end-time questions with this small group of His trusted disciples. It is also interesting to note that with the exception of the parable of the fig tree, the end-time parables are confined to this group and not shared with the wider audience publicly earlier in the Temple.

The Fig Tree will be considered in Part 3 below. The 'sheep and goat nations' will be considered in Chapter 12. The remaining advice and parables concern how those living in the end-times should respond, and are discussed in Chapter 13.

These five parables together with the teaching on 'days of Noah' and 'sheep & goat nations' are in response to questions 3, 4 and 5. They have nothing to do with the sacking of Jerusalem in AD70 and are in relation to the end of the age.

Now we understand the premise of the questions, we may progress to see how Jesus addressed them.

Part 3 – Jesus' End-Time prophecy and His Return

The accounts in Matthew, Mark and Luke all describe a time when Jerusalem will be surrounded by armies. But is the siege described in Matt 24.9-20 and Mark 13.9-17 the same siege as Luke 21.12-24? The short answer is no.

At face value, the siege of Jerusalem in Luke seems to be the same as described in

Chapter Two

Matthew and Mark. However, further study shows that we are actually seeing two different events. There are three arguments that support this view:

- in Luke 21.12 Jesus uses the phrase *'before all these things'* i.e. *'these things'* will occur before the 'labour pains' of the end-times. Let us remember that *'these things'* refer 'back' to:

  - Jerusalem surrounded by armies
  - those in Judaea to flee
  - great distress and wrath to come upon the people
  - the people to fall by the sword
  - **the people to be led away captive into all nations**
  - **Jerusalem would be trampled by the Gentiles until the times of the Gentiles be fulfilled**

  The first four signs are similar to those described in Matthew and Mark. It is highly likely that these were characteristic of every siege of Jerusalem throughout history. However, the last two signs (highlighted in bold) are not, and are unique one-off events which by their nature could never be repeated. They took place in AD70 and will not be repeated (albeit the trampling of the Gentiles is still happening).

- If we take up the prophecy from Matthew 24.15-22 and Mark 13.14-20, Jesus identifies the Abomination of Desolation[9] as the trigger that begins the Great Tribulation (and the final siege of Jerusalem). Of this tribulation He says *'such as has not occurred **since the beginning of the world until now, nor ever will'***. Jesus could not be more emphatic that this is to be a one-off and unique end-time event. It has not happened yet, whereas the AD70 captivity / Diaspora, and sacking of Jerusalem would have happened.

- The table shown below shows that Jerusalem has been besieged at least 30 times in history. We should not be surprised that Jesus described another two distinct and separate sieges. It had happened before. It would happen again. And again.

---

9. This will discussed at length in later chapters

Various Sieges / Battles of Jerusalem

Standard Chronology date	Siege	ref
c1150	Tribe of Judah against the Jebusites,.	Judg. 1:8
c1010	David against the Jebusites	2Sam. 5:6-10; 1Chron. 11:4-7
c926	Shishak king of Egypt against Rehoboam	1Kings 14:25, 26. 2Chron. 12:2-12
c852-48	Philistines, Arabians, and Ethiopians, against Jehoram	2Chron. 21:16, 17
c793	Jehoash king of Israel, against Amaziah king of Judah	2Kings 14:13, 14
c735	Rezin king of Syria, and Pekah king of Israel, against Ahaz	2Chron. 28
c701	Sennacherib king of Assyria against Hezekiah	2Kings 24:10-16
c605-597	Nebuchadnezzar king of Babylon, against Jehoiakim	2Chron. 36:6-7
	Nebuchadnezzar, against Jehoiakim	2Chron. 36:10
	Nebuchadnezzar, against Zedekiah	2Chron. 36:17-20
c320	Ptolemy Soter king of Egypt, against the Jews	
c201	Antiochus the Great,	
c199	Scopus a general of Alexander	
c167	Antiochus IV Epiphanes	Foretold Dan. 11
c162	Antiochus V against Judas Maccabaeus	
c137	Antiochus VII against John Hyrcanus	
c63	Pompey against Aristobulus,	
39BC	Herod besieged the city with a Roman army	
70AD	Titus	Foretold Luke 21.20-24
135	The Romans against Bar-Kochba. City was obliterated, and renamed Aelia Capitolina	
614	Persian army led by Shahrbaraz against the Christian inhabitants	
636-7	The Caliph Omar against Heralius	
1098	Afdal, the Vizier of the Caliph of Egypt, besieged two rival factions of Moslems, and pillaged the city	
1099	The army of the first Crusade	
1187	Saladin for seven weeks	
1244	Kharezmian Tartar hordes captured and plundered the city	
1834	Arab rebels march on Ibrahim Pasha	
1917	British General Allenby against Ottoman army	
1948	Jordanian Army against new State of Israel resulting in divided city	
1967	Jordanian army against Israel – Israel won and city was re-united	

CHAPTER TWO

General Note on Chronology

Since Christ came it has been relatively straightforward to identify dates for historical events, based on the BC and AD notations, working forward or back to the fixed point in history of His birth. However, before His birth it was trickier, as clearly, historians in the 'BC' period would not have known He was going to be born and would lack this absolute fixed point to work towards. The subject of chronology in pre-history (before Christ) is hotly debated amongst historians and archaeologists.

The Christian has three potential systems on which to base the dating of events in the ancient history of the Middle East:

- **Internal Bible Chronology** – the Bible contains a significant amount of information about the timing and duration of events. Theologians such as Bishop Ussher have built whole chronologies from this information. I have to say that some of these are more reliable than others. I have found the work of EW Bullinger particularly thought-provoking and detailed. Whilst I wholly accept the authority and accuracy of scripture, we need to treat its *interpretation* by well-meaning individuals with a certain caution. Bullinger for example had to anchor his chronology to the historical calendar of the late 19th / early 20th centuries, since when knowledge has advanced significantly.

- Most professional historians and archaeologists base their studies on the **Standard Chronology of the Ancient Near East.** This system is based on certain 'anchors', or events in which there is a level of confidence. However, from time to time, the basis of this timeline is challenged and amended when better, more reliable information emerges. This standard chronology is the consensus of the professional 'Establishment' and clearly evolves over time.

- A more recent system is the **New Chronology**. A group of archaeologists and historians has proposed that the timeline of ancient Egyptian chronology has been miscalculated by over 300 years and cite evidence from a wide variety of written and physical sources. The writings and TV documentaries of David Rohl are a good place to start as an introduction to this system. His findings actually confirm much internal Bible chronology, allowing for example the identification of Joseph's tomb in Egypt, and both Saul and David (whose existence are questioned by those using the standard chronology). I am very much persuaded by this approach. At the time of this thinking, Rohl was not a Christian, and had certainly not developed the New Chronology to justify any religious belief on his part, yet found himself able to explain certain chronological discrepancies that had been raised by more traditional Bible critics. In effect, those using the standard chronology were looking 'in the right places' but 'at the wrong time' or archaeological level in the ground. If I may get technical for a moment, their stratigraphical assumptions were wrong.

One can imagine the level of academic debate around these dating systems. Disdainful secular historians and archaeologists like to discredit Bible-based dating systems, whilst 'creationists' claim the planet is only 6,000[10] years old. The New Chronology too has come in for criticism from the Establishment. I believe actually in all three 'systems', but my final authority is my Bible and I am unaware of any historical or archaeological evidence that has yet disproved it. Since the Age of Enlightenment,[11] the majority of scientific academics look down on Bible-based thinking. They will not take it seriously, and actually consider it a threat to their credibility.

End-Time Prophetic Sequence

Let us now start to address and summarise the end-time chronology prophesied by Jesus. With the exception of the Book of Revelation (which we will consider in Chapters 3 & 4 and elsewhere) this is the longest prophecy in the New Testament. A cursory look shows use of terms such as 'when', 'then', 'immediately after', 'these things must come first' and so forth. The events described are sequential and each

---

10. This figure was calculated by Ussher by adding the lives of the genealogies from Adam to Jesus, then calculating forwards. There are a number of problems around this thinking however. One is the so-called 'Gap' theory, which holds that there is an unspecified period of time, potentially many millions of years, between Genesis 1.1 and 1.2. This provides plenty of time from the Creation to the advent of man for dinosaurs, for example. The other uncertainty we face is the length of the seven days of creation. Are they 24 hours, or (more probably) a much longer but less specific period of time?
11. The Age of Enlightenment took place in the 17th-18th centuries, where intellectuals sought to reform thinking based on scientific method. It was strongly sceptical of any faith-based thinking, and prevails in academia and education today. It is as if one can believe in science, or faith, but not both. As a Christian, I do believe in science, but where the Bible differs, it is placed first.

Chapter Two

is dependent upon the start or completion of a preceding activity. They form an obvious schedule and have been described as the 'Spine of Biblical Prophecy' by Bible scholars. The fact that we have a '3D' image from the 3 gospel accounts ties down the level of certainty still further.

When building a reliable project schedule, a project manager will normally begin by identifying all the discrete activities associated with the project. Once this is achieved, the next step is to establish the relationship between them by asking certain questions: which is first? Which comes last? How do they relate to each other? and how long does each event last?

The student of end-time prophecy must take the same disciplined approach.[12] We have the most reliable source for our thinking. Jesus is not called *Alpha* and *Omega*[13] for no reason. He is the First and the Last and He has identified the fundamental building blocks for our schedule. It is clear, simple, and reveals an obvious series of consecutive signs that we are to look for. Once fixed in place, other sources may then be added to supplement the picture. It would be a major error to start with these other scriptural sources and attempt to fit the spine onto these signs. This would allow the tail to wag the dog, create error and confusion, and require us to force discrepancies into place. If we rightly divide God's word, we will never have to 'shoe-horn' events into a sequence. Like the pieces of a well-made jigsaw, they will drop easily and neatly into place.

Read from first to last, the Spine provides us with a clear and definite sequence of events. These are summarised below. The prophecies from Matthew and Mark have been combined, as they are sourced from the same discourse on the Mount of Olives. Where Luke describes the same event, this has been aligned according to the same '4 Laws' defined in Chapter 1.

---

12. This lack of discipline accounts for much of today's popular literature on eschatology, where cutting and pasting to fit preconceived ideas can 'explain' almost any order of events. Usually, in my experience, the order chosen is the one that will sell the most books!
13. The first and last letters of the Greek alphabet. Even the word alphabet is taken from the Hebrew letters for A and B

Chapter Two

The Spine: basic sequence of end-time prophetic events

	1st Prophecy Given earlier in the Temple courts Luke 21		**2nd Prophecy** Given later on Mount of Olives Matt 24 & Mark 13			
	Luke		Matt		Mark	
See Ch 6	8-11a	**(beginning of Sorrows)** • False Christs • War / State of disorder • Ethnic conflict • earthquakes • Famine • Pestilence	4-8	**beginning of Sorrows** • False Christs #1 • Wars • Ethnic conflict • Earthquakes • Famine • Pestilence	5-8	S O R R O W S
		(Luke does not describe these events as 'the beginning of sorrows' or labour pains; however they are identical in nature and order to those described in Matthew and Mark.)				
	11b	• fearful sights (Greek: *Phobetron*. The 'Phobetron' will be explained in detail in Chapter 10) • great signs from heaven				P H O B E T R O N
See Ch 2	12-24	**(PARENTHESIS)** *'Before all these things…'* i.e. the events leading up to the Roman destruction of Jerusalem in AD70 • Religious persecution • Betrayal • Martyrdom • Hated by all • Jerusalem surrounded by armies • Days of vengeance • Killed by the edge of the sword • Led away captive • Jerusalem trampled by Gentiles until "Times of Gentiles" fulfilled				

Chapter Two

	1st Prophecy Given earlier in the Temple courts Luke 21			2nd Prophecy Given later on Mount of Olives Matt 24 & Mark 13			
	Luke			Matt		Mark	
See Ch 10				9-14	**Tribulation #1** • Tribulation • Martyrdom • Hated by all nations • Many offended, betraying & hating • False prophets & deception #2 • Lawlessness abounds • Agape / love of many grows cold • Gospel goes world-wide	9-13	T R I B U L A T I O N
See Ch 10				15-20	**Tribulation #2** • abomination of desolation in the Holy place	14-18	
See Ch 10				21-28	**Tribulation #3** • unparalleled worldwide, severe trouble • false Christs / prophets #3 now with great supernatural signs	19-23	
See Ch 10	11b & 25-26	**Tribulation #4** • signs in the Sun • signs in the Moon • signs in the stars Worldwide distress Sea / waves roaring Fearful heart attacks Powers of heaven shaken		29	**Tribulation #4** • Sun darkened • Moon dimmed • Stars fall Powers of heaven shaken	24-25	
See Ch 12	27	**Return of Christ** • Son of Man returns with power and great glory		30-31	**Return of Christ** • Sign of the Son of Man appears • all tribes of earth will mourn • Son of Man returns with power and great glory His elect are gathered	26-27	R E T U R N

The above table gives us our first full view of the foundational chronology of the end-times:

THE SPINE:

> **Beginning of sorrows / birth pangs / labour pains**
>
> **Phobetron**
>
> **Tribulation part #1 - Martyrdom**
>
> **Tribulation part #2: The Abomination of Desolation**
>
> **Tribulation phase #3 – worldwide persecution**
>
> **Tribulation #4 - signs in the heavens**
>
> **The Return of Christ**

We will consider 'progress' against each of these areas in Chapter 6.

The Fig Tree

The parable of the Fig Tree is a separate thought from Jesus' end-time schedule given in the preceding verses. It is meant to provide us with a different perspective of the end-times.

As I write, it is spring time and I have planted nearly 100 trees over the winter: apple, pear, ash, hazel and willow amongst others. When trees are not in leaf, it is difficult to tell them apart. However, once the leaves on my trees started to appear, each showed a distinctive shape and colour that were typical to and characteristic of that type of tree, thus revealing its identity. It is now possible to tell one type from another. The seasonal change in temperature and moisture, together with the tree's internal 'clock' have stimulated it to put forth its leaves, some earlier (as hazel), and some later (as ash).

Chapter Two

Figure 13. Unripe Figs from Israel.

Trees have significance in scripture. The fig tree is used as a type of Israel's national privileges.[14] When Jesus talks of the fig tree *'putting forth its leaves'*, He is saying that Israel, coming from a time of concealed dormancy, is starting to come to life and reveal its identity. On May 14th 1948, after a vote at the United Nations and a 'dormancy' of some 1900 years, Israel became a nation again. No nation has ever been recreated in such fashion, nor ever shall, and it is unique to Israel. The emergence of Israel is a miracle in itself, a plain sign for all those who are willing to see. Those who have no wish to see will remain blind to God's purposes. The present-day media for example claim that the nation of Israel is a mere 60 years old. God sees it differently.

Isaiah 66.8 states:

> *Who has heard such a thing? Who has seen such things?* ***Can a land be born in one day?*** *Can a nation be brought forth all at once? As soon as Zion travailed, she also brought forth her sons*

Israel was truly born in one day.

---

14. Mentioned some 38 times in the Bible, the context of fig trees is always associated with Israel, and normally to demonstrate God's provisions to Israel (food and shelter), but also His judgements upon her.

It is interesting that a few days before this prophecy was given Jesus had cursed the fig tree[15] when it had provided no fruit for him. The disciples were amazed at this display of Jesus' judgmental power. They had seen little of this aspect of His nature over the previous three years. This was a foretaste of what was to happen to Israel as a nation and what could happen to other nations who fail to produce fruit to satisfy Him. The event would still be very much fresh in the disciples' minds as Jesus gave His prophecy, and is surely linked.

Most fig trees produce new fruit twice a year. New shoots fruit in the spring and are usually harvested in the summer. The second showing of fruit appears in late summer and is normally ready for harvest the following spring. It was this second (spring) crop that Jesus was looking for when He cursed the tree.

Jesus now uses the phrase *'and all the trees'*. This term 'trees' is figurative for other nations, so we need to look for the emergence of more nations in the same season of Israel's re-appearance i.e. the mid 20th century.

We will start the 'clock' in 1897, with Herzl's pronouncement of a future State of Israel. I suggest that this is the point at which the 'Israel clock' started to tick again, after nearly 2000 years in abeyance. From the year 1900 to the present day, a total of 164 new nations declared independent statehood. Before World War 2, only 14 had appeared, whilst between 1948 and 2011, 131 more nations had emerged. This represents a strongly significant rise in nationhood, and the correlation of these 'trees' to the emergence of the 'fig tree' in 1947/48 is astonishing.

This rise in the emergence of nations is of further interest to us. The vast majority of these nations came out of the demise of two principal empires, the British and the Soviet. Both set themselves in opposition to the fledgling State of Israel.[16] It is outside the scope of this book to explore this topic, but the facts are well documented. In Genesis, the Lord God promises to Abraham that those who blessed him would be blessed, and those who cursed him would be cursed. He further promised through the prophet Zechariah that those who meddle with Jerusalem would be severely bruised. History confirms this warning.

As a patriotic Englishman it grieves my heart to see the decline of my country.

---

15. Matthew 21.19
16. In fact the USSR actually voted for the creation of Israel in 1947, but only to embarrass the UK and USA. Its activity has been generally hostile though throughout the 20th century.

Chapter Two

But I am not surprised and it will continue unless there is repentance on a national scale. British Zionists certainly encouraged the re-establishment of Israel in the nineteenth century, but with the coming of men like Ernest Bevin the policy changed. That prejudice against Israel is deep-seated and prevails today in UK government policy and attitude.

Another force however was at work in Britain. In the latter part of the 20th Century the British Church, once a friend of Israel and the Jews, turned against her. The Church of England and Methodist Church now effectively treat Zionism as a political crime against the Palestinians. They forget that their Saviour was (and still is) a Jew, who dwelt in the so-called 'West Bank' of Judaea, Samaria and Jerusalem. Thankfully some fellowships within these denominations are pro-Israel, but these are very much in the minority.

Both the British government and Church are together committed to the creation of a Palestinian State in Judaea and Samaria, and the division of Jerusalem. Britain is now reaping what she has sown. The irony is that as she tries to divide Jerusalem, she herself is being divided

- politically, through ineffective, weak and confused government, where no political party has a clear mandate from the electorate

- nationally, through the devolution of the Scottish and Welsh Parliaments / Assemblies and

- ethnically, through uncontrolled immigration and the imposition of a de facto state of Sharia Law from the UK's highly influential Muslim community.

I find it interesting that what Britain plans for Israel (i.e. to become an Arab State under Sharia Law) is happening to her. The first chapter of Proverbs describes how what we intend for others will come upon us. Jesus commanded us to do to others what we would have them do for us. It is the Royal Law and has consequences. Any nation that plans evil towards Israel should take note of the British example. We reap what we sow and America needs to watch and learn. I fear it is already too late for the UK.

CHAPTER TWO

We have now established a firm foundation for our prophetic panorama. It is now time to open the Book of Revelation.

Chapter Two

Chapter 3   The Revelation of Jesus Christ

I, John, your brother and fellow partaker in the tribulation and kingdom and perseverance which are in Jesus, was on the island called Patmos because of the word of God and the testimony of Jesus

Revelation 1.9

Figure 14. John on Patmos.

Part 1 – Patmos 96AD

Patmos is a small, mountainous island in the Aegean Sea some 35 miles off the western coast of modern-day Turkey. This was the setting for the Book of Revelation, the longest prophecy of the New Testament.

The fathers of the early church are unanimous that it was written by John,[1] the

---

1. Attested by Melito 170AD, Eusebius and Irenaeus 180AD, Clement of Alexandria 200AD, Tertullian 220AD, Origen 233AD,

CHAPTER THREE

disciple whom Jesus loved.[2] Now, nearly 70 years after His ascension, Jesus would reveal a stunningly detailed vision of the future to this old man. This was the same John who had spent that final afternoon on Olivet with His Lord and Saviour and been briefed there on the events of the end-time. It is likely that John would by now have been the oldest and last surviving of the Apostles, and would therefore be the final remaining eye-witness to the Cross, resurrection and ascension.

The Church historian Eusebius informs us that Revelation was written down around 96AD, at the close of the reign of the Emperor Domitian. This was 26 years after Jerusalem had been laid waste by Titus, an event John knew that Jesus had prophesied. Vespasian had died in 79AD, at which point his son Titus became Caesar. Domitian was Vespasian's second son, and succeeded Titus after Titus' brief reign ended with his death in 81AD. Domitian was a cruel and ruthless tyrant and was murdered in 96, but not before he had initiated the second great persecution of the Christians,[3] which had probably resulted in John's exile to Patmos.

Emperor	Ruled
Vespasian	AD69-79
Titus	AD79-81
Domitian	AD81-96

Patmos is an interesting location for the recording of the Revelation, due to its relative proximity to seven churches just across the sea on the mainland. The old man John was in the Spirit when he became the first human to preview the end of days. Of all living believers at that time, he was the best qualified to receive it. Others such as Isaiah[4] and Ezekiel[5] had found themselves in this heavenly state, but yet none had seen what John now saw. The Revelation (Greek: *apokalypsis*) is an unveiling, or disclosure of something that could not otherwise have been known. It was addressed to the seven churches and was sent from the Head of the Church, Jesus Christ. It is, quite simply, a blueprint for the end of the age.

You will find below the whole Book of Revelation. The text is based on the King James Version with nothing added or taken away, with the exception of selective sub-headings to highlight particular sections that we will be addressing. It has

---

    and Hippolytus 240AD
2. John 20.2
3. The first had been under Nero (64-68AD) and is traditionally associated with the deaths of Peter and Paul
4. Isaiah 6.1
5. Ezekiel 1.26

been edited only to adjust the old English words to the more modern versions e.g. *readeth* becomes *reads*.

Bible manuscripts over the last 800 years were broken into chapters and verses. These did not appear in the original manuscript, but were added later by Stephen Langton (chapters in the 13th Century) and Stephanus (verses in the 16th Century). Whilst they are convenient for quick reference, these artificially introduced breaks can often mislead, disrupt the flow and tend to encourage us to read a few verses rather than longer portions of scripture. It is also worth noting that the original Greek texts do not use punctuation, so these arbitrary additions are based on human judgement, not Divine authority. The version you are about to read removes these breaks, formats the book into logical sections and (hopefully) improves the punctuation.

The various section breaks reflect my own interpretation of the passages. The letters to the churches, seals, trumpets and bowls have been presented as tables.[6] You will note that there are passages which seem to interrupt the seals, trumpets and bowls. These are believed to be parenthetical (i.e. in brackets). I have highlighted these passages by placing a line across the page and starting and finishing them in a larger font. Each has a particular message for us.

Obvious lists have been indented. This reveals various patterns of numbers and allows us to understand more readily. If you look carefully you will find more.

You can form your own opinion as to whether my formatting is helpful. Maybe you could produce your own version from one of the many computer-based Bible texts. All I would warn is that you should be careful to add or remove nothing:

> *if anyone adds to them, God will add to him the plagues which are written in this book; and if anyone takes away from the words of the book of this prophecy, God will take away his part from the tree of life and from the holy city, which are written in this book*
>
> Rev 22.18-19

Before you start to read, let us consider a few keys to help your understanding. As mentioned above, Revelation is a book of numerical patterns, the most predominant of these being 7, 10 and 12 in the occurrence of individual words, lists and numbers.

---

[6]. Bear in mind when you read the tables that text flows from the bottom of one column to the top of the next, and that some columns span a number of pages

Chapter Three

What does this tell us?

The Number Seven: (Hebrew: *shevah*) and based on the word *savah* which means to be full, satisfied or be sufficient. It is interesting that *El Shaddai* means the 'all sufficient God'. These words begin with the Hebrew letter 'shin' ש which is used to denote God's name. A Jewish priest will form this shape with his hands when commanding the priestly blessing.[7] The shape of ש also maps perfectly onto a plan view of the Tyropaean, Hinnom and Kidron valleys of Jerusalem, 'I have chosen Jerusalem that My name might be there[8]. The Sabbath (Hebrew: Shabbat) is taken from the same root, and speaks of God's rest when He had created the heavens and earth, and was fully satisfied that it was perfect and complete. Nothing could be added or removed without somehow spoiling it. Seven, therefore, speaks of

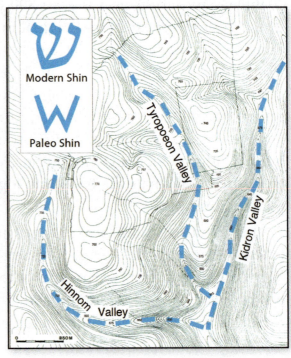

Figure 15. The Valleys of Jerusalem and the Name of God.

perfection or completion. It is no coincidence then that Revelation completes the Canon. It is fascinating also that there are seven colours in the spectrum and seven notes on the musical scale. You can't improve or add to either without spoiling them. One example of the occurrence of seven in Revelation is that we are presented with seven titles of Christ:

- 1.13 and 14.14 as 'The Son of Man'

- 1.8 as 'The Almighty'

- 3.8 and 22.6 as 'The Lord God'

---

7. Star Trek's Mr Spock (the Jewish actor Leonard Nimoy) performs a single-handed version of this blessing with the words "live long and prosper"!
8. See Ezra 6.12; 2 Chronicles 6.6

- 1.11 & 17, 2.8 and 22.13 as 'The First and the Last'
- 1.5 as 'The Ruler (or Prince) of the Kings of the Earth'
- 1.4 as 'The Coming One'
- 1.18 as 'The Living One'

The Number Ten: Ten starts a new sequence of numbers. It signifies completeness or perfection of Divine order, where nothing is found to be missing. Examples include the 10 Commandments and the 10 clauses of the Lord's Prayer (which we will consider in Chapter 13).

The Number Twelve: Twelve is associated with governmental perfection or completeness, and is concerned with ruling. Jesus had twelve apostles and there were twelve tribes of Israel. The Sun rules the earth's twelve hours of day; the Moon and stars rule the twelve hours of the night. Twelve is the product of 4 x 3, where four is earthly (the four corners of the earth, the four points of the compass, the four winds) and three is the number of Divinity (God is Three yet One).

Combining insights from these three numbers provides us with a useful key to understanding Revelation: it is a book which will make the full and perfect completion of God's plan, fulfil Divine order and replace human government with His own. With this in mind, take time now to read the whole book. There is a blessing for those who do!

Chapter Three

Part 2 – The Book of Revelation

The Revelation of Jesus Christ

THE PURPOSE OF REVELATION

Which God gave unto him, to show unto his servants things which must shortly come to pass; and he sent and signified *it* by his angel unto his servant John: Who bore record of the word of God, and of the testimony of Jesus Christ, and of all things that he saw.

Blessed *is* he that:

- <u>reads</u>, and they that
- <u>hear</u> the words of this prophecy, and
- <u>keep</u> those things which are written therein

for the time *is* at hand.

John to the seven churches which are in Asia: Grace *be* unto you, and peace,

- from Him which is, and which was, and which is to come, and
- from the seven spirits which are before his throne, and
- from Jesus Christ, *who is* the
  - faithful witness, *and*
  - the first begotten of the dead, and
  - the prince of the kings of the earth

Unto Him that:

- loved us, and
- washed us from our sins in his own blood, and

- has made us kings and priests unto God and his Father;

to Him *be* glory and dominion forever and ever. Amen.

Behold, He comes with clouds, and every eye shall see Him, and they *also* which pierced Him. And all kindreds of the earth shall wail because of Him. Even so, Amen.

I am:

- Alpha and
- Omega, the
- beginning and the
- ending, says the Lord,
- which is, and
- which was, and
- which is to come,
- the Almighty.

I John, who also am your brother, and companion in tribulation, and in the kingdom and patience of Jesus Christ, was in the Isle that is called Patmos, for the word of God, and for the testimony of Jesus Christ. I was in the spirit on the Lord's day, and heard behind me a great voice, as of a trumpet, Saying, I am:

- Alpha and
- Omega, the
- first and the
- last, and

what you see, write in a book, and send it unto the seven churches which are in Asia:

- unto Ephesus, and
- unto Smyrna, and
- unto Pergamos, and
- unto Thyratira, and
- unto Sardis, and
- unto Philadelphia, and
- unto Laodicea.

And I turned to see the voice that spoke with me. And being turned, I saw seven golden candlesticks. And in the midst of the seven candlesticks *one* like unto the Son of man, clothed with a garment down to the foot, and girt about the breast with a golden girdle.

- His <u>head</u> and *his* hairs *were* white like wool, as white as snow; and
- his <u>eyes</u> *were* as a flame of fire; And
- His <u>feet</u> like unto fine brass, as if they burned in a furnace; and
- His <u>voice</u> as the sound of many waters. And
- He had in his <u>right hand</u> seven stars: and
- out of His mouth went a sharp two-edged sword: and
- His <u>countenance</u> *was* as the sun shines in his strength.

And when I saw Him, I fell at His feet as dead. And he laid His right hand upon me, saying unto me, fear not:

I am:
- the first and
- the last

I am:

- He that lives, and
- was dead, and behold

I am alive for evermore, Amen. And:

- have the keys of hell and of death.

Write the:

- things which you have seen, and the
- things which are, and the
- things which shall be hereafter

The mystery of the seven stars which you saw in my right hand, and the seven golden candlesticks. The seven stars are the angels of the seven churches, and the seven candlesticks which you saw are the seven churches.

Chapter Three

The letters to the churches

Unto the angel of the church of **Ephesus**	And unto the angel of the church in **Smyrna**	And to the angel of the church in **Pergamos**	And unto the angel of the church in **Thyatira**	And unto the angel of the church in **Sardis**	And to the angel of the church in **Philadelphia**	And unto the angel of the church of the **Laodiceans**
write: These things says He that holds the seven stars in His right hand, who walks in the midst of the seven golden candlesticks;	write: These things says the first and the last, which was dead, and is alive;	write: These things says He which has the sharp sword with two edges;	write: These things says the Son of God, who has His eyes like unto a flame of fire, and His feet *are* like fine brass;	write: These things says He that has the seven Spirits of God, and the seven stars	write: These things says He that is holy, He that is true, he that has the key of David, He that opens, and no man shuts; and shuts, and no man opens;	write: These things says the Amen, the faithful and true witness, the beginning of the creation of God
I know your works, and your labour, and your patience, and how you can not bear them which are evil: and you have tried them which say they are apostles, and are not, and have found them liars: And have borne, and have patience, and for my name's sake have laboured, and have not fainted.	I know your works, and tribulation, and poverty, (but you are rich) and *I know* the blasphemy of them which say they are Jews, and are not, but are the synagogue of Satan. Fear none of those things which you shall suffer: behold, the Devil shall cast *some* of you into prison, that ye may be tried; and you shall have tribulation ten days. Be faithful unto death, and I will give you a crown of life.	I know your works, and where you dwell, *even* where Satan's seat *is*: and you holds fast my name, and have not denied my faith, even in those days wherein Antipas *was* my faithful martyr, who was slain among you, where Satan dwells.	I know your works, and charity, and service, and faith, and your patience, and your works; and the last *to be* more than the first.	I know your works, that you have a name that you are alive, and are dead. Be watchful, and strengthen the things which remain, that are ready to die	I know your works: behold, I have set before you an open door, and no man can shut it: for you have a little strength, and have kept My word, and have not denied My name. Behold, I will make them of the synagogue of Satan, which say they are Jews, and are not, but do lie; behold, I will make them to come and worship before your feet, and to know that I have loved you. Because you have kept the word of my patience, I also will keep you from the hour of temptation, which shall come upon all the world, to try them that dwell upon the earth. Behold, I come quickly: hold that fast which you have, that no man take your crown.	I know your works, that you are neither cold nor hot: I would you were cold or hot. So then because you are lukewarm, and neither cold nor hot, I will spew you out of my mouth. Because you say, I am rich, and increased with goods, and have need of nothing; and know not that you are wretched, and miserable, and poor, and blind, and naked: I counsel you to buy of Me gold tried in the fire, that you may be rich; and white raiment, that you may be clothed, and *that* the shame of your nakedness do not appear; and anoint your eyes with eye salve, that you may see. As many as I love, I rebuke and chasten: be zealous therefore, and repent. Behold, I stand at the door, and knock: if any man hear My voice, and open the door, I will come in to him, and will sup with him, and he with Me.

Chapter Three

Unto the angel of the church of Ephesus	And unto the angel of the church in Smyrna	And to the angel of the church in Pergamos	And unto the angel of the church in Thyratira	And unto the angel of the church in Sardis	And to the angel of the church in Philadelphia	And unto the angel of the church of the Laodiceans
Nevertheless I have *somewhat* against you, because you have left your first love. Remember therefore from whence you are fallen, and repent, and do the first works; or else I will come unto you quickly, and will remove your candlestick out of his place, except you repent. But this you have, that you hate the deeds of the Nicolaitans, which I also hate		But I have a few things against you, because you have there those that hold the doctrine of Balaam, who taught Balak to cast a stumbling block before the children of Israel, to eat things sacrificed unto idols, and to commit fornication. So have you also them that hold the doctrine of the Nicolaitans, which thing I hate. Repent; or else I will come unto you quickly, and will fight against them with the sword of My mouth.	Notwithstanding I have a few things against you, because you suffer that woman *Jezebel*, who calls herself a prophetess, to teach and to seduce My servants to commit fornication, and to eat things sacrificed unto idols. And I gave her space to repent of her fornication; and she repented not. Behold, I will cast her into a bed, and them that commit adultery with her into great tribulation, except they repent of their deeds. And I will kill her children with death. And all the churches shall know that I am He who searches the minds and hearts, and I will give unto every one of you according to your works. But unto you I say, and unto the rest in Thyratira, as many as have not this doctrine, and which have not known the depths of Satan, as they speak; I will put upon you none other burden. But that which ye have *already* hold fast till I come.	for I have not found your works perfect before God. Remember therefore how you have received and heard, and hold fast, and repent. If therefore you shall not watch, I will come on you as a thief, and you shall not know what hour I will come upon you. You have a few names even in Sardis which have not defiled their garments; and they shall walk with me in white: for they are worthy		
He that has an ear, let him hear what the Spirit says unto the churches	He that has an ear, let him hear what the Spirit says unto the churches;	He that has an ear, let him hear what the Spirit says unto the churches;				
To him that overcomes will I give to eat of the tree of life, which is in the midst of the paradise of God.	He that overcomes shall not be hurt of the second death.	To him that overcomes will I give to eat of the hidden manna, and will give him a white stone, and in the stone a new name written, which no man knows saving he that receives *it*.	And he that overcomes, and keeps My works unto the end, to him will I give power over the nations: And he shall rule them with a rod of iron; as the vessels of a potter shall they be broken to shivers: even as I received of my Father. And I will give him the morning star.	He that overcomes, the same shall be clothed in white raiment; and I will not blot out his name out of the book of life, but I will confess his name before My Father, and before His angels.	Him that overcomes will I make a pillar in the temple of my God, and he shall go no more out: and I will write upon him the name of My God, and the name of the city of My God, *which is* new Jerusalem, which comes down out of heaven from my God: and *I will write upon him* my new name.	To him that overcomes will I grant to sit with Me in My throne, even as I also overcame, and am set down with My Father in his throne.
			He that has an ear, let him hear what the Spirit says unto the churches.	He that has an ear, let him hear what the Spirit says unto the churches.	He that has an ear, let him hear what the Spirit says unto the churches	He that has an ear, let him hear what the Spirit says unto the churches.

Chapter Three

After this I looked, and, behold, a door *was* opened in heaven: and the first voice which I heard *was* as it were of a trumpet talking with me which said

> "Come up here, and I will show you things which must be hereafter"

And immediately I was in the spirit, and behold

- a throne was set in heaven, and *one* sat on the throne. And He that sat was to look upon like a jasper and a sardine stone
- and *there was* a rainbow round about the throne, in sight like unto an emerald.
- And round about the throne *were* four and twenty seats: and upon the seats I saw four and twenty elders sitting, clothed in white raiment; and they had on their heads crowns of gold.
- And out of the throne proceeded lightnings and thunderings and voices
- and *there were* seven lamps of fire burning before the throne, which are the seven Spirits of God.
- And before the throne *there was* a sea of glass like unto crystal
- and in the midst of the throne, and round about the throne, *were* four beasts full of eyes before and behind. And the
    - first beast *was* like a lion, and the
    - second beast like a calf, and the
    - third beast had a face as a man, and the
    - fourth beast *was* like a flying eagle.

And the four beasts had each of them six wings about *him*, and *they were* full of eyes within, and they rest not day and night, saying,

> "Holy, holy, holy, Lord God Almighty, which was, and is, and is to come".

And when those beasts give glory and honour and thanks to him that sat on the throne, who lives forever and ever, The four and twenty elders fall down before him that sat on the throne, and worship him that lives forever and ever, and cast their crowns before the throne, saying:

> *"You are worthy, O Lord, to receive glory and honour and power: for you have created all things, and for your pleasure they are and were created".*

And I saw in the right hand of Him that sat on the throne a book written within and on the backside, sealed with seven seals. And I saw a strong angel proclaiming with a loud voice,

> *"Who is worthy to open the book, and to loose the seals thereof?"*

And no man in heaven, nor in earth, neither under the earth, was able to open the book, neither to look thereon. And I wept much, because no man was found worthy to open and to read the book, neither to look thereon. And one of the elders says unto me:

> *"Weep not. Behold, the Lion of the tribe of Judah, the Root of David, has prevailed to open the book, and to lose the seven seals thereof."*

And I beheld, and, lo, in the midst of the throne and of the four beasts, and in the midst of the elders, stood a Lamb as it had been slain, having seven horns and seven eyes, which are the seven Spirits of God sent forth into all the earth. And He came and took the book out of the right hand of Him that sat upon the throne. And when He had taken the book, the four beasts and four *and* twenty elders fell down before the Lamb, having every one of them harps, and golden bowls full of odours, which are the prayers of saints. And they sung a new song, saying,

> *"You are worthy to take the book, and to open the seals thereof: for you were slain, and have redeemed us to God by your blood out of every*
>
> - *kindred, and*
> - *tongue, and*

Chapter Three

- *people, and*
- *nation;*

And have made us unto our God kings and priests, and we shall reign on the earth".

And I beheld, and I heard the voice of many angels round about the throne and the beasts and the elders: and the number of them was ten thousand times ten thousand, and thousands of thousands; Saying with a loud voice:

"*Worthy is the Lamb that was slain to receive*

- *power, and*
- *riches, and*
- *wisdom, and*
- *strength, and*
- *honour, and*
- *glory, and*
- *blessing"*

And every creature which is in heaven, and on the earth, and under the earth, and such as are in the sea, and all that are in them, heard I saying:

- *"Blessing, and*
- *honour, and*
- *glory, and*
- *power,*

be unto

- *Him that sits upon the throne, and unto*

- *the Lamb*

forever and ever"

And the four beasts said, *"Amen"*. And the four *and* twenty elders fell down and worshipped Him that lives forever and ever.

Chapter Three

THE SIX SEALS

And I saw when the Lamb opened the...

first of the seals	second seal	third seal	fourth seal	fifth seal	sixth seal
and I heard, as it were the noise of thunder, one of the four beasts saying, Come and see.	I heard the second beast say, Come and see.	I heard the third beast say, Come and see.	I heard the voice of the fourth beast say, Come and see.	I saw under the altar the souls of them that were slain for the word of God, and for the testimony which they held:	and, lo, there was a <ul><li>great earthquake; and the</li><li>Sun became black as sackcloth of hair, and the</li><li>Moon became as blood; And the</li><li>stars of heaven fell unto the earth, even as a fig tree casts her untimely figs, when she is shaken of a mighty wind. And the</li><li>heaven departed as a scroll when it is rolled together; and every</li><li>mountain and island were moved out of their places. And the</li><li>kings of the earth, and the great men, and the rich men, and the chief captains, and the mighty men, and every bondman, and every free man, hid themselves in the dens and in the rocks of the mountains; And said to the mountains and rocks, Fall on us, and hide us from the face of him that sits on the throne, and from the wrath of the Lamb: For the great day of his wrath is come; and who shall be able to stand?</li></ul>
And I saw, and behold a white horse: and he that sat on him had a bow; and a crown was given unto him: and he went forth conquering, and to conquer. And when He had opened the	And there went out another horse *that was* red: and *power* was given to him that sat thereon to take peace from the earth, and that they should kill one another: and there was given unto him a great sword. And when He had opened the	And I beheld, and lo a black horse; and he that sat on him had a pair of balances in his hand. And I heard a voice in the midst of the four beasts say, A measure of wheat for a penny, and three measures of barley for a penny; and *see* you hurt not the oil and the wine. And when He had opened the	And I looked, and behold a pale horse: and his name that sat on him was Death, and Hell followed with him. And power was given unto them over the fourth part of the earth, to kill with sword, and with hunger, and with death, and with the beasts of the earth. And when He had opened the	And they cried with a loud voice, saying, How long, O Lord, holy and true, dost you not judge and avenge our blood on them that dwell on the earth? And white robes were given unto every one of them; and it was said unto them, that they should rest yet for a little season, until their fellow servants also and their brethren, that should be killed as they *were*, should be fulfilled. And I beheld when He had opened the	

CHAPTER THREE

THE FIRST PARENTHESIS

(And after these things I saw four angels standing on the four corners of the earth, holding the four winds of the earth, that the wind should not blow on the earth, nor on the sea, nor on any tree.

And I saw another angel ascending from the east, having the seal of the living God: and he cried with a loud voice to the four angels, to whom it was given to hurt the earth and the sea, saying

> *"Hurt not the earth, neither the sea, nor the trees, till we have sealed the servants of our God in their foreheads."*

And I heard the number of them which were sealed: *and there were* sealed a hundred *and* forty *and* four thousand of all the tribes of the children of Israel:

- Of the tribe of Judah *were* sealed twelve thousand.
- Of the tribe of Reuben *were* sealed twelve thousand.
- Of the tribe of Gad *were* sealed twelve thousand.
- Of the tribe of Aser *were* sealed twelve thousand.
- Of the tribe of Nepthalim *were* sealed twelve thousand.
- Of the tribe of Manasses *were* sealed twelve thousand.
- Of the tribe of Simeon *were* sealed twelve thousand.
- Of the tribe of Levi *were* sealed twelve thousand.
- Of the tribe of Issachar *were* sealed twelve thousand.
- Of the tribe of Zabulon *were* sealed twelve thousand.
- Of the tribe of Joseph *were* sealed twelve thousand.
- Of the tribe of Benjamin *were* sealed twelve thousand.

Chapter Three

After this I beheld, and, lo, a great multitude, which no man could number, of all

- Nations, and
- kindreds, and
- people, and
- tongues,

stood before the throne, and before the Lamb, clothed with white robes, and palms in their hands, and cried with a loud voice, saying,

"*Salvation to our God which sits upon the throne, and unto the Lamb.*"

And all the angels stood round about the throne, and *about* the elders and the four beasts, and fell before the throne on their faces, and worshipped God, Saying,

"*Amen:*

- *Blessing, and*
- *glory, and*
- *wisdom, and*
- *thanksgiving, and*
- *honour, and*
- *power, and*
- *might, be unto our God forever and ever. Amen.*"

And one of the elders answered, saying unto me, What are these which are arrayed in white robes? And where did they come from? And I said unto him, Sir, you know. And he said to me, these are they which came out of Great Tribulation, and have washed their robes, and made them white in the blood of the Lamb. Therefore they are before the throne of God, and serve him day and night in his temple, and He that sits on the throne shall dwell among them. They shall hunger no more, neither thirst anymore; neither shall the Sun light on them, nor any heat. For the Lamb which is in the midst of the throne shall feed them, and shall lead them unto living fountains of waters: and God shall wipe away all **tears from their eyes**)

THE SEVENTH SEAL

And when He had opened the...

seventh seal
there was silence in heaven about the space of half an hour
And I saw the seven angels which stood before God; and to them were given seven trumpets.
And another angel came and stood at the altar, having a golden censer; and there was given unto him much incense, that he should offer *it* with the prayers of all saints upon the golden altar which was before the throne.
And the smoke of the incense, *which came* with the prayers of the saints, ascended up before God out of the angel's hand. And the angel took the censer, and filled it with fire of the altar, and cast *it* into the earth: and there were • voices, and • thunderings, and • lightnings, and an • earthquake.

Chapter Three

THE SIX TRUMPETS

And the seven angels which had the seven trumpets prepared themselves to sound. The…

first angel sounded	second angel sounded	third angel sounded	fourth angel sounded	fifth angel sounded	sixth angel sounded
and there followed hail and fire mingled with blood, and they were cast upon the earth: and the third part of trees was burnt up, and all green grass was burnt up. And the	and as it were a great mountain burning with fire was cast into the sea: and the third part of the sea became blood; And the third part of the creatures which were in the sea, and had life, died; and the third part of the ships were destroyed. And the	and there fell a great star from heaven, burning as it were a lamp, and it fell upon the third part of the rivers, and upon the fountains of waters; And the name of the star is called Wormwood. And the third part of the waters became wormwood; and many men died of the waters, because they were made bitter. And the	and the third part of the sun was smitten, and the third part of the moon, and the third part of the stars; so as the third part of them was darkened, and the day shone not for a third part of it, and the night likewise. And I beheld, and heard an angel flying through the midst of heaven, saying with a loud voice, Woe, woe, woe, to the inhabiters of the earth by reason of the other voices of the trumpet of the three angels, which are yet to sound! And the	and I saw a star fall from heaven unto the earth: and to him was given the key of the bottomless pit. And he opened the bottomless pit; and there arose a smoke out of the pit, as the smoke of a great furnace; and the Sun and the air were darkened by reason of the smoke of the pit. And there came out of the smoke locusts upon the earth: and unto them was given power, as the scorpions of the earth have power. And it was commanded them that they should not hurt the grass of the earth, neither any green thing, neither any tree; but only those men which have not the seal of God in their foreheads. And to them it was given that they should not kill them, but that they should be tormented five months: and their torment *was* as the torment of a scorpion, when he strikes a man. And in those days shall men seek death, and shall not find it; and shall desire to die, and death shall flee from them. And the shapes of the locusts were like unto horses prepared unto battle; and on their heads *were* as it were crowns like gold, and their faces *were* as the faces of men. And they had hair as the hair of women, and their teeth were as *the teeth* of lions. And they had breastplates, as it were breastplates of iron; and the sound of their wings *was* as the sound of chariots of many horses running to battle. And they had tails like unto scorpions, and there were stings in their tails: and their power *was* to hurt men five months. And they had a king over them, *which is* the angel of the bottomless pit, whose name in the Hebrew tongue *is* Abaddon, but in the Greek tongue has *his* name Apollyon. One woe is past; *and*, behold, there come two woes more hereafter. And the	and I heard a voice from the four horns of the golden altar which is before God, Saying to the sixth angel which had the trumpet, Loose the four angels which are bound in the great river Euphrates. And the four angels were loosed, which were prepared for an hour, and a day, and a month, and a year, for to slay the third part of men. And the number of the army of the horsemen *were* two hundred thousand thousand: and I heard the number of them. And thus I saw the horses in the vision, and them that sat on them, having breastplates of fire, and of jacinth, and brimstone: and the heads of the horses *were* as the heads of lions; and out of their mouths issued fire and smoke and brimstone. By these three was the third part of men killed, by the fire, and by the smoke, and by the brimstone, which issued out of their mouths. For their power is in their mouth, and in their tails: for their tails *were* like unto serpents, and had heads, and with them they do hurt. (And the rest of the men which were not killed by these plagues yet repented not of the works of their hands, that they should not worship devils, and idols of gold, and silver, and brass, and stone, and of wood: which neither can see, nor hear, nor walk: Neither repented they of their murders, nor of their sorceries, nor of their fornication, nor of their thefts) And I saw another mighty angel come down from heaven, clothed with a cloud: and a rainbow *was* upon his head, and his face *was* as it were the sun, and his feet as pillars of fire: And he had in his hand a little book open: and he set his right foot upon the sea, and *his* left *foot* on the earth, And cried with a loud voice, as *when* a lion roars: and when he had cried, seven thunders uttered their voices. And when the seven thunders had uttered their voices, I was about to write: and I heard a voice from heaven saying unto me, Seal up those things which the seven thunders uttered, and write them not). And the angel which I saw stand upon the sea and upon the earth lifted up his hand to heaven, And swore by him that lives forever and ever, who created heaven, and the things that therein are, and the earth, and the things that therein are, and the sea, and the things which are therein, that there should be time no longer:

But in the days of the voice of the seventh angel, when he shall begin to sound, the mystery of God should be finished, as he has declared to His servants the prophets.

THE SECOND PARENTHESIS

(And the voice which I heard from heaven spoke unto me again, and said, Go *and* take the little book which is open in the hand of the angel which stands upon the sea and upon the earth. And I went unto the angel, and said unto him, Give me the little book. And he said unto me, Take *it*, and eat it up; and it shall make your belly bitter, but it shall be in your mouth sweet as honey. And I took the little book out of the angel's hand, and ate it up; and it was in my mouth sweet as honey: and as soon as I had eaten it, my belly was bitter. And he said unto me, You must prophesy again before many

- peoples, and
- nations, and
- tongues, and
- kings.

And there was given me a reed like unto a rod, and the angel stood, saying, Rise, and measure the temple of God, and the altar, and them that worship therein. But the court which is outside the temple leave out, and measure it not, for it is given unto the Gentiles. And the holy city shall they tread under foot forty and *two* months.

And I will give *power* unto My two witnesses, and they shall prophesy a thousand two hundred *and* threescore days, clothed in sackcloth. These are the two olive trees, and the two candlesticks standing before the God of the earth. And if any man will hurt them, fire proceeds out of their mouth, and devours their enemies: and if any man will hurt them, he must in this manner be killed. These have power to shut heaven, that it rain not in the days of their prophecy, and have power over waters to turn them to blood, and to smite the earth with all plagues, as often as they will.

And when they shall have finished their testimony, the beast that ascends out of the bottomless pit shall make war against them, and shall overcome them, and kill them. And their dead bodies shall lie in the street of the great city, which spiritually is called Sodom and Egypt, where also our Lord was crucified. And they of the

- people and
- kindreds and
- tongues and
- nations

shall see their dead bodies three days and an half, and shall not suffer their dead bodies to be put in graves. And they that dwell upon the earth shall rejoice over them, and make merry, and shall send gifts one to another; because these two prophets tormented them that dwelt on the earth.

And after three days and an half the Spirit of life from God entered into them, and they stood upon their feet; and great fear fell upon them which saw them. And they heard a great voice from heaven saying unto them, Come up hither. And they ascended up to heaven in a cloud; and their enemies beheld them.

And the same hour was there a great earthquake, and the tenth part of the city fell, and in the earthquake were slain of men seven thousand, and the remnant were frightened, and gave glory to the God of heaven.

The second woe is past; *and*, behold, the third woe comes quickly).

CHAPTER THREE

THE SEVENTH TRUMPET

And the

> **seventh angel sounded**
>
> and there were great voices in heaven, saying, The kingdoms of this world are become *the kingdoms* of our Lord, and of his Christ; and he shall reign for ever and ever.
>
> And the four and twenty elders, which sat before God on their seats, fell upon their faces, and worshipped God, Saying, We give you thanks, O Lord God Almighty, which are, and was, and are to come; because You have taken to You Your great power, and have reigned. And the nations were angry, and Your wrath is come, and the time of the dead, that they should be judged, and that You should give reward unto Your servants the prophets, and to the saints, and them that fear Your name, small and great; and should destroy them which destroy the earth.
>
> And the temple of God was opened in heaven, and there was seen in his temple the ark of His testament: and there were
> - lightnings, and
> - voices, and
> - thunderings, and an
> - earthquake, and
> - great hail

THE THIRD PARENTHESIS

(And there appeared a great wonder in heaven; a woman clothed with the Sun, and the Moon under her feet, and upon her head a crown of twelve stars: And she, being with child cried, travailing in birth, and pained to be delivered.

And there appeared another wonder in heaven; and behold a great red dragon, having seven heads and ten horns, and seven crowns upon his heads. And his tail drew the third part of the stars of heaven, and did cast them to the earth: and the dragon stood before the woman which was ready to be delivered, for to devour her child as soon as it was born. And she brought forth a man child, who was to rule

Chapter Three

all nations with a rod of iron: and her child was caught up unto God, and *to* his throne. And the woman fled into the wilderness, where she has a place prepared of God, that they should feed her there a thousand two hundred *and* threescore days.

And there was war in heaven. Michael and his angels fought against the dragon; and the dragon fought and his angels, and prevailed not, neither was their place found any more in heaven. And the great dragon was cast out, that old serpent, called the Devil, and Satan, which deceives the whole world. He was cast out into the earth, and his angels were cast out with him.

And I heard a loud voice saying in heaven, Now is come salvation, and strength, and the kingdom of our God, and the power of His Christ: for the accuser of our brethren is cast down, which accused them before our God day and night. And they overcame him by the blood of the Lamb, and by the word of their testimony; and they loved not their lives unto the death. Therefore rejoice, *you* heavens, and you that dwell in them. Woe to the inhabiters of the earth and of the sea! For the Devil is come down unto you, having great wrath, because he knows that he has but a short time.

And when the dragon saw that he was cast unto the earth, he persecuted the woman which brought forth the man *child*. And to the woman were given two wings of a great eagle, that she might fly into the wilderness, into her place, where she is nourished for a time, and times, and half a time, from the face of the serpent. And the serpent cast out of his mouth water as a flood after the woman, that he might cause her to be carried away of the flood. And the earth helped the woman, and the earth opened her mouth, and swallowed up the flood which the dragon cast out of his mouth. And the dragon was angry with the woman, and went to make war with the remnant of her seed, which keep the commandments of God, and have the testimony of Jesus Christ.

And I stood upon the sand of the sea, and saw a beast rise up out of the sea:

having seven heads and ten horns, and upon his horns ten crowns, and upon his heads the name of blasphemy.

And the beast which I saw was like unto

- a <u>leopard</u>, and
- his <u>feet</u> were as *the feet* of a <u>bear</u>, and
- his <u>mouth</u> as the mouth of a <u>lion</u>:

and the dragon gave him his

- power, and his
- seat, and
- great authority.

And I saw one of his heads as it were wounded to death, and his deadly wound was healed, and all the world wondered after the beast. And they worshipped the dragon which gave power unto the beast. And they worshipped the beast, saying, "Who *is* like unto the beast? Who is able to make war with him?" And there was given unto him a mouth speaking great things and blasphemies, and power was given unto him to continue forty *and* two months.

And he opened his mouth in blasphemy against God, to blaspheme

- His name, and
- His tabernacle, and
- them that dwell in heaven.

And it was given unto him to make war with the saints, and to overcome them: and power was given him over all

- kindreds, and
- tongues, and
- nations.

And all that dwell upon the earth shall worship him, whose names are not written

Chapter Three

in the Book of Life of the Lamb slain from the foundation of the world.

If any man has an ear, let him hear. He that leads into captivity shall go into captivity: he that kills with the sword must be killed with the sword. Here is the patience and the faith of the saints.

And I beheld another beast coming up out of the earth, and he had two horns like a lamb, and he spoke as a dragon.

And he

- exercises all the power of the first beast before him, and
- causes the earth and them which dwell therein to worship the first beast, whose deadly wound was healed. And he
- does great wonders, so that he makes fire come down from heaven on the earth in the sight of men, And
- deceives them that dwell on the earth by *the means of* those miracles which he had power to do in the sight of the beast, saying to them that dwell on the earth, that they should make an image to the beast, which had the wound by a sword, and did live. And he
- had power to give life unto the image of the beast, that the image of the beast should both speak, and cause that as many as would not worship the image of the beast should be killed. And he
- causes all, both small and great, rich and poor, free and bond, to receive a mark in their right hand, or in their foreheads: And that no man might buy or sell, save he that had the mark, or the name of the beast, or the number of his name. Here is wisdom. Let him that has understanding count the number of the beast: for it is the number of a man; and his number *is* Six hundred threescore *and* six.

And I looked, and, lo, a Lamb stood on the mount Zion, and with him an hundred forty *and* four thousand, having his Father's name written in their foreheads.

And I heard a voice from heaven, as the voice of many waters, and as the voice of a great thunder. And I heard the voice of harpers harping with their harps. And they sung as it were a new song before the throne, and before the four beasts, and the elders, and no man could learn that song but the hundred *and* forty *and* four thousand, which were redeemed from the earth. These are they which were not defiled with women; for they are virgins. These are they which follow the Lamb wheresoever he goes. These were redeemed from among men, *being* the first fruits unto God and to the Lamb. And in their mouth was found no guile, for they are without fault before the throne of God. And I saw another angel fly in the midst of heaven, having the everlasting gospel to preach unto them that dwell on the earth, and to every

- nation, and
- kindred, and
- tongue, and
- people,

Saying with a loud voice,

"Fear God, and give glory to him; for the hour of his judgment is come: and worship him that made heaven, and earth, and the sea, and the fountains of waters".

And there followed another angel, saying,

"Babylon is fallen, is fallen, that great city, because she made all nations drink of the wine of the wrath of her fornication".

And the third angel followed them, saying with a loud voice,

"If any man worship the beast and his image, and receives his mark in his forehead, or in his hand, the same shall drink of the wine of the wrath of God, which is poured out without mixture into the cup of his indignation. And he shall be tormented with fire and brimstone in the presence of the holy angels, and in the presence of the Lamb. And the smoke of their torment ascends up

Chapter Three

forever and ever: and they have no rest day or night, who worship the beast and his image, and whosoever receives the mark of his name.

Here is the patience of the saints: here are they that keep the commandments of God, and the faith of Jesus".

And I heard a voice from heaven saying unto me,

"Write, Blessed are the dead which die in the Lord from henceforth. Yea, says the Spirit, that they may rest from their labours; and their works do follow them".

And I looked, and behold a white cloud, and upon the cloud *one* sat like unto the Son of man, having on his head a golden crown, and in his hand a sharp sickle.

And another angel came out of the temple, crying with a loud voice to him that sat on the cloud

"thrust in your sickle, and reap, for the time is come for you to reap, for the harvest of the earth is ripe".

And he that sat on the cloud thrust in his sickle on the earth; and the earth was reaped. And another angel came out of the temple which is in heaven, he also having a sharp sickle. And another angel came out from the altar, which had power over fire, and cried with a loud cry to him that had the sharp sickle, saying,

"thrust in your sharp sickle, and gather the clusters of the vine of the earth; for her grapes are fully ripe".

And the angel thrust in his sickle into the earth, and gathered the vine of the earth, and cast *it* into the great winepress of the wrath of God. And the winepress was trodden outside the city, and blood came out of the winepress, even unto the horse bridles, by the space of a **thousand *and* six hundred furlongs)**

And I saw another sign in heaven, great and marvellous, seven angels having the seven last plagues, for in them is filled up the wrath of God. And I saw as it were a sea of glass mingled with fire: and them that had gotten the victory over the beast, and over his image, and over his mark, *and* over the number of his name, stand on the sea of glass, having the harps of God. And they sing the song of Moses the servant of God, and the song of the Lamb, saying

> *"Great and marvellous are your works, Lord God Almighty; just and true are your ways, you King of saints. Who shall not fear you, O Lord, and glorify your name? For you only are holy: for all nations shall come and worship before you; for your judgments are made manifest"*

Chapter Three

THE SEVEN BOWLS

And after that I looked, and, behold, the temple of the tabernacle of the testimony in heaven was opened. And the seven angels came out of the temple, having the seven plagues, clothed in pure and white linen, and having their breasts girded with golden girdles. And one of the four beasts gave unto the seven angels seven golden bowls full of the wrath of God, who lives forever and ever. And the temple was filled with smoke from the glory of God, and from his power, and no man was able to enter into the temple till the seven plagues of the seven angels were fulfilled. And I heard a great voice out of the temple saying to the seven angels

"Go your ways, and pour out the bowls of the wrath of God upon the earth".

And the...

Chapter Three

first	second angel	third angel	fourth angel	fifth angel	sixth angel	seventh angel
went, and poured out his bowl upon the earth; and there fell a noisome and grievous sore upon the men which had the mark of the beast, and *upon* them which worshipped his image. And the	poured out his bowl upon the sea; and it became as the blood of a dead *man*: and every living soul died in the sea. And the	poured out his bowl upon the rivers and fountains of waters; and they became blood. (And I heard the angel of the waters say, You are righteous, O Lord, which are, and was, and shall be, because You have judged thus. For they have shed the blood of saints and prophets, and You have given them blood to drink; for they are worthy. And I heard another out of the altar say, Even so, Lord God Almighty, true and righteous *are* Your judgments) And the	poured out his bowl upon the sun; and power was given unto him to scorch men with fire. And men were scorched with great heat, and blasphemed the name of God, which has power over these plagues: and they repented not to give him glory. And the	poured out his bowl upon the seat of the beast; and his kingdom was full of darkness; and they gnawed their tongues for pain, And blasphemed the God of heaven because of their pains and their sores, and repented not of their deeds. And the	poured out his bowl upon the great river Euphrates; and the water thereof was dried up, that the way of the kings of the east might be prepared. And I saw three unclean spirits like frogs *come* out of the mouth of the dragon, and out of the mouth of the beast, and out of the mouth of the false prophet. For they are the spirits of devils, working miracles, *which* go forth unto the kings of the earth and of the whole world, to gather them to the battle of that great day of God Almighty. (Behold, I come as a thief. Blessed *is* he that watches, and keeps his garments, lest he walk naked, and they see his shame). And he gathered them together into a place called in the Hebrew tongue Armageddon.) And the	poured out his bowl into the air; and there came a great voice out of the temple of heaven, from the throne, saying, It is done. And there were voices, and thunders, and lightnings; and there was a great earthquake, such as was not since men were upon the earth, so mighty an earthquake, *and* so great. And the great city was divided into three parts, and the cities of the nations fell, and great Babylon came in remembrance before God, to give unto her the cup of the wine of the fierceness of his wrath. And every island fled away, and the mountains were not found. And there fell upon men a great hail out of heaven, *every stone* about the weight of a talent, and men blasphemed God because of the plague of the hail, for the plague thereof was exceeding great

CHAPTER THREE

BABYLON

And there came one of the seven angels which had the seven bowls, and talked with me, saying unto me

> *"Come here; I will show unto you the judgment of the great whore that sits upon many waters: With whom the kings of the earth have committed fornication, and the inhabitants of the earth have been made drunk with the wine of her fornication".*

So he carried me away in the spirit into the wilderness: and I saw a woman sit upon a scarlet coloured beast, full of names of blasphemy, having seven heads and ten horns. And the woman was

- arrayed in purple and scarlet colour, and
- decked with gold and precious stones and pearls,
- having a golden cup in her hand full of abominations and filthiness of her fornication:

And upon her forehead *was* a name written, "MYSTERY, BABYLON THE GREAT, THE MOTHER OF HARLOTS AND ABOMINATIONS OF THE EARTH". And I saw the woman drunken with the blood of the saints, and with the blood of the martyrs of Jesus: and when I saw her, I wondered with great admiration.

And the angel said unto me,

> *"Why did you marvel? I will tell you the mystery of the woman, and of the beast that carries her, which has the seven heads and ten horns. The beast that you saw was, and is not; and shall ascend out of the bottomless pit, and go into perdition: and they that dwell on the earth shall wonder, whose names were not written in the book of life from the foundation of the world, when they behold the beast that was, and is not, and yet is.*

And here is the mind which has wisdom:

- *The seven heads are seven mountains, on which the woman sits.*

- *And there are seven kings:*
    - *five are fallen, and*
    - *one is, and*
    - *the other is not yet come; and when he comes, he must continue a short space.*
- *And the beast that was, and is not, even he is the eighth, and is of the seven, and goes into perdition.*
- *And the ten horns which you saw are ten kings, which have received no kingdom as yet; but receive power as kings one hour with the beast. These have one mind, and shall give their power and strength unto the beast. These shall make war with the Lamb, and the Lamb shall overcome them: for he is Lord of lords, and King of kings: and they that are with him are called, and chosen, and faithful".*

And he said to me

"The waters which you saw, where the whore sits, are

- *peoples, and*
- *multitudes, and*
- *nations, and*
- *tongues.*
- *And the ten horns which you saw upon the beast, these shall hate the whore, and shall make her desolate and naked, and shall eat her flesh, and burn her with fire. For God has put in their hearts to fulfil his will, and to agree, and give their kingdom unto the beast, until the words of God shall be fulfilled.*
- *And the woman which you saw is that great city, which reigns over the kings of the earth"*

And after these things I saw another angel come down from heaven, having great power; and the earth was lightened with his glory.

Chapter Three

And he cried mightily with a strong voice, saying:

"Babylon the great is fallen, is fallen, and is become the habitation of devils, and the hold of every foul spirit, and a cage of every unclean and hateful bird. For all nations have drunk of the wine of the wrath of her fornication, and the kings of the earth have committed fornication with her, and the merchants of the earth are waxed rich through the abundance of her delicacies".

And I heard another voice from heaven, saying:

"Come out of her, my people, that ye be not partakers of her sins, and that ye receive not of her plagues. For her sins have reached unto heaven, and God has remembered her iniquities. Reward her even as she rewarded you, and double unto her double according to her works: in the cup which she has filled fill to her double. How much she has glorified herself, and lived deliciously, so much torment and sorrow give her: for she says in her heart, I sit a queen, and am no widow, and shall see no sorrow. Therefore shall her plagues come in one day, death, and mourning, and famine; and she shall be utterly burned with fire: for strong is the Lord God who judges her. And the kings of the earth, who have committed fornication and lived deliciously with her, shall bewail her, and lament for her, when they shall see the smoke of her burning, Standing afar off for the fear of her torment, saying, Alas, alas, that great city Babylon, that mighty city! For in one hour is your judgment come. And the merchants of the earth shall weep and mourn over her; for no man buys their merchandise any more: The merchandise of

- *gold, and*
- *silver, and*
- *precious stones, and of*
- *pearls, and*
  - *fine linen, and*
  - *purple, and*

- *silk, and*
  - *scarlet, and all*
- *thyine wood, and*
- *all manner vessels of ivory, and*
- *all manner vessels of most precious wood, and of*
  - *brass, and*
  - *iron, and*
  - *marble, And*
- *cinnamon, and*
  - *odours, and*
  - *ointments, and*
  - *frankincense, and*
- *wine, and*
- *oil, and*
- *fine flour, and*
- *wheat, and*
  - *beasts, and*
  - *sheep, and*
  - *horses, and*
- *chariots, and*
  - *slaves, and*
  - *souls of men.*

Chapter Three

And the fruits that your soul lusted after are departed from you, and all things which were dainty and goodly are departed from you, and you shall find them no more at all. The merchants of these things, which were made rich by her, shall stand afar off for the fear of her torment, weeping and wailing, And saying, Alas, alas, that great city, that was clothed in

- *fine linen, and*
- *purple, and*
- *scarlet, and*
- *decked with gold, and*
- *precious stones, and*
- *pearls!*

For in one hour so great riches is come to nought. And every shipmaster, and all the company in ships, and sailors, and as many as trade by sea, stood afar off, And cried when they saw the smoke of her burning, saying, What city is like unto this great city! And they cast dust on their heads, and cried, weeping and wailing, saying, Alas, alas, that great city, wherein were made rich all that had ships in the sea by reason of her costliness, for in one hour is she made desolate. Rejoice over her, you heaven, and ye holy apostles and prophets; for God has avenged you on her".

And a mighty angel took up a stone like a great millstone, and cast it into the sea, saying:

Thus with violence shall that great city Babylon be thrown down, and shall be found no more at all.

- *And the voice of harpers, and musicians, and of pipers, and trumpeters, shall be heard no more at all in you; and*
- *no craftsman, of whatsoever craft he be, shall be found any more in you*

Chapter Three

- *and the sound of a millstone shall be heard no more at all in you*
- *And the light of a candle shall shine no more at all in you*
- *and the voice of the bridegroom and of the bride shall be heard no more at all in you*

for your merchants were the great men of the earth, for by your sorceries were all nations deceived. And in her was found the blood of prophets, and of saints, and of all that were slain upon the earth".

And after these things I heard a great voice of much people in heaven, saying:

"Alleluia; Salvation, and glory, and honour, and power, unto the Lord our God: For true and righteous are his judgments: for he has judged the great whore, which did corrupt the earth with her fornication, and has avenged the blood of his servants at her hand".

And again they said, *"Alleluia"*. And her smoke rose up forever and ever.

And the four and twenty elders and the four beasts fell down and worshipped God that sat on the throne, saying

"Amen; Alleluia".

And a voice came out of the throne, saying,

"Praise our God, all ye his servants, and ye that fear him, both small and great."

And I heard as it were the voice of a great multitude, and as the voice of many waters, and as the voice of mighty thunderings, saying:

"Alleluia, for the Lord God omnipotent reigneth. Let us be glad and rejoice, and give honour to him: for the marriage of the Lamb is come, and his wife has made herself ready. And to her was granted that she should be arrayed in fine linen, clean and white: for the fine linen is the righteousness of saints".

And he said to me

Chapter Three

> "Write, Blessed are they which are called unto the marriage supper of the Lamb"

And he said to me

> "These are the true sayings of God".

And I fell at his feet to worship him. And he said unto me

> "See you do it not. I am your fellow servant, and of your brethren that have the testimony of Jesus: worship God: for the testimony of Jesus is the spirit of prophecy".

THE RETURN OF CHRIST

And I saw heaven opened, and behold a white horse; and he that sat upon Him *was* called Faithful and True, and in righteousness he doth judge and make war.

- His <u>eyes</u> *were* as a flame of fire, and
- on His <u>head</u> *were* many crowns; and
- He had a <u>name</u> written, that no man knew, but He Himself.
- And He *was* clothed with a <u>vesture</u> dipped in blood: and His name is called The Word of God. And the armies *which were* in heaven followed Him upon white horses, clothed in fine linen, white and clean.
- And out of His <u>mouth</u> goes a sharp sword, that with it He should smite the nations
- and He shall rule them with <u>a rod of iron</u>. And He treads the winepress of the fierceness and wrath of Almighty God.
- And He has on His vesture and on His <u>thigh</u> a name written "KING OF KINGS, AND LORD OF LORDS."

And I saw an angel standing in the Sun, and he cried with a loud voice, saying to all the fowls that fly in the midst of heaven

"Come and gather yourselves together unto the supper of the great God; That you may eat

- *the flesh of kings, and the*
- *flesh of captains, and the*
- *flesh of mighty men, and the*
- *flesh of horses, and*
- *of them that sit on them, and the*
- *flesh of all men, both free and bond, both small and great".*

THE BEAST & FALSE PROPHET DESPATCHED

And I saw the beast, and the kings of the earth, and their armies, gathered together to make war against him that sat on the horse, and against his army. And the beast was taken, and with him the false prophet that wrought miracles before him, with which he deceived them that had received the mark of the beast, and them that worshipped his image.

These both were cast alive into a lake of fire burning with brimstone.

And the remnant was slain with the sword of him that sat upon the horse, which *sword* proceeded out of his mouth: and all the fowls were filled with their flesh.

SATAN IMPRISONED / THE MILLENNIUM

And I saw an angel come down from heaven, having the key of the bottomless pit and a great chain in his hand. And he laid hold on the dragon, that old serpent, which is the Devil, and Satan, and bound him a thousand years, And cast him into the bottomless pit, and shut him up, and set a seal upon him, that he should deceive the nations no more, till the thousand years should be fulfilled: and after that he must be loosed a little season.

And I saw thrones, and they sat upon them, and judgment was given unto them. And *I saw* the souls of them that were beheaded for

Chapter Three

- the witness of Jesus, and for
- the word of God, and
- which had not worshipped the beast,
  - neither his image,
  - neither had received *his* mark upon their foreheads,
  - or in their hands; and they lived and reigned with Christ a thousand years.

But the rest of the dead lived not again until the thousand years were finished.

This *is* the first resurrection. Blessed and holy *is* he that has part in the first resurrection: on such the second death has no power, but they shall be priests of God and of Christ, and shall reign with him a thousand years.

And when the thousand years are expired, Satan shall be loosed out of his prison, And shall go out to deceive the nations which are in the four quarters of the earth, Gog and Magog, to gather them together to battle: the number of whom *is* as the sand of the sea. And they went up on the breadth of the earth, and compassed the camp of the saints about, and the beloved city: and fire came down from God out of heaven, and devoured them. And the devil that deceived them was cast into the lake of fire and brimstone, where the beast and the false prophet *are*, and shall be tormented day and night forever and ever.

THE GREAT WHITE THRONE

And I saw a great white throne, and him that sat on it, from whose face the earth and the heaven fled away; and there was found no place for them. And I saw

- the dead, small and great, stand before God; and
- the books were opened: and another book was opened, which is *the book* of life: and the dead were judged out of those things which were written in the books, according to their works. And
- the sea gave up the dead who were in it; and
- death and hell delivered up the dead who were in them: and they were judged

every man according to their works.

And death and hell were cast into the lake of fire.

This is the second death. And whosoever was not found written in the book of life was cast into the lake of fire.

NEW HEAVENS, NEW EARTH, & NEW JERUSALEM

And I saw a new heaven and a new earth: for the first heaven and the first earth were passed away; and there was no more sea. And I John saw the holy city, new Jerusalem, coming down from God out of heaven, prepared as a bride adorned for her husband. And I heard a great voice out of heaven saying

"Behold, the tabernacle of God is with men, and he will dwell with them, and they shall be his people, and God himself shall be with them, and be their God. And God shall wipe away all tears from their eyes; and there shall be

- *no more death,*
- *neither sorrow,*
- *nor crying,*
- *neither shall there be any more pain*

for the former things are passed away.

And He that sat upon the throne said

"Behold, I make all things new".

And He said unto me

"Write, for these words are true and faithful".

And He said unto me

"It is done. I am Alpha and Omega, the beginning and the end. I will give unto him that is thirsty of the fountain of the water of life freely. He that overcomes

shall inherit all things; and I will be his God, and he shall be my son. But the

- *fearful, and*
- *unbelieving, and the*
- *abominable, and*
- *murderers, and*
- *whoremongers, and*
- *sorcerers, and*
- *idolaters, and all*
- *liars*

shall have their part in the lake which burns with fire and brimstone, which is the second death".

And there came unto me one of the seven angels which had the seven bowls full of the seven last plagues, and talked with me, saying

"Come here, I will show you the bride, the Lamb's wife".

And he carried me away in the spirit to a great and high mountain, and showed me that great city, the holy Jerusalem,

- descending out of heaven from God,
- having the glory of God and
- her light *was* like unto a stone most precious, even like a jasper stone, clear as crystal; and
- had a wall great and high, *and*
- had twelve gates, and at the gates
- twelve angels, *and names* written thereon, which are the names of the twelve

tribes of the children of Israel:

- On the east three gates;
- on the north three gates; on the
- south three gates; and on the
- west three gates.
- And the wall of the city had twelve foundations, and in them the names of the twelve apostles of the Lamb.

And he that talked with me had a golden reed to measure the city, and the gates thereof, and the wall thereof. And the city lies foursquare, and the length is as large as the breadth. And he measured the city with the reed, twelve thousand furlongs. The length and the breadth and the height of it are equal.

And he measured the wall thereof, an hundred *and* forty *and* four cubits, *according to* the measure of a man, that is, of the angel. And the building of the wall of it was *of* jasper, and the city *was* pure gold, like unto clear glass. And the foundations of the wall of the city *were* garnished with all manner of precious stones:

- The first foundation *was* jasper
- the second, sapphire
- the third, a chalcedony
- the fourth, an emerald
- the fifth, sardonyx
- the sixth, sardius
- the seventh, chrysolite
- the eighth, beryl
- the ninth, a topaz
- the tenth, a chrysoprasus

Chapter Three

- the eleventh, a jacinth
- the twelfth, an amethyst.

And the twelve gates *were* twelve pearls. Every several gate was of one pearl, and the street of the city *was* pure gold, as it were transparent glass.

And I saw

- no temple therein, for the Lord God Almighty and the Lamb are the temple of it. And the city had
- no need of the Sun,
- neither of the Moon, to shine in it, for the glory of God did lighten it, and the Lamb *is* the light thereof. And the nations of them which are saved shall walk in the light of it, and the kings of the earth do bring their glory and honour into it.

And the gates of it shall not be shut at all by day, for there shall be no night there. And they shall bring the glory and honour of the nations into it. And there shall in no wise enter into it anything that

- defiles, neither
- *whatsoever* works abomination, or
- *makes* a lie,

but they which are written in the Lamb's Book of Life.

And he showed me a pure river of water of life, clear as crystal, proceeding out of the throne of God and of the Lamb. In the midst of the street of it, and on either side of the river, *was there* the tree of life, which bare twelve *manner* of fruits, *and* yielded her fruit every month, and the leaves of the tree *were* for the healing of the nations.

And there shall be

- no more curse, but the throne of God and of the Lamb shall be in it, and his

- servants shall serve him. And they shall see his face, and his name *shall be* in their foreheads. And there shall be

- no night there, and they need no candle, neither light of the sun, for the Lord God gives them light. And they shall reign forever and ever.

And he said unto me

"these sayings are faithful and true, and the Lord God of the holy prophets sent his angel to show unto his servants the things which must shortly be done".

"Behold, I come quickly. Blessed is he that keeps the sayings of the prophecy of this book".

And I John saw these things, and heard *them*. And when I had heard and seen, I fell down to worship before the feet of the angel which showed me these things. Then he said to me

"See you do it not: for I am your fellow servant, and of your brethren the prophets, and of them which keep the sayings of this book. Worship God".

And he said to me

"Seal not the sayings of the prophecy of this book: for the time is at hand.

- *He that is unjust, let him be unjust still and*
- *he which is filthy, let him be filthy still and*
- *he that is righteous, let him be righteous still and he that is*
- *holy, let him be holy still".*

"And, behold, I come quickly; and my reward is with me, to give every man according as his work shall be. I am Alpha and Omega

- *the beginning and*

Chapter Three

- *the end,*
- *the first and*
- *the last.*

Blessed are they that do His commandments that they may have right to the tree of life, and may enter in through the gates into the city. For outside are

- *dogs, and*
- *sorcerers, and*
- *whoremongers, and*
- *murderers, and*
- *idolaters, and whosoever*
- *loves and makes a lie*

THE GREAT INVITATION

I Jesus have sent mine angel to testify unto you these things in the churches. I am the root and the offspring of David, and the bright and morning star.

- *And the Spirit and the bride say, Come.*
- *And let him that hears say, Come.*
- *And let him that is thirsty come.*

And whosoever will, let him take the water of life freely. For I testify unto every man that hears the words of the prophecy of this book, If any man shall add unto these things, God shall add unto him the plagues that are written in this book. And if any man shall take away from the words of the book of this prophecy, God shall take away

- *his part out of the book of life, and*

- *out of the holy city, and*
- *from the things which are written in this book.*

He which testifies these things says

"*Surely I come quickly.*" Amen.

Even so, come, Lord Jesus.

The grace of our Lord Jesus Christ be with you all.

Amen.

Chapter Three

Chapter 4   Revelation – an analysis

So I went to the angel, telling him to give me the little book. And he said to me, 'Take it and eat it; it will make your stomach bitter, but in your mouth it will be sweet as honey'

Revelation 10.9

Figure 16. The Sun.

Part 1 – Introduction

Our prophetic framework is taking shape. The previous chapters described the general end-time landscape based on the solid foundation of the Spine. If the Spine was Christ's first instalment of end-time prophecy, then Revelation, written down around 66 years later, was His second. We can expect full synchronicity with no contradiction between Spine and Revelation.

Chapter Four

The first three verses of Revelation tell us that:

- its purpose is to ***reveal things which will happen soon***
- there is a blessing for those who ***read, hear, and keep*** it and
- the time is ***near***

We might say that Revelation can be applied to three phases of history, each in a slightly different way:

- a direct letter to 1st century local churches in Asia
- specific guidance to the Church for the end-times (i.e. us)
- an end-time perspective for the church between those times, say 100-2000AD

Some have said that the letters to the seven churches represent the seven ages of the Church through history. I can find no basis for this. I suggest they are simply what they say they are: messages from Jesus Christ to His church in Asia, for their consumption in the 1st century. There are clearly lessons we can learn from them as with every epistle, and their message is not limited to predictive prophecy only. The predictive aspects of these letters are more fully developed in the later part of the Revelation.

The prophecy of Revelation was placed in the care of these churches for safe-keeping. They did a good job because we still have it today. However, our primary concern is the times of the end, and it is here that we will focus our attention. We will not go into a verse by verse exposition of Revelation. Instead, our aim is to look at significant passages that shed light on the prophetic plan for the end-times. We will concentrate primarily in this chapter on the seals, bowls and trumpets, which provide the chronological key to interpret the whole book. The remainder of Revelation will be addressed in later chapters.

Before we start, take a look at the Word Cloud for Revelation. Words that appear more frequently look bigger:

Figure 17. Revelation: Word Cloud.

Chapter Four

Outline of Revelation

Based on the previous chapter, we can see that Revelation breaks readily into a number of sections. The table below lists them and indicates where each area will be discussed.

Outline of Revelation

Topic	where discussed in End-Time Survivor'
The purpose of Revelation	Chapter 3
who it is addressed to, and who it is from	
an introduction from John to set the scene	
the letters to the churches	-
the *6 seals*	Chapter 4
(the 1st parenthesis: 144,000 of the tribes of Israel, and the martyrs from the tribulation)	
the *7th seal*	
the *6 trumpets*	
(the 2nd parenthesis: the two witnesses)	
the *7th trumpet*	
(the 3rd parenthesis: the woman; the dragon; the beast; and the false prophet)	Chapter 9
the *7 bowls*	Chapter 4
Babylon	Chapter 4
the return of Christ	Chapter 12
the Beast, his kings, armies, and the false prophet despatched	Chapter 9
Satan imprisoned / Millennium commences	Chapter 14
Millennium ends	
Satan released then condemned	
the Great White Throne Judgement	Chapter 11
New heaven and New earth	Chapter 14
the New Jerusalem	
the great invitation to 'come'	
the amen	

Chapter Four

Part 2 – Seals, Trumpets and Bowls

The seals, trumpets and bowls of Revelation depict 21 activities, presented as three sets of seven. How should we interpret them?

Let us first consider their meanings:

Seals were used on the majority of important documents in days gone by. Their purpose was to close up or seal them to demonstrate that the document was indeed from the person who had sent it. Most seals displayed an image of the owner, often with a message around the edge, which might describe something

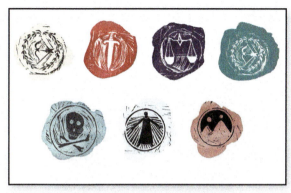

Figure 18. The 7 Seals.

about the person or their family. A Great Seal however was special. It belonged to the ruler and all important business had this Great Seal attached. If a document was sealed in this way, it had the ruler's 'seal of approval' and contained their edicts or commands, and carried with it their authority.

Figure 19. The 7 Trumpets.

So who was this document from that had the 'Seven Seals'? We know from Revelation that the only person worthy enough to open it was Jesus, so must assume that the scroll is from the Father Himself. This means that the events described in the document are His express wish. Not Satan's, not man's. That scroll is waiting in heaven right now to be handed to the Son.

Trumpets are generally associated with wakening, warning, worship and warfare in the Bible. So too in Revelation. In Hebrew they are known as *shofarim* and were made from a ram's horn and sounded by the priest. Their manufacture required

139

the death of the animal. The first occasion a shofar was blown was when the children of Israel assembled at Sinai. Joshua 6.2-5 recounts also how the *shofarim* were blown seven times to bring down the walls of the unholy city of Jericho. They would also be sounded at important occasions and ceremonies and are traditionally blown at Rosh Hashanah, the Jewish New Year, which might, possibly, give us a clue as to the timing of the 'last' trumpet.

Figure 20. The bowls.

Bowls (Greek: *phiale*) normally contain a libation (or fluid) to be poured out. The context is suggestive of a rapid emptying its contents and once emptied, the exercising of wrath is finished. The name of God Almighty, or *El Shaddai*, is translated as the 'all sufficient One', or the 'One who pours forth'. Jesus too poured Himself out[1] for us in His earthly ministry.

'God Almighty' is first used in Gen 17.1 when He appeared to Abraham to command him to walk before Him and be perfect. The name is used eight times in Revelation. El Shaddai is revealed in His power to supply His creature's needs, pouring Himself out for others. However, He can only give of Himself when the creature is empty and ready to receive. His power is perfected in our weakness. Abram at this time was 99 years old, a man of faith and yet a failure, as he had no heir and no country, but was soon to become the father of a multitude.

This pouring out can also refer to an act of judgment, as with the seven bowls.

When we read Revelation we cannot fail to be struck by the combination of real events and intense symbolism. But what is real and what is symbolic? And how are we supposed to arrange the events described? In studying the book, the problem is

---

1. See Titus 3.6; Is 53.12; and Philippians 2.17-18

that, unlike the Spine, Revelation does not present an unbroken 'start-to-finish' chronology. We therefore require a disciplined scheduling methodology. Let me explain…

There are clearly different groupings of activities which must be arranged. A cursory study of the events described under the seals, trumpets and bowls reveals marked similarities to those we have already seen in Jesus' great prophecy in Matthew 24, Mark 13 and Luke 21. There are a number of theories regarding the relationship of the events pictured under each 'category' and it is of particular importance that we place them in the right order. I suggest 5 Laws are used to ensure consistent and accurate arrangement of the seals, trumpets and bowls.

5
5 laws of Revelation

The 5 Laws of Revelation

Revelation Law 1 'first and last'	Jesus is the first and last, alpha and omega, the beginning and the end. It is He, and He alone that is 'worthy' to open the seals. It seems reasonable to assume that the overall end-time schedule commences with the 1st seal and concludes with the last. In this manner, Jesus is truly 'the first and the last' for the history of earth and the seals provide the drumbeat for the end of the age.
Revelation Law 2 'seals pre-eminent'	The seals are given first, before the revelation of the trumpets and bowls. This is another reason that we should give them pre-eminence i.e. each seal will always precede the same numbered trumpet or bowl e.g. the events described at the 2nd trumpet cannot precede those of the 1st seal; the 3rd bowl cannot precede the 2nd trumpet, and so on.
Revelation Law 3 'the Spine defines the order'	The 'Spine of Biblical Prophecy' is defined by Matt 24, Mark 13 and Luke 21. Here, Jesus describes to His disciples the general schedule for end-time events. He would not deny Himself, so it is safe to use this as the template for arranging the events under the seals, trumpets and bowls.
Revelation Law 4 'simple chronology'	Clearly the 2nd seal must come after the 1st seal and the 4th seal after the 3rd and so on. The 2nd trumpet must come after the 3rd trumpet and the 4th after the 3rd. So too with the bowls.
Revelation Law 5 'trumpets and bowls co-incident'	The events described by the 1st bowl/1st trumpet seem identical; so too with the 2nd trumpet / 2nd bowl and so on. We therefore take the position that the events described at each 'stage' for trumpets and bowls are co-incident unless obviously different.

Careful application of the 5 Laws now allows us to map seals, trumpets and bowls into both a logical and chronological arrangement. The right hand column of the table below shows a clear correlation with the phases we identified in the prophecy

Chapter Four

of the Spine. The order is identical to the Spine in every respect, without any need for manipulation to make events fit. This provides us with our 'chronological key', and allows us to confidently unlock the book, and to understand the timing of Revelation.

Chronological Key: arrangement of Seals, Trumpets and Bowls

seals		trumpets (3 Woes)		bowls (plagues)		comments	
1st	Conflict					The events described in the 1st 4 seals are different to those of the 1st four trumpets and bowls. However, their order is identical to the series of events described in the Spine (**Law 3**). Consequently the seals are placed first	S O R R O W S
2nd	Killing						
3rd	Famine						
4th	Death						
		1st	The Earth	1st	The Earth	There is a clear similarity between events described by the 1st four trumpets & bowls. It seems reasonable to assume these pairings are co-incident and identical i.e. 1st trumpet = 1st bowl; 2nd trumpet = 2nd bowl etc. (**Law 5**)	P H O B E T R O N
		2nd	The Sea	2nd	The Sea		
		3rd	Rivers and Springs	3rd	Rivers and Springs		
		4th	The Heavens	4th	The Heavens		
5th	Martyrs					The 5th seal bears no similarity to the 5th trumpet or bowl. Therefore, applying **Law 1**, it is assumed that the 5th seal precedes the 5th trumpet / bowl	T R I B U L A T I O N
		5th	Demonic outpouring	5th	Beast's Kingdom smitten	The events of the 5th trumpet and bowl seem different to one another. However, if they did not occur together they would be the only pairing of trumpets and bowls to occur separately, and are thus assumed to coincide (**Law 5**)	
		6th	Gathering at Armageddon	6th	Gathering at Armageddon	Key event: Armageddon, thus occurring at the same time (**Law 5**)	
6th	Great Day of His Wrath					Co-incident with 7th Trumpet and Bowl (**Laws 1 & 2**)	
7th	Saints' Prayers instigate God's Fire	7th	Jesus' Return	7th	Jesus' Return	Key event: Lightning, thunder, voices and an earthquake. The last seal or 'Omega' as **Law 1**	R E T U R N

Having established synchronicity with the Spine, we can now confidently map the activities described onto our timeline. We should be mindful that it was Jesus who gave us the Spine and the same Jesus who later gave us the Revelation. The two prophecies must align and we are now in a position where we can do this. Above all, they are 'safe' for our primary purpose of understanding the timing of the last days.

We will examine each stage in turn, confining our thoughts for the present primarily to the events described in Revelation. We will integrate and develop these with the Spine in the next chapter. The Tribulation, Jesus' return, Judgment and the Millennium are the subjects of later chapters.

Taken together, the seals, trumpets and bowls reveal four general phases or groups of activity:

- the beginning of sorrows
- the 'Phobetron'
- the Tribulation
- Jesus' return

Let us briefly consider each activity:

<u>Seals 1-4: 'the beginning of birth pangs / sorrows': war, famine & death</u>

It is Jesus Himself who opens the seals. These then are the 'Alpha and Omega' events, the first and the last according to Law 1. We commence the end-time sequence with a seal and it will be finished with a seal. It is left to His angels to blow the trumpets and pour out the bowls to enact further events. This fits the divine pattern revealed often in scripture, whereby an event is initiated by God Himself with the angels then enacting the judgments.[2]

The order of the first four seals (conflict, killing, famine and death) is totally consistent with the events in the 'beginning of sorrows' in the Spine. Seals 5 and 6 (martyrs, and the great day of His wrath) also fit the order of the Spine. There

---

2. For example, when the children of Israel were enslaved in Egypt, God appeared to Moses to foretell their deliverance. However, it fell to the Angel of Death to enact God's judgement on the firstborn

can be no doubt then that what was revealed by Jesus in His great prophecy of the Spine is identical to the pattern from Revelation. This reinforces and confirms our interpretation of the general timeline for the end-times.

We will consider where we are in relation to these events in Chapter 5:

Trumpets / Bowls 1-4: the 'Phobetron' - Earth, seas, rivers / springs and heavens smitten

The events described in Seals 1-4 do not correlate to the 1st 4 trumpets or bowls, but their order is identical to those of the Spine. Thus, respecting Law 2 (seals pre-eminent) the 1st four trumpets and bowls must follow on after the 4th seal.

They describe how creation is to be shaken and smitten on a global and unprecedented scale. It will feel very much like we are living in a Hollywood disaster movie. For this reason it is clear that we have not yet entered this period. It is however possible that we are seeing its foreshadowing in certain natural phenomena such as earthquakes, tsunamis and unusual weather patterns.

The key signs described by the first four trumpets and bowls are:

- #1: hail, fire and blood; a third of all the trees and grass burnt; sores come upon those bearing the mark of the Beast and who worship him (interim judgment #1)

- #2: a great burning mountain cast into the sea; a third of the sea becomes blood; a third of the sea creatures die; a third of the ships destroyed; the death of all at sea[3]

- #3: a third of the rivers and springs become bitter; rivers become blood

- #4: a third part of the sun, moon and stars becomes darkened; the sun scorches men causing them to blaspheme God (interim judgment #2)

You may remember that in Chapter 2 we placed *'the Phobetron'* before the Tribulation. The rationale for placing the commencement of Trumpets/Bowls 1-4

---

3. One possible scenario: scientists believe that the Cumbre Vieja volcano on the Island of La Palma in the Canaries is overdue for eruption. The islands themselves are unstable, and scientists believe that a resultant landslide could trigger a mega-tsunami which could devastate the eastern coast of the USA and affect those at sea, whilst the volcanic plume contaminates the atmosphere.

into our chronology here is found in Luke 21.11b:

there will be 'Phobetron' and great signs from heaven

The Greek word ***'phobetron'*** is used only once in the Bible and means the 'terrifying sights' or 'things that fill with fear' that are often experienced by an individual when seriously ill, rather like hallucinations, nightmares or feverish visions. I would therefore suggest that the Phobetron of Luke 21.11b, the 'fearful sights and great signs', are one and the same as the first 4 trumpets and bowls. It follows the 'birth pangs', and precedes the tribulation, so is a logical fit.

This sequence of seemingly natural events will further prepare the ground for the Tribulation, weakening and destabilising nations, spreading panic, and setting the stage for a new world order in government.

We can speculate about these events, but can add nothing that would explain them. I am often amused by TV 'documentaries' that explain for example how Moses led Israel out of Egypt, and it is suggested that a fortunately-timed earthquake caused the sea to 'part'. We can look for natural events to explain the cause of the miraculous and there are times when the Lord will use natural phenomena to achieve His ends. However the Almighty needs no favours from nature. He controls it, is not subject to it and does as He pleases. Many of the signs described above have occurred before (e.g. the Nile became blood under Moses), but never on this global scale. Remember that under the previous phase we saw the '*beginning* of sorrows'. This is the next instalment of sorrows.

It is possible that we are even now seeing the first indications of the shaking up of creation prophesied by the writer to the Hebrews:

See to it that you do not refuse Him who is speaking. For if those did not escape when they refused him who warned them on earth, much less will we escape who turn away from Him who warns from heaven. And His voice shook the earth then, but now He has promised, saying, 'Yet once more I will shake not only the earth, but also the heaven.' This expression, 'Yet once more,' denotes the removing of those things which can be shaken, as of created things, so that those things which cannot be shaken may remain

Heb 12.25-27

Over the last 20 years, we have seen instances of record hottest and coldest temperatures, precipitation and flooding. I am no scientist, but it does seem

CHAPTER FOUR

that somehow nature is in spasm. I believe this has nothing to do with so-called Anthropogenic Global Warming (AGW) and will discuss this further in Chapter 6.

If we factor in the tsunami from Boxing Day 2004 (230,000 deaths in 14 countries), and the Icelandic volcanic eruption of Eyjafjallajökull in 2010 where 250 Million M3 of ash (causing the largest flight disruption in Europe since WW2), we can begin to appreciate the scope and scale of the Phobetron. Interestingly, geologists believe that Iceland may experience more such events in the future. Eyjafjallajökull's big brother, the volcano Katla, is believed to be overdue for eruption. Also, the whole of the Yellowstone National Park is one great 'supervolcano'. Who knows if this has a part to play.

Figure 21. The ash plume of Eyjafjallajokull, Iceland.

Creation is groaning, awaiting the revelation of its sons and daughters as prophesied in Romans 8.19-22. This is fascinating, because these events are not originated by Satan, but happen as a result of creation preparing for an end-time event. We can take encouragement in this – no birth pangs, no birth. The birth is imminent, the Kingdom is coming.

Notice how the 1st bowl and 4th trumpet bring interim judgment upon those who bear the mark of the Beast and worship his image. Life might be hard for Jews and Christians, but it is certainly no bed of roses for the world either. This also shows us that the Phobetron will not commence properly until the rise of Antichrist and his false prophet.

The 4th trumpet and bowl will take away a third of the light from sun, moon and stars. This may possibly be caused by atmospheric pollution from volcanoes. This, together with an increase in sunspot activity or breakdown of the ozone layer would allow solar radiation to burn men. Since the coming of the space age, satellites have been affected by high levels of radiation as they passed over the South Atlantic. It has been discovered that these anomalies are caused by fluctuations in the earth's magnetic field, which in turn have been caused by a destabilisation of molten rock within the earth's crust. Were this effect to increase, it may degrade the earth's magnetic shield which presently protects us from solar radiation.

We should note that this 'dimming' of sun, moon and stars is a different event from the full-on 'darkness' in the heavens that is to occur immediately before Jesus' return.

Seal 5: the Tribulation begins - martyrs

The 5th seal signals the beginning of the Tribulation. We know that the Tribulation will last for precisely 7 years. This will be explored in detail in chapter 10. Note well though who instigates it: not Satan, not the Antichrist, but the Lord Jesus Christ with the opening of the 5th seal. We should take comfort that at every stage He commands and dictates the pace of events, and we can be confident that the 'end is near'. It is unusual for prophecy to provide us with timescale or duration. The fact that we are told of the 7 years of the Tribulation is to help us manage our expectations in dealing with the savage intensity of this period. Once we are in it, we will know that the clock is ticking and the end is rapidly approaching.

We are told that the martyrs come from *every* tribe, tongue and people and nation. This includes Christian and Jew. The persecution will be systematic, organised and efficient.

Chapter Four

At some stage during this period it is likely that the 144,000 Jewish witnesses, taken from the tribes of Israel, will now be active, fearlessly proclaiming the coming Kingdom. This will instigate the great ingathering of the Jews (see chapter 7).

<u>Trumpet / bowl 5 & 6: the Tribulation continues</u> – demonic outpouring; interim judgment on the Beast's followers; Armageddon

Respecting Law 5, all other trumpets and bowls were co-incident i.e. each numbered bowl happened at the same time as the same numbered trumpet. However, a comparison of the 5th trumpet and 5th bowl shows no similarity between the events described. We are therefore seeing two separate events, so must ponder which comes first. It may be that the 5th bowl happens first, as it is logical that the judgement described in the 5th bowl could be a consequence of the demonic activity in the 5th trumpet. However the trumpet is uttered before the bowl. We will just have to wait and see.

This demonic outpouring reminds us very much of the prophet Joel:

> *Blow a trumpet in Zion, and sound an alarm on My holy mountain!*
>
> *Let all the inhabitants of the land tremble, for the day of the Lord is coming;*
>
> *Surely it is near, a day of darkness and gloom, a day of clouds and thick darkness.*
>
> *As the dawn is spread over the mountains, so there is a great and mighty people;*
>
> *There has never been anything like it, nor will there be again after it to the years of many generations.*
>
> *A fire consumes before them and behind them a flame burns. The land is like the garden of Eden[4] before them but a desolate wilderness behind them, and nothing at all escapes them. Their appearance is like the appearance of horses, and like war horses, so they run. With a noise as of chariots they leap on the tops of the mountains, like the crackling of a flame of fire consuming the stubble like a mighty people arranged for battle.*
>
> *Before them the people are in anguish, all faces turn pale. They run like mighty men, they climb the wall like soldiers, and they each march in line. Nor do they deviate from their paths.*

---

4. This is suggestive of modern-day Israel. The land has been systematically restored to bear a rich variety of produce. A veritable Eden indeed.

Chapter Four

They do not crowd each other, they march everyone in his path.

When they burst through the defences, they do not break ranks.

They rush on the city, they run on the wall. They climb into the houses; they enter through the windows like a thief. Before them the earth quakes, the heavens tremble, the sun and the moon grow dark, and the stars lose their brightness.

The Lord utters His voice before His army. Surely His camp is very great, for strong is he who carries out His word. The day of the Lord is indeed great and very awesome, and who can endure it?

'Yet even now,' declares the Lord, 'return to Me with all your heart, And with fasting, weeping and mourning, and rend your heart and not your garments.'

Now return to the Lord your God, for He is gracious and compassionate, slow to anger, abounding in lovingkindness, and relenting of evil. Who knows whether He will not turn and relent and leave a blessing behind Him, even a grain offering and a drink offering for the Lord your God?

Blow a trumpet in Zion, consecrate a fast, proclaim a solemn assembly, gather the people, sanctify the congregation, assemble the elders, gather the children and the nursing infants.

Let the bridegroom come out of his room, and the bride out of her bridal chamber.

Let the priests, the Lord's ministers, weep between the porch and the altar, and let them say, 'Spare Your people, O Lord, and do not make Your inheritance a reproach,

A byword among the nations. Why should they among the peoples say, 'Where is their God?'
Joel 1.1-17

I have heard this passage described by some Christian teachers as an army of overcoming Christian believers, before which nothing can stand. This interpretation was used as the basis for a popular chorus in the 1980's. I don't buy this explanation, and would offer an alternative:

- Joel 2.25 describes this as an army of locusts: *Then I will make up to you for the years that the swarming locust has eaten: the creeping locust, the stripping locust and the gnawing locust, My great army which I sent among you.* Locusts are always figurative of demons in the Bible and never used as referring to believers. Their work is wholly destructive and judgmental, never creative. The term locust may possibly refer to heavily demonised people who have been endued with supernatural physical power. This is God's great army, a demonic army with a purpose. But what purpose could it be?

- Note how *'a day of darkness and gloom, a day of clouds and thick darkness. As the dawn is spread over the mountains'* precedes the invasion. This is the **phobetron** and fits perfectly with the preceding phases of events that we have described above.

- Note also how *'the earth quakes, the heavens tremble, the Sun and the Moon grow dark, and the stars lose their brightness'*. Where have we heard that before? We know that before Christ returns we will see signs in the heavens, with the sun, moon and stars darkened. Thus the demonic affliction is terminated by the appearance of signs in the heavens, and the return of Christ.

It is a terrible thing to fall into the hands of the living God. Joel's prophecy is clearly directed at Israel and its purpose is to make them 'Turn to *Him* with all their hearts, with fasting, with weeping and with mourning. So rending 'their *hearts* and not their *garments*'. This dreadful event will, finally, cause Israel to return to their God and look upon the One whom they have pierced.

Notice again though: it is the Lord's army. They do His bidding. He is the author of the trouble. It is not Satan ultimately who commands, but God. Truly, through much tribulation we must enter the Kingdom of God![5]

A further possibility should be considered: Joel mentions priests who minister to the Lord *'between the porch and the altar'*. This suggests the existence of a Temple at the time of these terrible events and is also necessary if there is to be 'an abomination of desolation' in the Holy of Holies. More on this in Chapter 8.

I recommend that you take time out to read the whole of Joel in this new light and reflect on the judgement and mercy of God and His plan for His chosen people, Israel. This will be considered further in Chapter 7.

The demonic army also 'stings' those who have not been sealed by God - yet another interim judgment on those in the world. It isn't just the Church and Israel that will suffer here. The judgments steadily increase, with darkness coming upon

---

5. Acts 14.22

the kingdom of the Beast, men gnawing their tongues in pain, blaspheming, yet not repenting from their evil ways. This is a third direct interim judgment on those who follow the Beast.

Before we move onto the next section, we should consider another army. This is the army of '200 million' which will be gathered at Armageddon to destroy Israel. An army of this size could not be assembled without support from China and possibly India. The mention of 'kings' indicates that a confederation of nations is involved. This will be discussed in Chapter 10.

The gathering around Armageddon defines the high water mark of organised iniquity and rebellion and brings us to the end of the 7 years of Tribulation. At this point, the cup of iniquity is so full that God must judge. His patience is at an end with those who have rejected Him. They have had ample opportunity to repent, but have not.

It is likely that the two witnesses of Revelation appear in this phase, as the conflict moves ever deeper into the realm of a supernatural battle between the Beast and those of faith, a clash of heaven and earth.

Seals 6 & 7; trumpet / bowl 7: Jesus' return – the great day of His wrath

So Jesus returns. This is not His 2nd Coming, as He has been to earth many times before: He appeared to Adam in Eden; to Moses on Sinai and within the Tabernacle; and to Abraham by the oaks of Mamre. He wrestled with Jacob. I find it interesting that even up to a few hours before His return, neither Jesus nor the angels will know the precise timing. He told His disciples that *'But of that day or hour no one knows, not even the angels in heaven, nor the Son, but the Father alone.'*[6]

The 'great day of His wrath' is a term that describes a number of acts of judgment, retribution, righteous anger, and justice. It is a day that God's chosen have long awaited: the terrified Jewish child entering the gas chamber; the Christian pastor martyred for preaching the gospel. We will consider the full picture of Christ's return in chapter 11.

'Vengeance is mine' said the Lord *'I will repay'*. This is when that repayment begins, and it will end with the final judgment.

---

6. Mark 13.32

Chapter Four

Notice that up to now it is always the Lord Jesus Christ who has determined the timing of end-time events. He alone is worthy to open the seals. His absolute authority is one of the key messages we need to take from Revelation. For the final act however, He waits until the prayers of men, His chosen, redeemed, ransomed, blood-washed children fill the censer, thus triggering the end. Each prayer adds a little more until the censer is full. This is a foretaste of the influence and responsibility that the Lord will bestow on His elect now and in the Millennium. Be sure and know that your prayers have a very real effect on events, both now and at the end of the age.

Jesus now takes back the title deeds of earth from Satan, who had been up to this point the 'god of this world'. Christ will then establish His earthly Kingdom until the end of the Millennium, when the earth will be dissolved by fire.

At *'the last trumpet.... we will be changed...'* (1Cor15.52). This is the moment that we shall receive our resurrection bodies. Fit, healthy, perfectly restored. In this sense we shall be 'like Jesus', for when we see Him we shall be like Him.[7]

The Lord's shout of 'it is done' signals the end of the Church age and the imminent start of the Millennium.[8]

It is also going to become very noisy: lightning, thunder, voices and the most powerful earthquake that the world has ever seen. We will now witness massive tectonic activity on a global scale. If we imagine the earth as the size of an apple, then its crust would be around half as thick as the skin. What lies underneath the thin crust is a fluid mass of molten magma. We therefore shouldn't be surprised by the power that is to be unleashed at this time. That power is there now, but is being constrained. Colossians 1.17b tells us that *'in Him, all things hold together'*. It is only God's restraining hand that presently keeps creation in its relatively stable state. This quake will change the surface of the earth, elevating Jerusalem and opening up a spring that will flow east and west.

These events will be further discussed in chapters 11, 12 and 14.

---

7. 1 John 3.2-3
8. At Calvary Jesus cried "it is finished' to signal the end of the Dispensation of Law, and the beginning of the age of Grace or Church age. This will be discussed in the next chapter

CHAPTER FOUR

Part 3 – Babylon

Revelation 17 and 18 describe a city yet to emerge. Babylon is a mystery[9] yet to be revealed. However, we have sufficient information in the prophecy from which we can assemble a picture.

It is important to understand that cities in the Bible are sometimes given figurative names. Jerusalem for example is called both Sodom and Egypt.[10] If we study the history of the city we would see that these titles are entirely appropriate. We also know that the ancient city of Babylon (in present day Iraq) is never again to be inhabited, but will be a lair of wild animals.[11] It cannot therefore be the city which Revelation describes, but is rather a prototype, a foreshadowing of what is to come in the future.

Again, we cannot accurately locate its position, but we do know that it will be on or near the coast:

And every shipmaster and every passenger and sailor, and as many as make their living by the sea, stood at a distance, and were crying out as they saw the smoke of her burning, saying, 'What city is like the great city?'

Revelation 18.17-18

So much for its location, but what about its nature?

I chose not to watch the London Olympics, but could not help but be aware of the much-celebrated opening ceremony. Vastly expensive, at a time when the UK was experiencing record levels of indebtedness, it seemed to sum up the days in which we live. The design of the event was wholly Godless, elevating human achievement in a riot of politicians, celebrities, media, music and party spirit. It married together cavorting ghouls and demons, against music from Mike Oldfield, who had earlier written the soundtrack for the movie The Exorcist. The birth of a giant baby symbolised the event. Jacques Rogge, the President of the IOC, had been requested to mark a minute's silence in memory of the 40 years since 11 Israeli athletes were murdered by Palestinian terrorists at the 1972 Munich Olympics. He

---

9. A mystery in Biblical terms is something that is currently hidden, but will be revealed at the appropriate time. An example would be the Church, hidden under the Law, but revealed through Christ
10. Revelation 11.8
11. Jeremiah 51.37

Chapter Four

refused and made no mention of them in his speech, but did find time to mention the victims of the London 7/7 bombings.

This is the spirit of Babylon, and the world is ready for it. It hates the God of the Bible, the Jews and Christians. The ceremony provided a foretaste of what is to come and was euphemistically called the Olympic Spirit. I do not doubt for a minute that many fine Christian athletes competed, or that many people of integrity were involved, but we need to be aware what we are dealing with here.

I cannot tell you when or where Babylon will appear, or what it will be called, but appear it must. It will be wholly humanist, and infested with demons. It will meld pleasure, business, sexual immorality, politics and entertainment into an abominable mixture, and the world will love and worship it. However, its destruction will come suddenly, in one 60 minute period, and will be performed by the ten kings (horns) that serve the Antichrist. Before this, believers who reside there will be warned to leave, much like they left Jerusalem in 66AD. The smoke rising from the devastation of Babylon will precede Armageddon. Revelation describes how merchants and kings will mourn its destruction. I would suggest that certain cities in the modern age have already tasted God's judgment. He is gracious and warns us to repent. Both New Orleans and Atlantic City ('Sin City') were devastated by hurricanes, one in the south, the other in the east. Is the west coast next?

Chapter 5   The Big Picture: an overall end-time chronology

*He said, 'Go your way, Daniel, for these words are **concealed and sealed up until the end time.** Many will be purged, purified and refined, but the wicked will act wickedly; and none of the wicked will understand, **but those who have insight will understand**'*

Daniel 12.9-10

Figure 22. Earthrise

Part 1 – Introduction

Having now examined the two major end-time prophecies of Jesus, it is time to combine them into an overall chronology. In looking forward, there are 'definites', of which we can be certain and 'possibles', where we must prayerfully speculate. If indeed we are entering the time of the end, we can expect to be given insight to

CHAPTER FIVE

understand the things that were hidden from previous generations. But according to Daniel's prophecy quoted above, these things will be hidden from the 'wicked', and we shouldn't be surprised when they ignore them. This chapter will consolidate our deliberations into the big picture, the grand panorama of end-time prophecy.

This will require some 'zooming out' to give us overall context of where we are and some 'zooming in', to understand the detail that scriptural prophecy provides.

Our journey through this chapter will be as follows:

- a general introduction to the dispensations of Bible chronology
- a detailed event-by-event comparison of the Spine and Book of Revelation
- a discussion of the Kingdoms of Daniel Chapters 2 and 7, which will provide us with a political perspective of the end times

Part 2 – the Bigger Picture: from everlasting to everlasting[1]

Before we proceed further, we need to step back and 'zoom out' from the end-times for a moment to get a bigger perspective and establish the context. This requires an understanding of dispensations. Dispensations provide us with insight into how God deals with mankind over different periods of history.

In Paul's letter to the Church at Ephesus, there are various references to different dispensations and 'ages':

- 1.10 *'an administration **(dispensation)** suitable to the fullness of the times'*
- 2.7 *'in the **ages** to come He might show...'*
- 3.2 *'the stewardship **(dispensation)** of God's grace'*
- 3.5 *'in other generations **(ages)**'*
- 3.9 *'...the mystery which for **ages** has been hidden'*

The writer to the Hebrews (1.1-2) states that

---

1. This phrase is drawn from Psalm 41.13, and is associated with the God of Israel. Israel is very much part of God's eternal plan

Chapter Five

> *God, after He spoke long ago to the fathers in the prophets in many portions (times) and in many ways, in these last days has spoken to us in His Son, whom He appointed heir of all things, through whom also He made the **worlds**. (Greek: aion = **ages**)*

Jesus spoke specifically of the 'age to come', describing how things would be different at that time.[2] On many occasions He used the word '*aion*' to describe either this present world age or eternity. It is clear that dispensations and ages are a legitimate reality in scripture. The principal dispensations or ages are identified in the table below and take a slightly different interpretation from those identified by others.

Biblical Dispensations - a notional framework

Dispensation or Age	Relates to	Ref	When
1. ETERNITY PAST	Father, Son and Holy Spirit	Gen 1.1-25 Prov 8.22-31 John 1.1-3	'In the beginning'. From **EVERLASTING** to Adam
2. INNOCENCE	Adam & Eve in Eden	Gen 1.26 - 2	From Adam to the Fall
3. PATRIARCHAL	All Mankind	Gen 2 - Ex 20	From the Fall to the Law
4. LAW	Israel Only	Ex 20 - Cross	From the Law to the Cross
5. GRACE or CHURCH	Israel & Church	Cross - Return	From the Cross to Jesus' Return
6. MILLENNIUM	All Mankind	Rev 20	From Jesus' Return for a period of 1000 years
7. ETERNITY FUTURE	All Mankind	Rev 21-22	From end of Millennium to **EVERLASTING**. New Heavens and New Earth

These references show that God may speak at different times in history in different ways. He spoke differently to the patriarchs of Israel than He is doing to us right now. As a general rule the Lord spoke face to face with Moses and Abraham; He spoke to Israel through His prophets; He speaks to His Church through the Holy Spirit, either directly to our spirit, or through other believers. It is important to note that God hasn't changed and never will. Jesus told us that He was the same yesterday, today and forever.[3] Past, present and future, from everlasting to

---

2. Matthew 12.32; Mark 10.31; Luke 18.30
3. Hebrews 13.8

everlasting,[4] He is the same God.

The Greek word for dispensation is **oikonomia**, the same word we use today for economy (political, domestic or social). It means literally the management or administration of a household.

Dispensations

Our English word for dispensation is based on the Latin **dis** (apart) and **pendere** (to weigh out), rather like a medical dispensary. The Oxford Dictionary defines it as *a divinely ordained system prevailing at a particular period of history.*

It is important before we progress further that we understand something of dispensational truths. For example, some truths may be read across different dispensations and relate to the nature of God:

- Jesus Christ is the same yesterday, today and forever
- God is three yet one
- all things hold together in Him (Christ)

The above statements were and are equally true for Adam and Eve, Israel under the Law of Moses, the Church age or age of grace, the Millennium and eternity future. As God said, 'I change not.'[5]

However, other truths may be limited in their application to particular dispensations and vary due to man's condition at that prevailing time and the system under which he must relate to God. Examples would include:

- Adam and Eve were able to walk naked in Eden only because of their innocence, but since that time man cannot do this because of his fallen nature. Even in the age of eternity to come we will be clothed. Naturists are in rebellion towards God!
- Israel was the only nation placed under the Law of Moses. It cannot be applied to any people other than the Jews (or converts to Judaism) or to any time other than the Dispensation of Law, which ended with the Cross. Many

---

4. Psalm 90.2
5. Malachi 3.6

Christians get into trouble by somehow seeking to earn their salvation and righteousness by adopting elements of the Mosaic Law and trying to obey a set of rules that was never designed for them. This is known as legalism and brings the individual a sense of condemnation and a curse (read Galatians for Paul's teaching). Our salvation is a free gift and can never be earned by our actions or self-worth.

- The aspiration of 'Swords into ploughshares' is for the Millennium, and may not be read into any other dispensation. Peace campaigners who attempt to apply it today are taking it out of context and will be disappointed. It is true but not yet a reality. Lions lying down with lambs also come to mind here – a wonderful thought but not yet.

In some dispensations certain truths were hidden. For example the Church was hidden until Jesus revealed it to Peter and it must have come as a shock to Satan. Satan thought that by killing Jesus he could take His place. He didn't know about the resurrection, and was unaware that the Church, Christ's body, would fulfil His work on earth until He returns. We can and should expect therefore that God will still have further revelations for us as we proceed into the last days, although this will never contradict His word as revealed in the Bible. For example, in Chapter 14 we will look at the Millennium. We have a significant amount of insight into this period, but there are undoubtedly many things currently concealed from our gaze.

It is vital that we rightly divide the Word of God and do not arbitrarily read truth from one dispensation into another. In my experience, those who claim that the Bible contradicts itself have not understood dispensational truth and pick and choose verses at random to suit their argument. This approach can get the Bible to say almost anything, as it would if we were to apply this methodology to any book on your shelf. Dispensationalism is a subject that means different things to different people and I have heard many different opinions regarding its content and scope. The simple classification defined above reflects my views and has helped frame my understanding of scripture, although I suspect there is room for flexibility in its interpretation.[6]

---

6. The dispensations described show the general rule – however, there are certainly exceptions. For example, Ruth was a

CHAPTER FIVE

Our primary focus here is the final three dispensations:

- the age of Grace (or Church age)
- the Millennium
- eternity future

The key prophecies of the Spine and Revelation were given to us early in the current age of Grace, in order to warn and prepare the Church for the end-time. When we talk about the 'end of the age' it is therefore the age of Grace that is being referred to as being 'ended'. This will precede the Millennium, after which come the New Heavens and New Earth of eternity future.

Part 3 – The Spine and Revelation combined

In chapter 2 we looked in detail at the Spine of Biblical prophecy and its order of events. In chapter 4 we took the same approach with the Book of Revelation. It is now time to meld the two prophecies together. This presents no difficulties as both were given by the same person, Jesus Christ. He cannot deny Himself, so we will find no problem areas.

As we place the two great prophecies from the Gospels and Revelation side by side, we will see that combining these two major prophetic sources provides a more detailed and comprehensive overview. There is no need to manipulate events to make them fit. However, we do need to be aware that in prophecy we are not generally privy to the dating or duration of future events.[7] We have though been provided with a clear and definite order, so we can build a safe and reliable chronology.

The table below:

- utilises the basic chronology of the Spine
- supplements this with the sequence of events described under the seals,

---

gentile, but became a Jewess under the age of Law. Under the 'Age of Grace', or Church age, we see the growth of Messianic Jewish fellowships. I would suggest we should not be over-dogmatic, but use the general principles of interpretation to frame our understanding of God's dealings with man through the ages

7. One interesting exception to this is in Daniel 9.24. We will examine the prophecy of the '70 x 7's' in chapter 10

trumpets and bowls

- goes beyond the events described by Spine/seals/bowls/trumpets, by completing the prophetic sequence with the events described in Revelation 19-21

    - the Millennium

    - Final Judgment

    - the creation of the New Heaven and Earth

- assigns each set of events with a Phase title and number. These will build on the general periods identified previously under the analyses of the Spine and Revelation in Chapters 2 and 4. The colour coding used for the beginning of sorrows, Phobetron, Tribulation and Return is consistent with that used earlier

Chapter Five

Prophetic Chronology - the Spine and Seals / Trumpets / Bowls combined

main theme	applies to	Matthew 24 Mark 13 Luke 21 'Spine of prophecy'	Revelation		
			Seals	Trumpets (3 Woes)	Bowls (Plagues)
PHASE 1 - BEGINNING OF SORROWS					
False Messiahs	God's people: the church and Israel	Many coming in Christ's name saying 'I am He' — Many deceived			
War — Ethnic conflict	Mankind in general	Wars and rumours of war — Nation v nation — Kingdom v kingdom	1st / 2nd - WAR — Conflict — Killing		
Famine / disease earthquakes		Famines and pestilences and earthquakes in various places	3rd - FAMINE — 4th - DEATH from sword, hunger and beasts		
PHASE 2 - PHOBETRON					
PHOBETRON Sights and signs from heaven – the earth, sea, rivers and heavens smitten and shaken	the land, sea and heavens	fearful sights and great signs from heaven (Luke 21.11b)		1st trumpet – THE EARTH • hail & fire & blood • 1/3 trees burnt • All green grass burnt — 2nd trumpet – THE SEA • Burning mountain cast into sea • 1/3 becomes blood • 1/3 creatures die • 1/3 ships destroyed — 3rd trumpet – RIVERS & SPRINGS • Great star Wormwood falls on them • 1/3 waters become wormwood • Many men die due to bitter waters — 4th trumpet – THE HEAVENS • 1/3 Sun smitten • 1/3 Moon smitten • 1/3 stars smitten • daylight lasts less than 1/3 • 3 Woes announced	1st bowl – THE EARTH • Sores upon those with 666 and who worship his image — 2nd bowl – THE SEA • Becomes as blood of dead man • every living soul on the sea dies — 3rd bowl – RIVERS & SPRINGS • become blood — 4th bowl – THE HEAVENS • poured out on Sun • men scorched with great heat • men blaspheme God's name • men don't repent

SORROWS

PHOBETRON

162

CHAPTER FIVE

main theme	applies to	Matthew 24 / Mark 13 / Luke 21 'Spine of prophecy'	Seals	Trumpets (3 Woes)	Bowls (Plagues)
PHASE 3 – TRIBULATION part #1 – MARTYRS					
SEE CHAPTER 10 'WAR ON THE SAINTS'. A time of worldwide persecution, betrayal, false prophecy, occult power A time for God's people to endure 'to the end' and so be saved keep proclaiming the Gospel to all nations	God's people: the Church / Israel	believers delivered up to tribulation hated by all nations for Jesus' sake many believers offended, betraying & hating one another. Betrayal within families many false prophets deceiving many lawlessness abounds Agape of many grows cold he who endures is saved This Gospel of the Kingdom preached to all nations then the end will come	5th – MARTYRS • under the altar • 'how long Oh Lord?' • white robes • rest for a while until full number of brothers killed'		
PHASE 3 – TRIBULATION part #2 – ABOMINATION OF DESOLATION					
Abomination of Desolation Unprecedented persecution and deception		Abomination of Desolation in the Holy place then there will great tribulation such as has never been seen many false Christs and prophets performing wonders			
PHASE 3 – TRIBULATION part #3 – DEMONIC OUTPOURING & BEAST'S KINGDOM SMITTEN					
interim judgment on the Beast, his kingdom and followers. These events serve to harden their hearts still further	the Beast, his kingdom and followers			5th – 5 MONTH DEMONIC OUTPOURING • 1st Woe - bottomless pit opened • locusts/demons released • sting those not sealed by God • don't touch trees or plants	

Chapter Five

main theme	applies to	Matthew 24 Mark 13 Luke 21 'Spine of prophecy'	Revelation		
			Seals	Trumpets (3 Woes)	Bowls (Plagues)
					5TH – BEAST'S KINGDOM SMITTEN • darkness upon his kingdom • men gnaw tongues in pain • men blaspheme • don't repent

PHASE 3 – TRIBULATION part #4 – ARMAGEDDON

main theme	applies to	Matthew 24 etc.	Seals	Trumpets	Bowls
the gathering together of the armies of the East at the valley of Megiddo in Israel. On their way there, they use their technology to kill 1/3 of men	Mankind in general			**6th – GATHERING AT ARMAGEDDON** • 2nd Woe - an army of 200 Million men cross the Euphrates from the east • they kill 1/3 of men by fire, smoke and brimstone • men still don't repent	**6TH – GATHERING AT ARMAGEDDON** • waters of Euphrates dried up to prepare way for Kings of the East • unclean spirits from mouth of Beast & False Prophet • men gather at Armageddon

PHASE 4 – THE GREAT DAY OF HIS WRATH – THE RETURN OF JESUS CHRIST

main theme	applies to	Matthew 24 etc.	Seals	Trumpets	Bowls
the heavens shaken ---------- SEE CHAPTER 12 "THE RETURN OF JESUS CHRIST" the return of Jesus Christ	land, sea and heavens ---------- mankind in general	immediately after the tribulation Sun darkened Moon dimmed Stars fall from heaven powers of heaven shaken hurricanes (Luke 21.25) ---------- sign of Son of Man appears in heaven all tribes of earth will mourn Jesus returns with power and great glory His angels sent out to gather the elect	**6th – HEAVEN SHAKEN** • great earthquake • Sun blackened • Moon becomes blood • stars fall to earth • sky recedes like a scroll • every mountain & island moved out of its place • men try to hide themselves from the great day of God's wrath ---------- **7th – PRAYERS INTO FIRE** • a 30m silence (pause ?) in heaven • the prayers of the saints poured out on the altar, instigating God to act • in response, the angel takes fire from the altar and casts it on the Earth • VOICES / THUNDER / LIGHTNING / EARTHQUAKE	**7TH – JESUS REGAINS THE EARTH** • great voices in heaven • Kingdoms of this world become the kingdoms of our Lord • He shall reign forever • 24 elders worship God • God destroys those that destroy the earth • the Temple of God opened, and the Ark revealed • LIGHTNING / VOICES / THUNDER / EARTHQUAKE • great hailstones	**7TH – JESUS REGAINS THE EARTH** • great voice from heaven: 'it is done' • VOICES / THUNDER / LIGHTNING • a great EARTHQUAKE such as has never been seen • the great city divided into 3 • the cities of the nations fall • God remembers Babylon, visits His wrath upon it • every island flees away • mountains not found • great hailstones fall on man

RETURN OF CHRIST

CHAPTER FIVE

main theme	applies to	Matthew 24 Mark 13 Luke 21 'Spine of prophecy'	Revelation		
			Seals	Trumpets (3 Woes)	Bowls (Plagues)
PHASE 5 – THE MILLENNIUM					MILLENNIUM
SEE CHAPTER 14 'THE MILLENNIUM & AFTER'	The Church and Israel				
The Millennium – Jesus Christ 1000 year earthly reign					
SEE CHAPTER 11 'JUDGEMENT'					
Final Judgement					
Satan freed to deceive the Nations					
Gog & Magog v the Saints in Jerusalem					
Devil cast into lake of fire					
Great White Throne					
Death & Hades into the lake of fire					
PHASE 6 - NEW HEAVENS & NEW EARTH					ETERNITY FUTURE
SEE CHAPTER 14 "THE MILLENNIUM & AFTER"					
'Eternity future - All things new'					
New Heaven and Earth					
New Jerusalem					

Chapter Five

Part 4 – End-Time Politics: The Kingdoms of Daniel 2 and 7

Our stated approach was to establish a safe and reliable foundation for our prophetic timeline. Having now achieved this goal, we may now delve into other prophetic material to supplement our picture. Our first such detour will be into Daniel Chapters 2 and 7 to gain a different prophetic perspective to the Spine / Revelation account. We have so far viewed the end-time as a series of events, but Daniel sheds light onto what will happen in the kingdoms of the world, the realm of global politics.

Daniel 2

As we saw in Chapter 2 of *End-Time Survivor* Daniel 2 identifies individual kingdoms that would exercise dominion over Jerusalem. We considered there the historical (or backward looking from our present day) perspective of these kingdoms. We can now complete the kingdoms of Nebuchadnezzar's dream in Daniel 2 by adding the forward-looking perspective i.e. those kingdoms from the present day and in the future.

We speculated there how certain kingdoms might trample Jerusalem, and are able to develop this idea here. The table below completes the picture and shows how Jerusalem will be 'trampled' until Jesus returns.

Chapter Five

'Times of the Gentiles' - Part 2: End of Gentile dominion over Jerusalem[8]

Temple Mount / 'Holy Place'		date(s) of captivity or reign over Jerusalem	Key figures affecting status of Jerusalem	Prophetic perspective of Kingdoms from Nebuchadnezzar's Vision (Daniel Ch 2)	Comments	Level of certainty in identifying nationality in prophecy?
under Jewish rule	under Gentile rule					
State of Israel / Islamic Waqf		Present day	Israeli government Mahmoud Abbas 'Quartet' of UN, USA, EU, & Russia	(no Kingdom 'ruling')	Israel is now a sovereign nation but the Temple Mount remains under Islamic Waqf i.e. Temple Mount is still 'trampled' by the Gentiles	Certain
State of Israel		shortly before Tribulation Stage #1		(no Kingdom 'ruling')	We must assume Jewish sovereignty over the Temple Mount in order to allow the Temple to be rebuilt (see Chapter 8)	Probable
	Antichrist's Kingdom	Tribulation Stage #2 3 ½ years	Antichrist	7th Kingdom ?	Follows the Abomination of Desolation	Certain
Millennial Reign of Christ from Jerusalem		Post-Tribulation	Jesus Christ	(8th Kingdom ?)		Certain

Our present position – where are we now?

We should attempt to reconcile the kingdoms of Daniel 2 with those in Daniel 7, such that we can understand what is to come regarding the dominion of Jerusalem. It would make things much clearer if we could determine our present position, our 'time now' in Daniel's prophecy. So what do we know?

Israel is a nation once more, because the 'Fig Tree' has 'put forth its leaves'. Furthermore, 'all the trees' are putting forth their leaves as many nations have come into being since 1948. This fulfilment alone puts us most definitely at the time of the end.

But can we be more specific as to our position in the timeline? I believe so. Let us first establish the historical 'certainties'. Looking back over the kingdoms that dominated Jerusalem we can be confident over the identity of Babylon, as this was

feet of iron & clay

---

8. 'Times of the Gentiles Part 1: Beginning of Gentile Dominion over Jerusalem' is found in Chapter 2

identified by Daniel. Medo-Persia, Greece and Rome followed in succession, so may be confidently named. The first time we are required to speculate is to identify the 'feet of iron and clay'. I believe that there is only one candidate that fits, and have already identified it as the Islamic powers that have subjugated Jerusalem since 637AD. As explained in Chapter 2, Jerusalem is still today 'trampled by gentiles'. I have taken the liberty of splitting the 'iron and clay' into two parts: the first under a wholly Islamic rule, and the second under a British / Islamic combination. The 'iron and clay' dominion will continue until the Gentiles no longer trample the Temple Mount.

Daniel Chapter 7

In Daniel 7, Daniel has further dreams and visions concerning certain kingdoms to come. As we saw in Daniel 2, Nebuchadnezzar's dream was to do with a number of kingdoms, starting with Babylon, which would come into *successive* possession of Jerusalem i.e. the *beginning* of gentile dominion. These kingdoms described in Daniel 2 concern the beginning of Gentile dominion over Jerusalem. We will demonstrate that those of Daniel 7 concern the *end* of this dominion.

Daniel 7 – The Vision of the Four Beasts

In the first year of Belshazzar king of Babylon Daniel saw a dream and visions in his mind as he lay on his bed; then he wrote the dream down and related the following summary of it.

Daniel said, 'I was looking in my vision by night, and behold, the four winds of heaven were stirring up the great sea. And four great beasts were coming up from the sea, different from one another.

The first was like a lion and had the wings of an eagle. I kept looking until its wings were plucked, and it was lifted up from the ground and made to stand on two feet like a man; a human mind also was given to it.

And behold, another beast, a second one, resembling a bear. And it was raised up on one side, and three ribs were in its mouth between its teeth; and thus they said to it, 'Arise, devour much meat!'

After this I kept looking, and behold, another one, like a leopard, which had on its back four wings of a bird; the beast also had four heads, and dominion was given to it.

After this I kept looking in the night visions, and behold, a fourth beast, dreadful and terrifying and extremely strong; and it had large iron teeth. It devoured and crushed and trampled down the remainder with its feet; and it was different from all the beasts that were before it, and it had ten horns.

While I was contemplating the horns, behold, another horn, a little one, came up among them, and three of the first horns were pulled out by the roots before it; and behold, this horn possessed eyes like the eyes of a man and a mouth uttering great boasts.

'I kept looking until thrones were set up, and the Ancient of Days took His seat.

His vesture was like white snow and the hair of His head like pure wool. His throne was ablaze with flames; its wheels were a burning fire. A river of fire was flowing and coming out from before Him. Thousands upon thousands were attending Him, and myriads upon myriads were standing before Him. The court sat, and the books were opened.

Then I kept looking because of the sound of the boastful words which the horn was speaking. I kept looking until the beast was slain, and its body was destroyed and given to the burning fire. As for the rest of the beasts, their dominion was taken away, but an extension of life was granted to them for an appointed period of time.

I kept looking in the night visions, and behold, with the clouds of heaven One like a Son of Man was coming, and He came up to the Ancient of Days and was presented before Him. And to Him was given dominion, glory and a kingdom that all the peoples, nations and men of every language might serve Him. His dominion is an everlasting dominion which will not pass away, and His kingdom is one which will not be destroyed.

As for me, Daniel, my spirit was distressed within me, and the visions in my mind kept alarming me. I approached one of those who were standing by and began asking him the exact meaning of all this. So he told me and made known to me the interpretation of these things:

'These great beasts, which are four in number, are four kings who will arise from the earth. But the saints of the Highest One will receive the kingdom and possess the kingdom forever, for all ages to come.'

Then I desired to know the exact meaning of the fourth beast, which was different from all the others, exceedingly dreadful, with its teeth of iron and its claws of bronze, and which devoured, crushed and trampled down the remainder with its feet, and the meaning of the ten horns that were on its head and the other horn which came up, and before which three of them fell, namely, that horn which had eyes and a mouth uttering great boasts and which was larger in appearance than its associates. I kept looking, and that horn was waging war with

CHAPTER FIVE

the saints and overpowering them until the Ancient of Days came and judgment was passed in favor of the saints of the Highest One, and the time arrived when the saints took possession of the kingdom.

Thus he said: 'The fourth beast will be a fourth kingdom on the earth, which will be different from all the other kingdoms and will devour the whole earth and tread it down and crush it. As for the ten horns, out of this kingdom ten kings will arise; and another will arise after them, and he will be different from the previous ones and will subdue three kings. He will speak out against the Most High and wear down the saints of the Highest One, and he will intend to make alterations in times and in law; and they will be given into his hand for a time, times, and half a time. But the court will sit for judgment, and his dominion will be taken away, annihilated and destroyed forever. Then the sovereignty, the dominion and the greatness of all the kingdoms under the whole heaven will be given to the people of the saints of the Highest One. His kingdom will be an everlasting kingdom, and all the dominions will serve and obey Him.'

At this point the revelation ended. As for me, Daniel, my thoughts were greatly alarming me and my face grew pale, but I kept the matter to myself.'

Keys for interpretation:

This prophecy uses figurative language, but we don't have to guess what is meant by these figures of speech. In Daniel, 'one who stands nearby' helps us; in Revelation, it is the angel who advises. These keys may be generally applied throughout Biblical prophecy where figurative language is used:

- '*Waters*' = peoples, multitudes, nations and tongues
- '*Sea*' = the nations of the world ('nations' are always Gentile, translated from the Hebrew 'goyim')
- '*Horns*' = kings, rulers, heads of state, presidents
- '*Heads*' = mountain

We saw in Daniel 2 how the nations follow one another with each beast standing up successively in the place of its predecessor e.g. Rome follows Greece. No such statement is made of those in Daniel 7. Here, Daniel sees the beasts one at a time, but the sequencing is less definite. We may thus infer that these kingdoms overlap and run concurrently. That this chapter refers to the time of the end is clear from the context (of vv17-18) because the four kings precede and build up to the final kingdom inherited by Messiah and His saints.

Biblical prophecy often 'goes quiet' when the Lord withdraws from Israel. There was silence from heaven towards Israel on a number of occasions, including:

- the period of the Egyptian bondage until Moses
- from the last Old Testament prophet, Malachi (c350BC), until the coming of John the Baptist
- from the Jews' rejection of the Kingdom of God until the modern era (see chapter 7)

As we have seen though, the 'Fig Tree' started to bud on or slightly before Theodor Herzl's declaration of the Jewish State in 1897, the first explicit statement of intent concerning a Jewish national homeland. Around this time, the Holy Spirit began to move again concerning Israel. It therefore seems reasonable to associate the 'budding' of Israel with the appearance of the three kingdoms described in Daniel 7. The kingdoms:

- had to appear *after* the kingdoms of Daniel 2, because of their association with the end-times
- but had to coexist[9] *at* or *by* the time of Israel's re-emergence, 1897-1948, as Israel is the great subject, the focus, of the prophecy

We will therefore take the approximate time of Herzl's announcement as our key for understanding the identity of the 3 beasts of Daniel 7. Using this date as our starting point, there are three potential candidates for identity of the first three beasts:

---

9. Because the Bible is not a general book of world affairs, but does prophesy a future in as much as it deals with Israel

Chapter Five

The First beast: The Lion with eagle's wings – Great Britain / USA

Figure 23. Lion with Eagles wings

The Lion that had eagle's wings may possibly (probably in my opinion) be identified as the British Empire and the subsequent transition of power to America. British emigration to the US was significant, and the two countries share many traditions, laws and customs. Culturally, there is no doubt that the UK has more in common with the US than Europe. The beasts have broadly similar 'DNA'. The Lion is the symbol of England and the Eagle that of the US. It is the simplest explanation, and fits with the facts of history.

Britain became the world superpower at the battle of Waterloo in 1815 and this lasted until World War 2. Britannia 'ruled the waves' and it was said that the 'Sun never set on the British Empire'. During 1943 however the balance of power shifted. One month Britain had more troops under arms, a month later the US had more than the British.[10] The cost of the war, the lend lease arrangement with the US and attrition, wore Britain down so much that the US overtook to become the global leader in a more or less seamless transition. As of today, the US still leads the world – just.

At the time of Herzl's pronouncement of Zionism, and throughout the first half of the 20th century Britain reigned supreme. America then took up the mantle of global stewardship. Both nations had considerable influence over the fledgling State of Israel. In 1917, Britain's Foreign Secretary Arthur Balfour made the declaration:

> *His Majesty's government view with favour the establishment in Palestine of a national home for the Jewish people, and will use their best endeavours to facilitate the achievement of this*

---

10. See *'After America'* by Mark Steyn for more on this theme

object, it being clearly understood that nothing shall be done which may prejudice the civil and religious rights of existing non-Jewish communities in Palestine, or the rights and political status enjoyed by Jews in any other country

Figure 24. The Balfour Declaration.

During this period, Britain was generally supportive towards a Jewish homeland in Palestine, but soon back-tracked and began a long policy of opposition which exists today. America was initially less supportive of Israel, but grew into a true friend and even today assists Israel's budget and defensive capability. The God of Israel kept His promise to Jacob to 'bless those who bless you, and curse those who curse you'. America has generally prospered, whilst the UK is a mere shadow of its former power, its empire a distant memory. However, under Barack Obama even America is now starting to harden its position against Israel.

The US was literally lifted up from the earth during the space programme, so this possibly explains that reference in Daniel 7.4. It could also refer to how the US

Chapter Five

became without question the first global superpower and the dollar became the basis for international trade.

That this beast stood on two feet like a man and had a man's heart given to it may speak of the massive rise in militant secular humanism in both the UK and US. Some believe that humanism has taken over the White House and human rights laws, political correctness and erosion of Bible values have radically diminished the influence of Judaeao-Christian principles throughout America.

We are warned that the beast's 'wings were plucked' i.e. It still possessed wings, but they were rendered ineffective for flight. This is a powerful picture of the present-day impotence of the UK. My once proud nation is increasingly unable to project herself on the world stage and is becoming limited to posturing. This impotence will also come to the US once the impact of her massive government debt hits home. No nation has ever been as indebted as the US is right now. Virtually all public spending (including welfare and defence) is being funded by loans from the Chinese.

The decline of the lion and eagle is seeing the sun setting on 200 years of supremacy, trade, military dominion, world politics and the global currency of the pound and dollar. The vast majority of the inhabitants of these nations are in denial over this reality, but the demise of the UK and US is inevitable.

Figure 25. The Bear.

The Second Beast: The Bear – Russia, USSR and Eastern Europe

One candidate stands out above all for the identification of the Bear, which is the national symbol of Russia. This would also include the Soviet-bloc nations and Eastern Europe. The ribs in its mouth speak of violent consumption, as it arises to devour 'much flesh'. Under Stalin as many as 50M people were killed. Add to this those deaths resulting from Soviet-funded conflict since WW2 and the number may be increased. Even today, Russia provides weapons and training for Islamist states such as Syria and Iran, whose leaders call for Israel's destruction. The reference to 'standing up on one side' may be that one part of this beast is elevated at later stage, which could refer to how Russia has risen as an economic superpower from the USSR whilst other Soviet bloc nations have declined. Russia (and China) together have generally opposed any attempts by the West to deal with rogue states such as Iraq, North Korea, Syria or Iran.

The Third Beast: The Leopard - Islamism

Figure 26. The Leopard

The Leopard is more problematical to identify, as unlike the previous two beasts, it is not the national symbol of any particular state. My view is that it represents Islamism, whether national or localised. It is ruthless, stealthy, fast moving and predatory.

It has wings, so is highly mobile and able to transcend national boundaries. These wings grant it the ability to project its influence almost anywhere in the world. Most of Europe is now in effect under Sharia law, with fatwas issued against any who speak against Mohammed (the author Salman Rushdie and Dutch politician Geert Wilders being two such examples). Politicians appease Muslims in order to secure the votes of the rapidly increasing population, avoid confrontation and keep the oil taps open from the Middle East. Dominion has certainly been given to the Islamists of the Middle East (the Arab Spring), the Far East (Indonesia is the world's biggest Muslim state), Europe (East and West), Australia and the US.

Whilst the advent of Islam pre-dates both the British Empire and the US, the Leopard has really only became a factor on the global stage over the last fifty years. Its influence is now felt by most people around the world, where the impact of 9/11

CHAPTER FIVE

and subsequent security measures to counter terrorism affect us all. It has been estimated that by 2050, due to a high birth rate, over half of the UK's population will be Muslim. We may safely assume that Sharia will be a reality in Britain at least a decade before that. So whilst Islam has existed since the 7th century, its recent and dramatic increase may explain why it is the third beast to appear in Daniel 7, rather than the first.

Jesus Christ died for Muslims too and despite the level of persecution inflicted on the Church in Islamic countries, many are finding Christ as their Saviour, often in quite miraculous circumstances.

The Fourth Beast: Antichrist

This will be discussed in Chapter 9 'The Antichrist'

Timing

Daniel 7.7 describes how the Beast (i.e. Antichrist) deals with the 'residue' or rest of the kingdoms once he comes to power. The inference here is that he deals with them collectively, meaning they must co-exist at the time of their subjugation to him. However, the general order of the first three beasts appearing respects history, where first Britain, then the US, Russia then Islam have gradually risen, co-existed, but will eventually be crushed. Britain has nearly gone. The US is on the downward slope. We will watch and wait to see what befalls Russia. Islamists too will also be dealt with, as the Beast's secular humanist world takes shape.

'Dominion taken away'

Daniel 7.12 tells us that the rest of the beasts (i.e. the Lion/Eagle, Bear and Leopard) had their dominion (global influence) taken away, yet their lives (national identity and existence) were prolonged for a 'season and a time'. Are we seeing the start of this process right now? Britain and the USA are bankrupt, running on empty. In a few years the USA will lose its position as the world's No.1 economy to China. Russia's oil and gas make her currently strong economically, yet politically she is unstable with growing resentment against her government. The Islamists are growing in power in the West (Britain, Europe and the USA) yet the so-called

'Arab Spring' is destabilising the Middle East and weakening the Arab states.[11] All these circumstances are combining to form what I have shown as a *'transitionary period'* on the table below. This season of instability, unrest, conflict and economic turmoil is a necessary step required to weaken and erode the power of nations like the EU, UK, US and Russia and set the world stage for the kingdom of the 4th beast, Antichrist. All this is being engineered by Satan, the god of this world, yet permitted by the Lord God of Israel and revealed to us by His prophets.

I believe that this 'transitionary period' is where we are right now.

The Beast or Antichrist will tolerate the first three beasts for a season, but then take away their 'lives' i.e. he will destroy their national power and identity, maybe in much the same way that Hitler suddenly subjugated countries like Czechoslovakia and Poland in 1939. Daniel 7.23 says the kingdom of the beast will *'be **different** from all the other kingdoms and will devour the whole earth and tread it down and crush it.'* Ultimately then the beast will change the nature of global government, but will start by breaking these three. More of this in chapter 9.

The 10 horns

The 10 horns of Daniel 7 are 10 kings that will arise at the time of the end and precede the Beast's global government. In order to assess this we need to understand the current 'who's who' of global power. We are presently witnessing massive change in the world order:

- the **USA** is presently the world No1 Superpower, but losing ground quickly to **China**

- **Britain**, once the global superpower, is in rapid decline, politically impotent, economically bankrupt, losing her armed forces and ability to project her dwindling power. With the exception of Queen Elizabeth II, a committed Christian, her government is largely godless. Prince Charles has already stated that when he accedes to the throne he would like to become the 'defender of faiths' rather than 'defender of *the* Faith'

---

[11]. Their artificial national borders were imposed largely by the Sykes-Picot Agreement, ignoring tribal, cultural and ethnic divisions. With the onset of the 'Arab Spring' these divisions are re-surfacing with violent consequences in countries such as Egypt, Libya, and Syria

CHAPTER FIVE

- the humanistic **EU** is experiencing massive economic turmoil and it is likely that it may be restructured with a smaller number of more committed nations into a single political and economic entity

- The Islamic **Arab States** are wealthy with oil revenues, but divided by unrest and factions, with distrust on every side

- **Turkey**, once had cordial relations with Israel, but has now become hostile. The Ottoman Empire is beginning to stir again

- The so-called **'BRICS'** nations are an association of fast-growing countries, whose economies are giving them new found power and influence:

  - Brazil

  - Russia

  - India

  - China (will become world No.1 c2015)

  - South Africa

  This axis of the 'new rich' will certainly change global politics and economics.

Based on the above discussion we may speculate the identity of the 10 kings. In postulating, we should take into account each nation's military capability and its economic power. The identity of the '10' is currently hidden from view but we can be confident that at least some of the nations in the list below will emerge amongst them:

- China

- India

- Russia

- a reconstituted EU

- USA

- Brazil

- an Arab confederation
- Turkey
- South Africa
- UK

One thing is for certain: when the 10 are revealed it will be clear to all, and we won't be guessing.

Daniel 7 tells us that 'another' (i.e. the antichrist) will arise after these 10. Clearly then, the rise of the 10 kingdoms / empires / nations must therefore pre-date the appearance of Antichrist.

We are told that the Beast will then subdue three kings, so it seems that either militarily or politically Antichrist will subjugate three nations. We will have to wait to see who these are, but are told that Antichrist will 'pluck them up by the roots'.

Speculative Timeline

So if we trust our speculation in identifying Britain, the US, Russia / Soviet-bloc and the Islamists as the beasts of Daniel, then we may present a general schedule based on Daniel 7. These are the global superpowers of the last 200 years, the time during which Israel was reborn. It is good to remind ourselves that the Bible, including the prophet Daniel, is God's revelation to His chosen people, Israel and the Church. The Lord God told us these things would happen and permits them to hasten His return, and sheds light on them so that we can watch, pray and prepare.

The table below summarises the kingdoms of Daniel 2 and 7, highlighting the characteristics of each. As we draw nearer the end, things will become clearer to those who study the Word and so show themselves approved to God.

Chapter Five

Daniel 2 and 7 compared: the beginning & end of gentile dominion over Jerusalem

	Kingdoms				Level of certainty in identifying nationality in prophecy
	Symbol	Features / Characteristics	Identified as		
The beginning of gentile dominion over Jerusalem (Daniel 2)	Head of gold		Babylon	successive kingdoms	Certain
	Breast & arms of silver		Medo-Persia		Certain
	Belly & thighs of brass		Greece		Certain
	Legs of Iron		Rome		Certain
	Feet of iron & clay		Islamist		Speculative
1897 – Herzl's pronouncement – the Israel 'clock' begins to tick again					
The end of gentile dominion over Jerusalem (Daniel 7)	Lion / Eagle	<ul><li>wings became plucked</li><li>lifted up from the Earth</li><li>feet like a man</li><li>a man's heart</li></ul>	Britain / USA?	concurrent / overlapping kingdoms	Speculative
	Bear	<ul><li>raised up on one side</li><li>3 ribs in its mouth</li><li>devours much flesh</li></ul>	USSR / Russia / E. Europe ex-Soviet bloc states?		Speculative
	Leopard	<ul><li>4 wings of a fowl</li><li>4 heads</li><li>dominion given to it</li></ul>	Islamism?		Speculative
	TRANSITIONARY PERIOD: *'As for the rest of the beasts, their dominion was taken away, but an extension of life was granted to them for an appointed period of time'* Dan 7.12				
	Beast	<ul><li>dreadful, terrible & strong</li><li>2 rows of iron teeth</li><li>nails of brass</li><li>devours, breaks in pieces & stamps on the rest of the beasts</li><li>the little horn comes from small beginnings</li><li>10 horns</li><li>unlike any other kingdom</li><li>devours the whole earth</li></ul>	Antichrist	successive	Certain
	Messianic		Jesus Christ		Certain

Chapter 6   The Gathering Storm : pre-requisites for the end

Who will take his stand for me against those who do wickedness? If the Lord had not been my help, my soul would soon have dwelt in the abode of silence. If I should say, 'My foot has slipped,' Your loving-kindness, O Lord, will hold me up. When my anxious thoughts multiply within me, Your consolations delight my soul.

Can a **throne of iniquity be allied with You, one which devises mischief by law?** *They band themselves together against the life of the righteous and condemn the innocent to death. But the Lord has been my stronghold, and my God the rock of my refuge.*

Psalm 94.16-22 (paraphrased)

Figure 27. Storm Clouds

Part 1 – Introduction[1]

Having established our prophetic frame of reference we must now consider our

---

1. The title of this chapter is borrowed from Winston Churchill. The author's claim to fame is that Winston's barber used to cut my hair when I was a child

Chapter Six

position in the timeline, so we may appreciate what lies behind and ahead. This chapter considers a number of significant developments that are required as precursors to the end. The 'thrones of iniquity' that the psalmist describes above are devising evil laws to prosecute the righteous. It is beyond doubt too that the world is deteriorating at an unprecedented rate, but certain key events have not yet occurred, such as the emergence of Antichrist, or the events of the Phobetron. In the previous chapter we suggested that we are currently in a 'transitionary period' that started with the emergence of Israel and will finish with the 'big-ticket' end-time events. This transition will prepare the ground, both physically and spiritually, to usher in the Phobetron.

Do you know how to boil a frog? I'm told (although wouldn't suggest you do this) that if you drop a frog into hot water, it simply jumps out. However, if you place it into cool water, and slowly increase the temperature, you will kill it. The moral is that small, incremental changes in our environment go unnoticed, but do affect our status. If you had been working in the wilderness for the last 15 years, cut-off from communication, then returned home to your busy city and switched on the news you might be shocked by what you saw. But those who had lived there through that time might not have noticed, as the insidious march of events crept up on them. This is why it is so important that we take time to watch and pray. Jesus rebuked the Jews over their inability to read the signs of the times, and we must be found ready and watchful.

I should also warn you that as events move on, this chapter will become outdated. It is vital that we stay in touch and not be overcome by fear or apathy. May I encourage you to stay the course. The world will get worse, but you will get better and better.

Chapter 6 will consider and examine two aspects of the landscape:

- Part 2: identification of twelve 'pillars' on which the stage will be built for the coming events

- Part 3: an assessment of where we are in relation to the 'beginning of sorrows' or 'birth pangs' prophesied by Jesus

Part 2 – Preparing the Stage – 12 Pillars

We will investigate here a number of separate but inter-related developments that have taken place over recent years. Taken together, they represent a significant shift in society and appear to be accelerating. They are not intended to provide an exhaustive study; neither should they be considered as the only factors that are preparing the ground for the times to come. This discussion is simply intended to provoke you to investigate and prayerfully consider the 'signs of the times' against the light of scripture.

Our 12 pillars are:

- apostasy
- anti-Zionism and anti-Semitism
- moral inversion of the legal system
- witchcraft
- secular-humanism and militant homosexuality
- debt
- demise of the family
- governance & regulation
- supra-national government bodies
- technological integration and electronic commerce
- celebrity worship
- weather and other natural events

Apostasy

The last two centuries have seen the established Church moving away from sound scriptural doctrine. The early church fathers fought hard to defend the canon of Christian belief. Just like a chameleon blends into its background, the leaders

Chapter Six

of many of today's denominations seem more interested in being conformed to the world in order that they may remain 'relevant' to society, rather than uphold scriptural truth and risk becoming marginalised or unpopular. This can be seen in a number of areas, but would include belief in the deity of Christ, the virgin birth, the physical resurrection of Christ, heaven and hell, marriage (between a man and a woman) and the authenticity of scripture. These central truths of Christian doctrine have been questioned, belittled and then denied by leaders of many of the mainstream denominations including the Church of England, the Methodist Church and the Quakers. Whereas the early Church had to resist error against those wanting to add[2] to scriptural doctrine, today's battle seems to be against those of a liberal disposition who want to cut away absolute truths.

Timothy warns us that:

> *...For the time will come when they will not endure sound doctrine; but wanting to have their ears tickled, they will accumulate for themselves teachers in accordance to their own desires, and will turn away their ears from the truth and will turn aside to myths*
>
> 2 Timothy 4.3-4

So-called evangelical and charismatic fellowships are not immune to this deception. Some have already denied the reality of Hell for example, or are introducing Celtic mysticism dressed up as Christianity. I remember the advice from one of my favourite Bible teachers, John Barr, who advised that we should always 'weigh the mixture' between truth and error. Sound advice then and now.

Global anti-Zionism and anti-Semitism

We will examine this topic more closely in Chapter 7. However for the sake of completeness we should delve briefly into this topic here.

The modern history of Israel began again in 1947-48 and this was met with great hostility from the surrounding nations, and resulted in several wars and much ongoing conflict. Even now, only a cold peace exists between Israel and Egypt and Jordan, but a state of war prevails between Israel and the other members of the Arab League.

---

2. Examples of this would include the adoption of a professional clergy, church buildings, and following a set of rules to gain salvation

A brief study of resolutions passed in the various UN Councils shows a highly disproportionate bias against Israel. However, she has been able to withstand this diplomatic assault because America stood by her. When Jesus said to His disciples that *you* will be hated by all nations, He was talking to Jewish believers. We know from our studies so far that one day Israel will stand entirely alone, with every other nation opposed to it. At present, American foreign policy is publicly supportive of Israel, but under Barack Obama we are seeing a shift. Most US Presidents don't visit Israel in their first term, but even so, he appears to have a relatively tense relationship with PM Netanyahu.

Obama has to be seen to support Israel, as there are nearly as many Jews in the USA as Israel[3] itself, and they wield considerable political power. However, a time will come when America too will stand against Israel and Jews within America (many of whose families fled the pogroms of Russia) will not be tolerated. I believe that the Lord will permit this to drive Jews into Israel. Across Europe we are presently seeing a significant rise in anti-Semitic attacks, vandalism of Jewish cemeteries and intolerance. Jewish Schools in the UK have to be guarded by specialist security teams against attack. This gets little media coverage, but is the grim reality.

Moral Inversion of the Legal System

Many column inches have been expended in newspapers about criminals who seem not just to get off lightly, but almost be rewarded for their activity. Liberal judges, human rights laws and wrong-headed politicians have combined to create a system where it seems there is little punishment for the guilty and no effective consequence for wrong-doing. On the other hand, Christians are losing their jobs and being hounded through the courts for standing by their beliefs. Isaiah pronounces a curse ('woe') on those who do this:

> 'Woe to those who call evil good, and good evil, who substitute darkness for light and light for darkness, who substitute bitter for sweet and sweet for bitter!'
>
> Isaiah 5.20

---

3. As I write in early 2013, this situation has just changed. For the first time in its modern history, Israel (6M) has now overtaken the USA (5.5M) as the largest population of Jews. There are however still collectively more Jews outside of Israel than resident there. I would suggest we should monitor the balance of the Jewish population as an end-time sign

Chapter Six

In the West, our legal system was built largely upon Judaeo-Christian principles. This is being systematically and aggressively dismantled piece by piece by secular humanists, and we are approaching a time when it will be difficult to be a Christian in public life. However, we should remember that this situation is already a reality for our brothers and sisters in the majority of the nations. We will consider this persecution in Chapter 10.

Witchcraft

Galatians 5 lists witchcraft as one of the fruits of the flesh. 2 Chronicles 33 tells us how Manasseh

> ...made his sons pass through the fire in the valley of Ben-Hinnom; and he practiced witchcraft, used divination, practiced sorcery and dealt with mediums and spiritists. He did much evil in the sight of the Lord, provoking Him to anger

We should be in no doubt that the Lord hates witchcraft and will judge those who practice it. It is not just a sin, but an abomination.

The Potter novels have sold over 450 million copies since 1997, making them the bestselling book series in history.[4] A whole generation has now literally come under their spell. Some children's books now actually describe how to cast spells. Many Christians have read these books and, showing a complete lack of discernment, encourage their children to read them. The fruit is rebellion (1 Sam 15.23), mental illness, fear, nightmares and opposition to God. What we sow, we shall reap and like any seed sown into the mind or spirit, it may spring up immediately, or at some later time. My advice to any who are reading this is to repent, do an 'Acts 19.19' and have a bonfire. You then need to seek ministry.

Remember that Antichrist and the False Prophet will come performing signs so as to deceive even the elect. Harry Potter is helping to lay the foundation.

---

4. The principle character has a lightning bolt on his forehead. Jesus told His disciples that Satan fell like lightning from heaven, and the thunderbolt is a symbol of his fall. The symbol was also used by the Nazi SS as an insignia on their collars, and figures in the artwork of a number of rock bands

CHAPTER SIX

Secular Humanism and Militant Homosexuality

There was a time in Western society when Christian tradition was considered normal. Your local town council might open a meeting with prayer. Every school day would begin with a Christian Assembly, the reading of scripture and a hymn. Society exhibited a respect for Godly traditions, even if it did not necessarily follow Him.

My grandfather, a pioneer of radio, was one of the original shareholders of the BBC in the early 1920's. The motto that appears in the lobby of the BBC's Broadcasting House in London reads:

> 'This Temple of the Arts and Muses is dedicated to Almighty God by the first Governors of Broadcasting in the year 1931, Sir John Reith being Director-General. It is their prayer that good seed sown may bring forth a good harvest, that all things hostile to peace or purity may be banished from this house, and that the people, inclining their ear to whatsoever things are beautiful and honest and of good report, may tread the path of wisdom and uprightness'

This has all changed now though. Christianity is being ruthlessly marginalised, schools are required to be inclusive (i.e. multi-faith) and the BBC is one of the world's foremost politically correct anti-Christian (and anti-Israel) broadcasters. It denies this of course with the typical arrogance of the humanist, which completely disdains those who hold any kind of religion.

That is not all though. The emergence of human rights legislation is beginning to criminalise our faith. This drives an increasing agenda of political correctness that does not recognise or respect Christianity or Judaism and elevates homosexual rights over the rest.[5] What underpins these developments is a spirit of highly militant, well organised secular 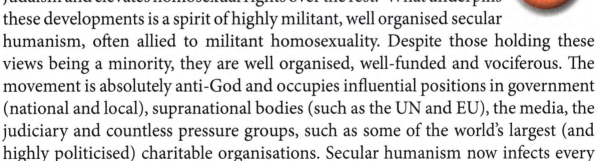 humanism, often allied to militant homosexuality. Despite those holding these views being a minority, they are well organised, well-funded and vociferous. The movement is absolutely anti-God and occupies influential positions in government (national and local), supranational bodies (such as the UN and EU), the media, the judiciary and countless pressure groups, such as some of the world's largest (and highly politicised) charitable organisations. Secular humanism now infects every

---

5. The fact that the exponents of human rights are strangely silent on the activities of Islamists is revealing. It shows that they originate from a similar spirit

Chapter Six

area of society and Christians can and should pray and resist whilst we are able.

The Bible is clear about this subject:

> *The fool has said in his heart, 'There is no God.' They are corrupt, they have committed abominable deeds. There is no one who does good*
>
> Psalm 14.1

The Church too is being overtaken by homosexuality. The Catholic Church has been beset by years of abuse, particularly towards vulnerable young people in its care. The Church of England is being torn apart by liberals who seek a place for homosexual bishops. Leading evangelicals and charismatics (from many denominations) are now stating that Jesus' message is one of 'reconciliation and inclusion' for the homosexual, and that the Church should recognise 'faithful and loving' homosexual relationships in a non-judgmental way.

Let us be absolutely clear on this: homosexuality is sin. Paul is unequivocal:

> *Or do you not know that the unrighteous will not inherit the kingdom of God? Do not be deceived; neither fornicators, nor idolaters, nor adulterers, nor effeminate,[6] nor homosexuals,[7] nor thieves, nor the covetous, nor drunkards, nor revilers, nor swindlers, will inherit the kingdom of God.*
>
> 1 Cor 6.9-10

Like all sinners, the homosexual can come to repentance, be forgiven and set free, but scripture is quite clear. Just like the sins of fornication, idolatry, adultery, thieving, covetousness, drunkenness, reviling and swindling – none who practise these things will inherit the Kingdom of God.

In Abraham's time, Sodom and Gomorrah were completely destroyed by God for the sin of rampant homosexuality. Later, under the Law, the children of Israel were warned:

> *You shall not lie with a male as one lies with a female; **it is an abomination**. If there is a man who lies with a male as those who lie with a woman, both of them have **committed a detestable act**; they shall surely be put to death. Their blood guiltiness is upon them*
>
> Leviticus 18.22 and 20.13

---

6. Greek '*malakos*'. Typically describing those men who have sexual relations with young boys, or who have homosexual relations with a man, who submit their bodies to unnatural lewdness, or who are male prostitutes
7. Greek '*arsenokoites*'. One who abuses or defiles one's self with men, or who lie with a male as with a female

Christians are not under law, but the warning is very clear. Lesbianism too is forbidden:

> *For this reason God gave them over to degrading passions; for their women exchanged the natural function for that which is unnatural, and in the same way also the men abandoned the natural function of the woman and burned in their desire toward one another, men with men committing indecent acts and receiving in their own persons the due penalty of their error*
>
> Romans 1.26-27

When Paul wrote to Timothy, he clearly warned him about false teachers, with particular reference to a number of sins, including homosexuality. We need to be on our guard and test these 'new doctrines' against the Bible to see what spirit these teachers are of.

> *For some men, **straying from these things, have turned aside to fruitless discussion, wanting to be teachers of the Law, even though they do not understand either what they are saying or the matters about which they make confident assertions**…But we know that the Law is good, if one uses it lawfully, realizing the fact that law is not made for a righteous person, but for those who are **lawless** and **rebellious**, for the **ungodly** and **sinners**, for the **unholy** and **profane**, for those who kill their fathers or mothers, for murderers and **immoral men and homosexuals** and kidnappers and liars and perjurers, and **whatever else is contrary to sound teaching**, according to the glorious gospel of the blessed God, with which I have been entrusted*
>
> 1 Tim 1.6-10

The warnings against homosexuality are stark, and encompass the dispensations of the patriarchs, Law and Grace. Check out the authors on your bookshelf and the speakers in your teaching library. No matter how big the name, don't be afraid to bin it if their teaching is contrary to the Word of God. Do it now. The Lord does not change His mind over sin.

We will see later in chapter 9 that anything that seeks to oppose or replace Christ is antichrist in nature. The present humanistic/homosexual 'conditioning' of society and Church is no coincidence and is laying the foundation for a religion that will worship a man. Ultimately, this movement will subjugate other religions too such as Islam and Buddhism and make a separation between those who follow Jesus Christ and those who don't.

CHAPTER SIX

Debt

As I write a massive economic storm is building over Europe and the USA, potentially greater in its impact than the Great Depression of 1929. Right now, within the USA, each citizen's share of the national debt is $200,000, making it the most indebted nation in history. Within the UK, the individual's share stands at £74,000 each. And this is merely the *national* debt of these countries (i.e. that borrowed from the international markets). If we add to this the average *personal* debt (such as credit cards and bank loans) then we have a disaster waiting to happen.

It does seem that the USA and Europe are in denial over the scale of this problem. Portugal, Ireland, Greece, Spain and the UK are all affected. The majority of public spending is being financed by loans from China, and who knows what the outcome will be. The savings of private individuals are being seized from bank accounts by the Cypriot government to cover their debts, much to the dismay of the Cypriot people.

This debt has seriously weakened the influence of western nations on the world stage. Military power may only be projected if their armed forces can back up their intentions with strong defence budgets, and I suspect that the next few years will see further erosion, the creation of an EU Army and the decline national armed forces.

It is of vital importance that wherever possible, Christians deal with debt. The Lord gives grace, but we must play our part by living within our means.

Paul's advice is:

> *Render to all what is due them: tax to whom tax is due; custom to whom custom; fear to whom fear; honor to whom honor. Owe nothing to anyone except to love one another...*
>
> Romans 13.7-8

Demise of the family

The family is one of the key pillars of society, along with the Church and local school. The family unit, led by a married father and mother, provides welfare, education, support and a moral framework for society. Increasingly the role of the family is being supplanted by the State, fatherhood is being devalued (spiritually and biologically) and the humanist/homosexual lobby is pushing for equality with same-sex marriages, led by politicians such as Barack Obama and David Cameron. Nearly half of the UK's 15 year olds live in a broken home and 3.8 million children are in the government's justice system. Never in history has the traditional family been under greater pressure. Equality and diversity legislation means that children may now be adopted by homosexual couples, whilst evangelical Christians are denied due to their faith. Schoolteachers may well lose their jobs if they refuse to teach that homosexual marriage is 'normal'.

Governance & Regulation

The last generation has witnessed a massive rise of rules and regulations in the west. In effect, the State has become bigger, and seized liberties from the individual. Much of this is presently benign, but its purpose is to establish mechanisms to outlaw what the State considers illegal and impose State control. From installing an electrical circuit in your home, to coaching a youth sports team, or even what you include in your child's lunchbox, there are regulations and areas of compliance that must be adhered to. Much is common sense, but clearly when your nation becomes secularised and requires for example that your small Christian hotel may not legally exclude homosexual couples, this becomes a problem.

This has been reinforced where professional disciplines have introduced accreditation and licensing systems, with the effect that those professionals who do not comply are ostracised and eventually excluded from participation. Again, whilst it appears a sensible step towards consistent professionalism, this is a concern for Christians practising in areas such as the Law or medicine. This relentless, insidious, gradual elevation of process and regulation over individual choice and discretion causes a sense of powerlessness, particularly for those working for large corporations or public sector bodies. Much of this dogma is flowed down from institutions like the secular-humanist EU, or the International Panel on Climate Change, so to object or fail to comply is to risk one's career and livelihood.

Christians in positions of influence can and should be salt and light in these areas to resist ungodly practices. However, we should also recognise that a time is coming soon where we will not be tolerated and may need to consider if we have become unequally yoked to

CHAPTER SIX

ungodly organisations. I do sense that now and in the coming days Christians may have to become a little streetwise in their dealings in this area and may have to adapt to find a profession that does not compromise their beliefs. The Lord is in control, and if one door shuts on your livelihood, you can be sure that he will open another. He is THE Door,[8] so this is no problem for Him.

A paraphrase of Psalm 94 offers an interesting insight:

> *Will those who sit influential positions and devise evil laws be able to fellowship with you? They congregate to come against the life of righteous people, and condemn the blood of the innocent. Nevertheless, the Lord defends me. God is the rock in which I take refuge*

Supra-National Government Bodies

There was a time in global politics where each nation's affairs were decided by its own sovereign government, whether democratically or by some other system. The last 50 years have seen a dramatic increase of supra-national government bodies, which extend control across borders.

An example of this occurred during November 2011, when the European Union[9] had baled-out the Italian economy. The political price for this was that the Italian government was replaced en-masse by EU technocrats, with not a single elected politician. A similar situation happened in Greece a few months later. In effect, both nations were then governed by the EU. They are certainly not accountable to the people and wield enormous power. This is even more significant when we recognise that the EU itself is not democratic. When Ireland for example voted to reject the EU's Lisbon Treaty, the EU manipulated the situation to make them vote again to get the 'right' result.

Individual countries are gradually but relentlessly ceding sovereign powers to organisations such as the Intergovernmental Panel on Climate Change (IPCC)[10] the EU Courts, International Criminal Court and the United Nations bodies. It is estimated that the UK Parliament at Westminster for example now decides only

---

8. John 10.9
9. The EU now possesses a single Parliament, single currency, single legal system, and single President. It is also moving towards a single banking system, and defence force as it strives for 'ever closer union'
10. In the author's opinion, the Climate Change movement, and so-called man-made global warming (AGW) is a deception, and very much driven by the move towards a single world government

25% of its laws, the remainder being under EU control. This includes control over borders, criminal and civil law, the environment and human rights. For example, the UK Courts may not expel terrorists because the terrorist then appeals to Brussels where the decision is overturned.

Supra-national rules decided by supra-national bodies are now given precedence over those of individual countries. It seems that we are moving, brick by brick, towards a single world government and this effect will be hastened by the governance and regulatory mechanisms considered above.

It is interesting that this system does not seem to take its authority from a single source, but is rapidly evolving, infecting every legal system and spawns many treaties and charters. It affects areas such as religious freedom, employment and commerce. It has been deployed without seeking permission from national citizens and is driven forward by activists in human rights, liberal judges, civil servants and ex-politicians who see opportunity for power and wealth in these entities. National governments and their opposition seem blind and powerless in the face of this rising tide, but Christians should be watching and praying. The spirit of antichrist is at work here and this is discussed further in Chapter 9.

Technological Integration & Electronic Commerce

In 1965, the co-founder of Intel, Gordon Moore, suggested that the number of transistors on a microchip would double every two years. Moore's Law, as it became known, now reasons that the price of technology halves every two years and its performance doubles. This is the reason we dispose of our mobile phones so frequently and why we feel pressured into upgrading our computers and other gadgetry. In 1899, the head of the US patent Office, Charles Duell declared that 'everything that can be invented has been invented'. People laugh at that now, but does it stop us from imagining what new technology may exist five years from now?

We live in a highly integrated age and the internet now means we can access knowledge with a few clicks of a mouse. Daniel prophesied that 'knowledge would increase' and that 'many would travel to and fro' and has been proved correct. It seems we have so much knowledge, but so little wisdom to use it.

However the march of technology has a sinister aspect. CCTV and other surveillance technologies are able to track us, recognise our faces, follow our car

Chapter Six

journeys and feed information into international databases for consumption by various national and supra-national bodies. In my local town, automatic number plate recognition cameras record your car's registration, immediately cross-check it with a database of insurance and road tax, and within seconds you may be stopped by the police. Whilst this is a good system, it could be abused in the hands of a secularist police state. We are also aware that every electronic commercial transaction is recorded and cash is becoming increasingly irrelevant, with the use of mobile phones to purchase items.

My pet dogs were 'chipped' to allow them to be more easily identified in the event of their loss. It is quite feasible to develop this technology to allow humans to make financial transactions and this is described in Revelation as the Mark of the Beast. This mark might somehow encode who we are (fingerprints, biometrics, DNA, social security number) with our financial assets.

A final thought here. At Babel,

> *The Lord said, 'Behold, they are one people, and they all have the same language. And this is what they began to do, and now nothing which they purpose to do will be impossible for them. Come, let Us go down and there confuse their language, so that they will not understand one another's speech'*

Gen 11.6-7

The internet combined with mobile phone and computer technology is restoring man's ability to communicate without barriers and do whatsoever he proposes, in a unified common voice.

Celebrity Worship

Celebrities have always been with us, from the time of Greece's Olympic champions or Rome's gladiators to today's TV personalities. However, it does seem that we are witnessing a massive rise in those who idolise them. The celebrity cult has all the trappings of a religion, and affects what their fans think, what they say, how they dress, how they spend their time and money, and their personal values.

A time is coming when a man will appear on the world stage who will be the ultimate celebrity. The conditioning that society has witnessed over the last twenty years or so has prepared his fan base and he will meet with little resistance. There was a time past when those in countries like the UK or USA possessed a measure of discernment, rooted in a predominantly Christian education, establishment and family values. However, as we have seen this has been largely eroded and marginalised, such that many today have no appreciation of biblical values. The majority of women in the UK for example now support same-sex marriages. This would never have happened say in the 1950's.

For these people, the Antichrist's appearance will tick all the right boxes. Again, as Christians it is important not only that we train our discernment now by making godly choices about what we let into our minds, but also warn people about God's righteousness. We have a choice and should exercise it. As we make righteous decisions, our discernment will improve.

Weather and other natural events

Backed by billions of dollars of funding, the Climate Change lobby has promulgated the message that our climate is being seriously damaged by the release of man-made CO_2 into the atmosphere. They claim that only a radical reduction in its emission will save the planet from drought, floods, loss of Arctic ice and consequent sea-level rise and the consequent impact on humans and animals. The campaign has been bought into by governments, and the Climate Change Act was the most expensive government Bill ever passed in the UK's Parliament. The lobby combines western governments with multi-million dollar pressure groups such as the World Wildlife Fund and Greenpeace. The International Panel on Climate Change co-ordinates the 'science' and resulting targets required to manage the problem.

However, there is a problem in that there has been no appreciable global warming since 1997, even though around a third of the world's CO_2 has been released since then. There has been virtually no rise in the sea-level, and no reduction in total global ice coverage. A growing body of sceptics has emerged, comprising many eminent scientists and climatologists, who now challenge the belief in Anthropomorphic Global Warming (AGW). The Climate Change lobby uses many tactics to attempt to close the debate down and the BBC for example, promotes the view that the 'science is settled', so has almost completely closed down the debate.

Whichever viewpoint one takes (I am a sceptic!), one cannot but help have noticed

Chapter Six

that the weather does appear to be behaving unusually. In the UK for example over the last 10 years we have seen a variety of hottest and coldest temperatures and unusually high rain and snowfall. The US too has experienced a number of significant weather events. 'Superstorm Sandy' that flooded parts of New York and devastated Atlantic City is but one example. Atlantic City, also known as 'Sin City', is famous for its gambling and prostitution. The storm hit the coast here and I suspect that God is sending a message to America.

These events are emphatically not driven by CO_2, so what then is the cause?

Figure 28. Asteroid DA14.

There are other signs too. During February 2013 astronomers warned of asteroid 2012 DA14 that would pass within 17,000 miles of the earth. Its path was north to south, and the scientific community seemed pleased with their foreknowledge. However, on the same day a 40 ton meteor slammed into the earth's atmosphere over Russia from the south at 40,000mph, with its shock wave causing over 1,000 injuries. The last similar major collision with the earth was in 1908 when Siberia was hit by a meteor 140' long. Having waited over 100 years, and with all its technological advances, science was duped into looking 180° the wrong way. Coincidence? I don't think so, and statistically it is virtually impossible. It has been estimated that the probability of two such meteors as the February 2013 event on the same day are around 100 million to one.

There are many who say that we cannot trust God in an age of science and that science has all the answers. Try blogging on creation, and watch the humanists appear.[11] I believe the Lord has just given the scientific community a wake-up call. We will see increasingly that men's predictions about the world, including the natural, economic and political arenas, will prove unreliable. The Latin word *scientia* (from which we derive science) means knowledge, and Paul's letter to

---

11. Their responses will follow a pattern: 1. They won't answer your questions 2. They will insult you 3. They will present unproven scientific theory as 'fact' for their argument

Corinth (a society steeped in man's scientific knowledge) tells us that

> *Knowledge makes arrogant, but love edifies. If anyone supposes that he knows anything, he has not yet known as he ought to know*
>
> 1 Corininthians 8.1-2

I am not knocking science – I love it. But it has its place and, since the age of enlightenment, men have sought to elevate science and reason over scripture. Where science and the Bible disagree we should put our trust in God's word, not man's. Cursed is the man who trusts in man.[12]

So, there we have it. The passage of time will no doubt result in others arising. We need to be sober and watchful, redeeming the days, for the time is indeed short.

Part 3 – The Beginning of Sorrows

We will now examine the events prophesied by Jesus as the beginning of sorrows or labour pains. These were clearly provided as milestones to watch for, so it is of vital importance that we understand where we are in relation to them.

Labour Pains

In Matthew 24.8 / Mark 13.8 Jesus says **all these** things are the beginning of sorrows. The word sorrows is the Greek word *odin*, meaning a birth pang, travail or pain. 'These things' refer back to this list of events.

On a personal note, my wife was a midwife. We have two children of our own. Like any parent who has experienced a normal birth, we understand the nature of labour pains. As the moment of birth nears, the labour pains (or sorrows or birth pangs) come faster and grow more intense. There is absolutely no doubt, no argument, no discussion, no more guessing for anyone involved that they have started. Once they have started they cannot be stopped (even if we wanted to!) until the baby is born. It is a frightening experience, but also encouraging. We know now that once we have got through the pain, there is a baby on the way. The point is that we don't have to guess if they have started, as it is obvious to all.

---

12. Jeremiah 17.5

Chapter Six

In Romans 8, Paul says:

> *For I consider that the sufferings of this present time are not worthy to be compared with the glory that is to be revealed to us. For the anxious longing of the creation waits eagerly for the revealing of the sons of God. For the creation was subjected to futility, not willingly, but because of Him who subjected it, in hope that the creation itself also will be set free from its slavery to corruption into the freedom of the glory of the children of God. For we know that* **the whole creation groans and suffers the pains of childbirth together until now.** *And not only this, but also we ourselves, having the first fruits of the Spirit, even we ourselves groan within ourselves, waiting eagerly for our adoption as sons, the redemption of our body*

Creation is indeed groaning and labouring whilst it awaits the revelation of the children of God. Maybe this explains the unusual climatic conditions and other natural phenomena the world is experiencing. If so, we should expect them to increase.

But what are these labour pains that we are to look for? Jesus lists them in both His prophecies given in Jerusalem, but only describes them as labour pains in His second prophecy on Olivet. There are six signs:

- False Christs
- War / State of disorder
- Ethnic conflict
- Earthquakes
- Famine
- Pestilence

These events are a collective group and are not apparently given in chronological order, as there are no 'then' statements between events. However, we shall examine their incidence to determine if such a pattern emerges.

As I write we see incidences of them all. Open your newspaper, check the TV and you will see them reported almost every day. However, although they have been occurring throughout history, it is the *rate* of incidence and intensity (i.e. how *often* and how *bad*) that we are interested in to determine if they are indeed 'birth pangs', or merely isolated one-off incidents.

Chapter Six

In the same way that labour pains come upon a woman suddenly, we don't know the actual time at which they will begin, or even if they have already begun. Jesus gave us no single event or sign to indicate the beginning of this phase. We therefore have to watch and pray to look for the signs. It may seem that nothing is happening, but as with the woman in labour, things may happen with alarming speed i.e. the 'beginning of sorrows' is in itself the milestone for the start of the sequence.

Let us take a look with an open mind at each type of labour pain. As we consider them, we should ask ourselves three questions:

- are they coming more **frequently**?
- are they becoming more **intense**?
- is there any doubt at all that they have **started**?

Christians would particularly like to believe that these things are happening, as it would justify our faith in the Bible. However, if we are to be truthful we must examine each condition objectively, dispassionately and carefully. If it isn't true yet, a time is coming when it will be beyond dispute.

I should mention here that we cannot rely on the world to keep us informed. Jesus said that 'the 'whole world lies in the evil one'. The media, government and academia all have their own agendas, and proving Bible truth isn't usually high on the list. The majority of such institutions are highly political and ruled by a strong spirit of secular humanism that seeks to deny, play-down or ridicule faith. Some even seek to criminalise our beliefs. We must 'watch and pray', reading 'the signs of the times' from a variety of trustworthy sources with a discerning heart, prayerfully forming our own opinion based on observation.

I have attempted below to provide you with a start to your investigation. Each topic is discussed briefly and basic, widely available statistics are provided. Under each topic I have also identified the largest accurately recorded occurrence. Make your own mind up and think for yourself. I am not a scientist nor have any expertise in these areas, but here is how I see it...

As with the discussion in part 2 of this chapter, we should associate the appearance of these signs with the re-emergence of Israel, the fig tree. We will thus focus our analysis from 1800 onwards.

False Christs

(Greek: *'pseudochristos'*): Christ means 'the anointed one'. False Christs are the leaders of counterfeit pseudo-Christian cults. They lay claim to the office and name of Christ, but distort His word and teaching. Examples of the most significant of these movements (as defined by number of followers) with approximate dates, would include the following:

False Christs

Commenced	Cult	Followers in 2011 (Millions)
1774	Unitarianism Universalist Assoc.	c0.5M
1820	Mormonism - The Church of Jesus Christ of Latter day Saints	14.1M (2010)
1853	Spiritualist Churches	unknown
1863	Seventh Day Adventists	25M+
1864	Christadelphians	c0.06
1879	Jehovah's Witnesses	7.7M
1879	Christian Science	c0.06
1934	Armstrongism the Worldwide Church of God	unknown
1954	Unification Church (Moonies)	5-7M
1968	Children of God	unknown
1968	Rastafarianism	0.6 – 1M

Clearly, doctrinal error and false religious movements existed before the 19th Century. However, it does seem that we have witnessed a significant upsurge in the number of followers from around the turn of the 1800's.

Our overall chronology in chapter 5 showed a number of incidences of deception. Here is the first wave (#1), whose principle 'surge' was during the 19th Century. We can expect two more such waves as we near the end of the age, one in the first phase of the Tribulation (#2 false prophets) and another in the second (#3 false prophets and false Christs). Interestingly, it appears that the emergence of these cults coincides with both the start of Zionism and the birth of modern Pentecostalism as evidenced by the Asuza St. Revival. The enemy always seeks to oppose, counterfeit and disrupt the plans of God.

There is one primary test that can be applied to reveal truth from error. Jesus said *'who do men say that I am?'* Every cult and false religion somehow denies or questions the divinity of Jesus Christ[13], or the nature of the Trinity. They might acknowledge that He was a good man, or a prophet, but the spirit operating within them seeks to oppose, replace or distort His deity, and His completed work on the Cross.[14]

These false Judaeo-Christian cults adopt some of the basic 'furniture' or language of the true faith, but deny some of the key tenets, for example the existence of hell, or work of the Holy Spirit. Even so-called 'charismatic' or evangelical Churches are not guaranteed to be free from error. Remember that rat poison is very tasty, and at least 99% of it is good food. It still kills the rat though.

With these false movements, what sometimes started out in the Spirit ended in the flesh. Even today, bona-fide movements still go wrong, such as an over-emphasis on 'shepherding' or 'discipleship' where leaders have undue levels of control over church members. Deception takes many forms so we must be vigilant and continue to test these with scripture. One such example is the recent rise of the Emergent Church, which discounts Hell, belittles sin, permits homosexuality, encourages Celtic mysticism and questions the authority of scripture. Beware.

Space does not permit a more detailed examination of error, but the epistles are full of warnings. The fact that these pseudo-Christian cults exist at all is thus further evidence of the reliability of scripture. I pray that the followers of these movements come into the true and saving knowledge of their Lord and God, Jesus Christ.

There are many good books out there that can help in this area.

---

13. The Gospel of John makes seven references to the deity of Christ
14. This test also applies to every other world religions. Secular Humanism however is different in that it does not recognise Jesus Christ at all. More of this in Chapter 9

Chapter Six

> **Labour Pain #1: Largest Cult**
>
> 7th Day Adventism instigated in 1863. Over 25M followers

War / State of Disorder

(Greek *'polemos'* : a war or battle) For consistency, this has been assumed to be between states, countries or nations. 'Conflict' within nations will be considered below.

War has been a constant throughout history and historical records improve over time. In order to understand if wars are increasing we will therefore consider the last 200 years, with a particular focus on the last century. We will consider the number and frequency of wars, then the number of casualties inflicted.

For the period 1816 to 2007[15] there have been some 650 wars. The chart below shows those between states as well as conflict within states, but makes no allowance for how big those wars were.

Frequency of Individual Wars

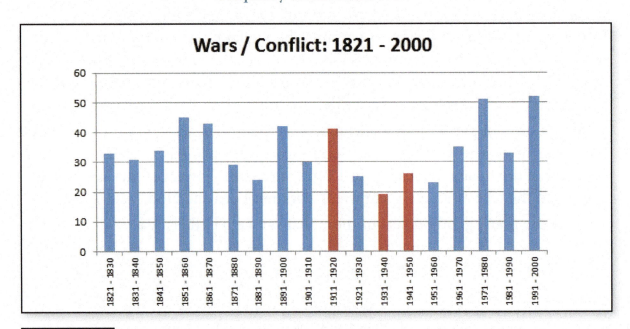

---

15. Sarkees, Meredith Reid and Frank Wayman (2010). *Resort to War: 1816 - 2007*. CQ Press.

Chapter Six

It is only in the 21st Century that we have coined the phrase 'World War'. The advent of the jet engine and other technologies has allowed man to project force across the globe in a way that was previously impossible. The bars in red show when there was a 'World War'. These World Wars had the effect of reducing the total numbers of wars in their decade, but resulted in a major shift in terms of their impact on world affairs and number of casualties.

Casualties of War

when	what	approx number killed
1939-45	Second World War	66M
1914-18	First World War	20M
1937-45	Second Sino-Japanese War	20M
1917-22	Russian Civil War	5-9M
1959-75	Vietnam War	4.2M
1950-53	Korean War	3.0M
1955-72 1983-2005	1st Sudanese War 2nd Sudanese War	2.6M
1977-78	Menghistu Haile Mariam	2.0M
1971	Benghali Genocide	1.5M
1967-70	Nigerian-Biafran War	1.0M
1977-92	Mozambique Civil War	0.8M
1935-41	Italo-Ethiopian War	0.75M

Based on the table above, we can clearly see a dramatic increase in the deaths from war in the 20th Century.

Taking the two charts together, I beleive that it is safe to say that we have seen a significant increase in the impact of war, particularly in the 20th Century. Although there has been no 'World War' in the last 50 years, the numbers of ethnic conflicts in such places as Africa have dramatically increased.

Chapter Six

> **Labour Pain #2: Largest recorded war**
>
> 1939-45 World War 2 killed 66M

Ethnic Conflict

(Greek '***ethnos***': a group of peoples from the same genus or tribe). This is where we get our word 'ethnic' from, and forms the basis of the new phrase of '*ethnic cleansing*'. This type of conflict is between ethnic groups rather than government against government.

Ethnicity has to do with religion, race, nationality, language and culture. There are roughly 14 *racial* groups. Estimates vary, but it is believed that there are potentially 10-25,000 *ethnic* groups.[16] We will define ethnic conflict as where this disagreement escalates into violence and killing. It might be possible to view WW2 on this level, as Hitler's Aryan vision sought to eradicate those who stood in his way, such as Jews and Poles. It could be argued that we are now seeing fewer inter-State wars and more conflict between ethnic groups.

Arguably, three modern events have had the most impact on the massive rise in ethnic conflict:

- the decline and dismantling of the British Empire in the mid-twentieth century
- the fall of the Soviet Union in the early 1990's
- the 'Arab Spring' in the Middle East

It is interesting that these events are firmly related to the three 'beasts' of Daniel 7 too. We should note that all are relatively recent and have occurred since the milestone of Herzl's 1897 proclamation of the State of Israel.

In Chapter 2, I mentioned how both 'empires' had been instrumental in opposing the birth of Israel, and her survival since then. The Soviet Union (rather like modern

---

16. See Fields of Fire by Stuart Notholt 2010

Russia) has maintained a cold peace with Israel, whilst actively supplying Israel's enemies with weapons and intelligence. Britain's foreign policy has generally been to elevate its Arab interests above the interests of the Jew. It is interesting that the demise of both the USSR and British control have resulted in such a dramatic rise of ethnic conflict, 'Nation rising against Nation', or 'ethnos against ethnos'. It seems the British and Soviet dominance had a restraining effect on policing local differences. Once this was removed, conflict ensued and accelerated.

The unfortunately named 'Arab spring' is the latest example of ethnic conflict sweeping through the Middle East and is impacting most of the countries created in the early 19th century by the Sykes-Picot agreement, most recently in Syria.

It is generally agreed that the world has seen a dramatic rise in the level of ethnic conflict since 1989. However this is difficult to establish statistically. Possibly the most significant is the ethnic violence starting in post-colonial Africa and peaking through the latter part of the 20th century.

> **Labour Pain #3: Largest ethnic conflict**
>
> Central Africa c1980-90
>
> approx 5M deaths

Earthquakes

(Greek: *seismos* – a shaking, commotion, tempest or earthquake). The US Geological Survey's website states quite categorically that earthquakes are not increasing. It offers the partial explanation that there are now significantly more  seismometers, better communications and a huge public interest for news, and these factors have contributed to an increase in *recorded* earthquakes.

I am unconvinced by this reasoning and would respectfully suggest that even over the last 30-40 years or so the technology must have stabilised so as to allow the scoping of the total number and magnitude of earthquakes with a high level of confidence. The graph below shows that even if we limit our view to this period

Chapter Six

and ignore what went before, we still see an increase in their occurrence. I would therefore respectfully suggest that this is an inconvenient truth for government geologists who have no desire to prove the Bible correct, much in the same way as 'Global Warmists' ignore the fact that there has been no significant warming since 1997. I am not suggesting any conspiracy here, merely a blindness, in part because it does not fit the scientific consensus, and few scientists wish to risk their professional reputations (or funding!) with such sensational claims.

Number of earthquakes Magnitude 6 and above by decade

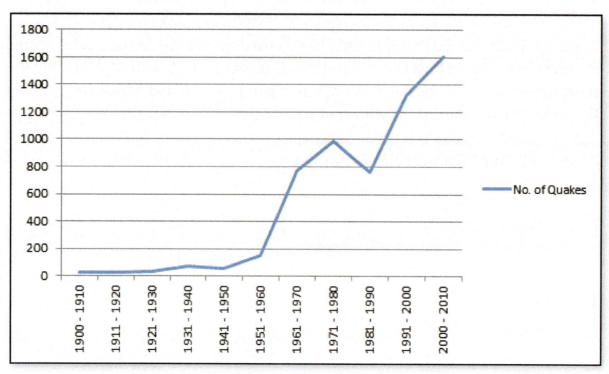

Figure 29. Significant earthquakes (based on USGS database)

CHAPTER SIX

> **Labour Pain #4: Most significant earthquake**
>
> Chile 1960 Magnitude 9.5

Famine

(Greek *limos* = famine, hunger or scarcity of harvest). Famine has many causes, including war (e.g. Leningrad) volcanic eruptions, or crop failure (e.g. the Irish potato famine). It marches hand in hand therefore with the other labour pains such as pestilence, war and earthquakes.

Most significant famines

when	what	approx number died
1996	North Korea	up to 3.5M
1960	China	up to 43M
	(This has been selected as the 'most significant' labour pain as the China famine in the early 19th Century was over a much longer duration)	
1947	USSR	up to 1.5M
1943	India	up to 1.5M
1941-43	Leningrad	1M
1936	China	5M
1932-33	Ukraine	10M
1921	Russia	5M
1845	Ireland	1.5M
1810-49	China	45M

The 'developed' world often looks on at countries such as Africa as they suffer from famine. However, it may be that famine will come to the West as the economic crisis deepens and harvests are reduced by shifting weather patterns and events. Trees in Europe have been affected significantly over the last 40 years, with Dutch Elm and Ash Dieback disease devastating our woodland. Colder weather patterns

CHAPTER SIX

have affected crops, with yields seeming to reduce.

The great tragedy of course is that in the world as a whole, there is sufficient food for all. It is man who fails to share it out.

> **Labour Pain #5: Most significant famine**
>
> China 1960 43M

Pestilence

(Greek *loimos* = pestilences or plagues i.e. contagious or infectious epidemic disease that is virulent and devastating. The modern word often used is a pandemic)

Due to the relatively recent and rapid development of medical science, it is difficult to obtain reliable statistics for pestilences beyond the last 100 years or so, so this will limit our assessment. However, there have been two major instances we should consider. The Pandemic of Spanish Flu that followed WWI had a global impact, affecting even young adults. Of the world's population at that time, it killed approximately 3% but actually infected around a quarter of the total.

A more recent 'plague' has been the human immunodeficiency virus infection / acquired immunodeficiency syndrome, also known as HIV/AIDS. It passes the infection through sexual intercourse, infected hypodermic needles used by drug addicts and from mother to child.

The table below summarises incidences of more than 100,000 deaths for the last century.

Pestilence and disease

Date	Outbreak	Approximate Deaths
1918-20	1918 Flu Pandemic	up to 50M
1957-58	Asian Flu	2M
1968-69	Hong Kong Flu	1M
1981 –present	HIV / AIDS	34M

> **Labour Pain #6: Most significant pestilence**
>
> 1918 Flu Pandemic 50M deaths

Part 4 - Summary

In Mathew 24.7 Jesus describes how the labour pains would occur in 'diverse' (or different) places. It can be seen that of the most significant instances described above, how His prediction has been fulfilled and the whole world impacted. Furthermore, when we consider the periodicity of occurrence, we cannot fail to notice how these major events occur in the same timeframe as the Herzl's 1897 proclamation and the rebirth of Israel in 1948. My opinion is therefore that these events are *indeed* the labour pains that Jesus foretold. When I began this study, my opinion had been that the labour pains were something to look for in the future, but that we might now just be seeing their *beginning*. My overwhelming sense now is that they are for the most part in the *past* and that we are now transitioning into the next phase (via the transitional period postulated in earlier chapters).

Personal Conclusion

When we combine:

- the incidence of birth pangs, with
- the 'pillars' discussed in Part 1 of this chapter,
- the emergence of the 'fig tree' and other trees, and
- the unveiling of the kingdoms of Daniel 7,

I would confidently propose that we must surely be entering the end-game of history.

Chapter 7 Israel – chosen people, promised land

Isaiah is very bold and says, 'I was found by those who did not seek Me, I became manifest to those who did not ask for Me.' But as for Israel He says, 'All the day long I have stretched out My hands to a disobedient and obstinate people.'

I say then, God has not rejected His people, has He?

May it never be!

Romans 10.20 – 11.1

Part 1 – Introduction

Why does Israel so inflame and divide world opinion? This tiny land with its small population is almost obsessively hounded by both media and the UN. Normally rational people begin to act very strangely when its name is mentioned and hold her to standards that they would not apply elsewhere.

Chapter Seven

Within the Church there is also a prevailing and long-held view that Israel is now irrelevant to God's purposes. This position holds that because Israel 'killed Christ', disobeyed God, rejected His kingdom and lost both its land and its temple, then now God must have discarded its people and given away its land. Surely then, all the promises made to Israel now belong to the Church. We will see. The vast majority of the world's secular and even Christian institutions see Israel's rebirth as an act of land theft from Palestinian Arabs. Is this true and what does the Bible have to say about it?

One thing all would agree on is that Israel is a divider of opinions. Between governments, academia, and even amongst friends, family and colleagues, there are few who sit on the fence. You are generally either for or against. As time goes by, it seems that the gulf that divides the pro and anti lobbies is widening. Is this God's purpose for Israel, and if so, why?

In Chapter 8 we will explore these questions, and in answering these issues there are three key relationships we must address:

- The God of Israel

- The Land of Israel

- Israel and the Church

One of the Lord's purposes for the State of Israel is to demand the world's attention. Psalm 78.5 tells us that *'He established a testimony in Jacob'*. This has proved to be a most effective strategy. There is something about human nature whereby once we know something of the Jews, Israel and the surrounding issues, it seems impossible to remain neutral. Jesus told us that He didn't come to bring peace, but a sword, and that He would even divide members of a household from one another. This is a classic example of that truth. As we approach the end of the age, it seems the fast-forward button has been pressed and the Lord is hastening the fulfilment of His prophetic word. We should not be surprised then by the pace of events and the days are coming when the Lord is going to answer a lot of prayers (from both Christian and Jew) very quickly indeed. Israel seems like a sharp knife, whose divine purpose is to divide and separate opinion and, in so doing, mankind. We have a choice before us: we can bless and support Israel; or we can curse, oppose and condemn her. There is no middle ground on offer here and as time moves on that choice will become more stark.

Israel is no bastion of morality however and we must not assume that God chose its people because they were more deserving than any other nation. Abortion, homosexuality and godlessness prevail as in many other nations. However, they are the people of the Bible, in which Israel is mentioned over 2,300 times and Jerusalem over 760 times.[1] Cut Israel out of your Bible and you would have just a few scraps of paper left. As Christians, we cannot ignore Israel or the Jews.

After they had left Egypt, and before they entered the Promised Land, the Lord gave the children of Israel a choice:

> *'I call heaven and earth to witness against you today, that I have set before you life and death, the blessing and the curse. So choose life in order that you may live, you and your descendants'*
>
> Deut 30.19

The Lord also promised Abraham:

> *'And I will bless those who bless you, and the one who curses you I will curse. And in you all the families of the earth will be blessed'*
>
> Gen 12.3

Israel's choice concerned life or death. Our choice today in our attitude and actions towards Israel also has consequences. As we move towards the second half of this book, we will see that God's will and word most definitely polarise mankind into two camps. *"Who is on the Lord's side?"* cried Moses and it is now time to make up your mind. Our God is a Master Scheduler and is engineering events so as to leave no middle ground, no ambiguity, and it is clear that Israel is absolutely central to His strategy.

I'll be honest with you: of all the chapters in this book, this was the most difficult to write. That is possibly because it is the most important. Why? Because the story of Israel is the story of us all. It tells how God selected and redeemed an apparently undeserving and 'stiff-necked' people to be His own special possession. Would you have chosen a double-dealer like Jacob and founded a nation upon him? Probably not, me neither. There really wasn't much to like about this difficult character.[2]

---

1. Interestingly, despite the Muslim's claims, Jerusalem is not mentioned once in the Koran
2. Jacob's one redeeming feature was his ambition, ruthlessness and cunning to grasp his spiritual birthright and blessing. It

Chapter Seven

But for the Christian, did God choose you because He liked you, or because you deserved it? Emphatically no. If we are honest, Christians are amazed that God chose and redeemed us from our sinful way of life. Also amazing is the daily miracle that He stays with us, knowing what is really in our hearts and continues to forgive and show us mercy.[3] We cannot apply one standard to Israel and another to the Church, because God is One. He is the same God, He doesn't change and isn't capable of showing two kinds of love, or two different standards towards these two peoples.

Not only did God choose Israel, but He also decided that His Son was to be incarnated in bodily form as a Jew and would grow up in obscurity amongst other Jews. Some would accept Him, but most would reject the Kingdom He came to offer. The Bible tells Jesus' story from everlasting to everlasting, and the Gospels describe how He lived, died and was resurrected to offer a way for every man, woman and child to enter that Kingdom. But He came first to Israel. When He returns, He will return as a Jew. And it will not be to London or Washington, Moscow or Mecca, but to Jerusalem. God hasn't finished with Israel yet.

Part 2 – The God of Israel

The children of Israel are God's chosen people. Ask any Jew and they will tell you that it is not easy to be chosen. They have endured more suffering than any other nation throughout history. If you follow the right news feeds, you will discover that even today Jew-hatred is a daily reality for Jewish communities world-wide. Of course, in our politically correct society, it is frowned upon to hate someone on the basis of their race. Anti-Semites get around this difficulty by venting their hatred on Israel and 'Zionists'. It amounts to the same thing though and there is no practical difference between anti-Semitism and hatred of Israel. Search any of the Israeli blog sites on the internet, and the question that continually arises is 'why does the world hate us?'

---

  may not seem right to us, but the Lord was evidently pleased with him. Esau, the father of the Arab nations, came off second best: still blessed, but not the son of the promise
3. One of the finest Bible teachers I have had the privilege of hearing was Dr Alan Redpath. An old man in his 80's, who confessed that there was 'not one sin that I am not capable of committing five minutes after this meeting'. As a 25 year old, I found that hard to believe. Into my 50's now, I am beginning to understand what he meant

Why God chose Israel

We cannot seek to understand this question on a natural, human or political level, and must look to the Bible for answers.

'For you are a holy people to the Lord your God. The Lord your God has chosen you to be a people for His own possession out of all the peoples who are on the face of the earth. The Lord did not set His love on you nor choose you because you were more in number than any of the peoples, for you were the fewest of all peoples, but because the Lord loved you and kept the oath which He swore to your forefathers, the Lord brought you out by a mighty hand and redeemed you from the house of slavery, from the hand of Pharaoh king of Egypt. Know therefore that the Lord your God, He is God, the faithful God, who keeps His covenant and His lovingkindness to a thousandth generation with those who love Him and keep His commandments, but repays those who hate Him to their faces, to destroy them. He will not delay with him who hates Him, He will repay him to his face. Therefore, you shall keep the commandment and the statutes and the judgments which I am commanding you today, to do them'

Deut 7.6-11

When Paul wrote to the Church at Corinth he gave us a key:

'Because the foolishness of God is wiser than men, and the weakness of God is stronger than men. For consider your calling, brethren, that there were not many wise according to the flesh, not many mighty, not many noble; but God has chosen the foolish things of the world to shame the wise, and God has chosen the weak things of the world to shame the things which are strong, and the base things of the world and the despised God has chosen, the things that are not, so that He may nullify the things that are, so that no man may boast before God'

1 Cor 1.25-29

God chose Israel because they were few in number, the 'least of all peoples', weak, base and despised. Why? So that no flesh could glory in His presence. Nobody would be able to say that He had chosen them because of any quality that they might possess. Rather, The Lord takes those who are weak and ordinary and transforms them into a 'special treasure'. Salvation is a gift – it can never be earned. Remind yourself of this the next time the Devil makes you feel inadequate!

When Paul was describing his 'thorn in the flesh' in his second letter to Corinth, the Lord said to him:

'My grace is sufficient for you, for power is perfected in weakness. Most gladly, therefore, I will rather boast about my weaknesses, so that the power of Christ

Chapter Seven

> *may dwell in me. Therefore I am well content with weaknesses, with insults, with distresses, with persecutions, with difficulties, for Christ's sake; for when I am weak, then I am strong'*
>
> 2 Cor 12.9-10

One of the key principles in the Christian life is that when we are weak, we are strong, because God can then act through us. Elijah told the prophets of Baal to pour water on the sacrificial bonfire on Mount Carmel to make it impossible to ignite. When they had done this four times, the fire fell from heaven. Humanly speaking, it was impossible. But nothing is too hard for our God. He delights in doing the impossible, because it results in more glory for Him. This is why the Lord, in His wisdom, chose Israel. It is also the reason why He chose you and me. He delights in redeeming and restoring that which is base and broken. The Son of Man came to seek and save that which is lost, not to those who think they have all the answers.[4] He wants the glory, so chooses failures, outcasts and the foolish things to shame those who are 'wise', and the weak ones to shame those who are mighty. So with Israel, so too with the Church, you and me.

The enemy of our souls

In Eden, the Lord had promised to bruise Satan's head[5] through the Seed of Eve. From that point on, Satan carefully studied Eve's descendants, looking for the ancestral line from which the Seed would emerge. As the Lord's plan to choose Israel was gradually revealed, so the intensity of the attacks from Satan increased. This has been true throughout history, with Satan seeking to destroy the Royal family line of Christ.

Once Christ had been born, Satan sought to destroy Him, through Herod's murder of the infants,[6] through a crowd seeking to throw Him off a cliff,[7] and then, finally, at the Cross. The surprise however was that though Christ died, He rose again. A further surprise was that Christ would not then operate through His own physical body, but through the Church. The Church then became a target for Satan. But what then of Israel? Did it still have a purpose?

---

4. The exception is sometimes true however. The Lord will take one who 'knows it all', like Saul of Tarsus, and so shake and break him that he will cry out for salvation. He also chose Moses, the 'Prince of Egypt', but who first had to endure the loneliness of rejection and the wilderness before he would be ready to serve his God
5. Genesis 3.15
6. Matthew 2.16
7. Luke 4.28-29

Chapter Seven

Jesus came to proclaim the Kingdom of God to the Jews, but was rejected then crucified. The kingdom was offered again to the Jews in Jerusalem by Peter's patient explanation of Christ's mission:

But the things which God announced beforehand by the mouth of all the prophets, that His Christ would suffer, He has thus fulfilled. Therefore repent and return, so that your sins may be wiped away, in order that times of refreshing may come from the presence of the Lord, and that He may send Jesus, the Christ appointed for you, whom heaven must receive until the period of restoration of all things about which God spoke by the mouth of His holy prophets from ancient time. Moses said, 'The Lord God will raise up for you a prophet like me from your brethren. To Him you shall give heed to everything He says to you. And it will be that every soul that does not heed that prophet shall be utterly destroyed from among the people.' And likewise, all the prophets who have spoken, from Samuel and his successors onward, also announced these days. It is you who are the sons of the prophets and of the covenant which God made with your fathers, saying to Abraham, 'And in your seed all the families of the earth shall be blessed.' For you first, God raised up His Servant and sent Him to bless you by turning every one of you from your wicked ways.

Acts 3.18-26

The chief priests and elders of Israel again rejected the kingdom. The book of Acts goes on to describe how the salvation spread to the Gentiles. Finally, in Acts we read:

When they had set a day for Paul, they came to him at his lodging in large numbers; and he was explaining to them by solemnly testifying about the kingdom of God and trying to persuade them concerning Jesus, from both the Law of Moses and from the Prophets, from morning until evening. Some were being persuaded by the things spoken, but others would not believe. And when they did not agree with one another, they began leaving after Paul had spoken one parting word, The Holy Spirit rightly spoke through Isaiah the prophet to your fathers, saying:

'Go to this people and say, "You will keep on hearing, but will not understand; And you will keep on seeing, but will not perceive. For the heart of this people has become dull, and with their ears they scarcely hear, and they have closed their eyes, otherwise they might see with their eyes, and hear with their ears, and understand with their heart and return, and I would heal them."'

Therefore let it be known to you that this salvation of God has been sent to the Gentiles; they will also listen

Acts 28.23-29

Chapter Seven

Throughout Acts we see a steady transition in focus from the Jews to the Gentiles, but this was the point where the Jews finally rejected the Kingdom that had been offered to them. The prophet Daniel sheds further light here too. Daniel 9 describes a period of 70 sets of seven years in the (then) future of Jerusalem. We will return to this prophecy more fully in Chapter 10, but Daniel makes it clear that Messiah would be cut off, the city and sanctuary would be destroyed and war and desolation would follow. There was to be a gap between the Messiah being cut off and this final period of seven years. This gap starts with Israel's rejection of the kingdom, where in effect Israel, though still God's chosen, had gone into a period of abeyance in His dealings with them.

But Jesus had prophesied that some time after His death the fig tree (the nation of Israel) would begin to 'put forth leaves' (i.e. re-emerge). Satan knew then that the return of Christ would be linked to the re-establishment of Israel and so acted to destroy, frustrate and confound God's chosen race through the judgment of Rome, pogroms of Russia, gas chambers of Europe and hatred of Islamists. He failed, despite inflicting a grievous wound on the Jews, and the State of Israel was eventually reborn in 1948. This did not stop Satan's determination to destroy Israel however. We will take this up below, when we consider Israel's relationship with the land. We will also look at why the Lord permitted this persecution in later chapters.

We read in Job[8] that Satan can do nothing without permission from God, so why did the Lord grant this permission? Again, we will consider this point below, as it is inextricably linked with the Covenant of Sinai and Israel's possession of the land. We have in previous chapters described the 'occupation' of the land of Israel by various empires, nations and kingdoms. We have already explored some of the reasons why the God of Israel allowed this destruction and exile. We will now explore Israel's relationship with the land.

Part 3 – The Land of Israel

It is 135AD, some 65 years after Titus had destroyed Jerusalem, and the 10th Legion remains stationed southwest of the ruined city. Little reconstruction has taken place during this period and the Temple Mount is still strewn with the white limestone

---
8. Job 1-9-12

rubble from the desolated sanctuary. Foxes hunt amongst the broken blocks, much like they had during the Babylonian captivity,[9] when the prophet Jeremiah cried out:

The joy of our hearts has ceased. Our dancing has been turned into mourning.
The crown has fallen from our head. Woe to us, for we have sinned!
Because of this our heart is faint. Because of these things our eyes are dim.
Because of Mount Zion which lies desolate. Foxes prowl in it.

Lamentations 5.15-18

The Emperor Hadrian now commands that Jerusalem is to be rebuilt as the new Roman city of Aelia Capitolina.[10] It will become a centre for pagan worship and administration for the eastern borders of the empire. He further decrees that henceforth the province will be known as *Syria Palaestinia*, named for the Philistines, the implacable foes of the Jews.

The seeds of Hadrian's decision were to be found in the aftermath of Titus' victory in AD70. Judaism and the Jewish people had been humiliated in the most public manner in the triumphal procession in Rome at which Vespasian and his son Titus were adulated. Vespasian had also imposed an annual Temple Tax on all Jews throughout the Empire. Not only were the Jews forbidden to rebuild their own temple, but now Rome required them to fund the reconstruction of a pagan shrine to Jupiter Capitolina. Jews throughout the empire began to be treated with contempt, suspicion and hostility. Because of their worship of a single God, Jehovah, who had no image, they were also treated as atheists by the Romans.

Following the death of Titus, His younger brother Domitian came to power and (yet) again the Jews were refused permission to rebuild their temple. This was in stark contrast to those other nations that had also been conquered by Rome, yet whose temples and shrines had been rebuilt and

Jewish Revolts	
1st Revolt	AD 70
2nd Revolt	AD 115-117
3rd Revolt	AD 135

who were permitted to openly and publicly worship their gods. Rome was most definitely singling out the Jews for special and spiteful treatment. Jewish resentment

---

9. The Temple Mount sifting project has found fox bones from the rubble of Solomon's Stables. Akiva, who was a Jewish rebel executed by the Romans in the 2nd century, was said to have visited the temple mount and watched a fox playing where once the Holy place was once sited
10. The name derives from Aelia, the emperor's family name, and the three Capitoline gods of Jupiter, Minerva and Juno

CHAPTER SEVEN

finally boiled over into violent uprisings in 115-117AD, and these were put down by Trajan. Despite this, Jewish resistance in Judaea continued to ferment and came to a head in the highly organised Bar Kochba revolt of 132-135AD. This war was just as violent and bloody as the conflict of AD70, and was the cause for Hadrian's terrible, unprecedented judgment on the Jewish people and the land of Judaea. Never before had any people been treated like this. Never again would any people be treated so: expelled from their land; their whole system of religion destroyed; and punitive taxation imposed on the exiles.

Despite the absolute totality of Hadrian's victory, no coins were minted to celebrate his campaign (unlike the *Judaea capta* coins issued after 70AD) nor was a triumph[11] held to mark the conquest. It was just as if neither Jerusalem nor Israel had ever existed, with millennia of Jewish history, religion, infrastructure and culture being erased by the Roman Empire and met with seeming indifference from Roman citizens. However, even during this period, Jews were still dwelling in Palaestina. They would no doubt be feeling that their God had abandoned them and it would be dangerous for them to openly demonstrate their faith or Jewish culture on pain of death. They were forbidden entrance to Aelia Capitolina, but it seems probable that some visited incognito. This climate of intimidation would likely have prevailed throughout the empire, thus there tends to be less evidence of Jewish activity in Palestine or the rest of the Empire until the early 4th century.

We will further explore the character and actions of Hadrian in Chapter 9, but by denying the Jews a country and their temple, he became responsible for laying the foundation for the modern politics of Palestine, which routinely ignore, deny and downplay the existence of the Jewish people and their right to the land of Israel. Media organisations and governments virtually ignore Israel's historical right to the land. Modern anti-Semitism,[12] treating the Jew as a suspicious outcast and as a land-thief, was also born here out of Roman religious prejudice. Once this attitude was in place, its cultural and spiritual momentum would transfer from the Roman Empire to the Church of Rome and thence to the wider Christian world and endures in today's media and politics.

---

11. A victory parade, held in Rome, to celebrate a conquest, and honour the military
12. This can take the most obscure forms. The cry of "hip, hip hooray" is based on the Roman cry for victory over Jerusalem of the first letters of 'Hierusylema Est Perdita' meaning Jerusalem is destroyed. Be careful what you confess!

CHAPTER SEVEN

The construction of Aelia Capitolina was typical for a new Roman town and its roads and structures form key parts of today's Jerusalem. The debris from Titus' destruction in AD70 provided ample building material for the Emperor's project and Jerusalem's tour guides today will point out Herodian and Roman material that has been adopted and recycled into later structures.

Fast-forwarding now to 326AD, the Emperor Constantine changed the name of Byzantium to Constantinople, which then became an administrative centre for the Eastern Roman Empire. Under this Byzantine rule, Jerusalem would see many physical changes resulting from Constantine's conversion to the Christian faith. His mother Helena oversaw the construction of a number of churches, including for example the Church of the Holy Sepulchre, which involved the demolition of Hadrian's Temple of Jupiter. During the Byzantine period (up to the Muslim conquest of 638[13]) Jerusalem became a predominantly Christian city where Jews were barely tolerated. Whereas Jews had persecuted Christians throughout the Empire in the first century,[14] the boot was now on the other foot, with Christians now very much looking down on the Jews. Christianity had by this time 'conquered' the Roman Empire and the Jews were bereft. Israel had disappeared as a nation. The Jews were by now widely scattered and persecuted, yet still retained their identity and culture as a people through the observance of their law and tradition.

It is not our purpose here to describe the highly complex history of the Jews and Jerusalem in detail, but it is helpful to have a little understanding to explain the tap-root of anti-Semitism. The reader may wish to delve deeper into this through reference to the titles in the bibliography.

For such a small country, Israel gets a lot of news coverage. I don't intend to go into a detailed examination of Israel's modern history, as others have done a more professional job than I am able or space would allow, but I will provide a brief overview of my own take on the situation.

The State of Israel – brief modern history

In the late 19th century the region of Palestine was under Turkish Ottoman rule, typically overseen by absentee landlords. The small population of Arabs and Jews

---

13. Until the 10th Century Muslims called the city 'Aelia', when it then became known as el-Quds
14. As described in the Acts of the Apostles

Chapter Seven

scratched a living from the largely barren and dusty landscape. Photographs and journals of the time show Jerusalem as little more than a run down and neglected village. Russian pogroms increased the flow of Jewish refugees fleeing persecution. With the coming of the First World War, the Turks sided with Germany. British forces under General Allenby swept up through Egypt, defeating them and capturing Jerusalem in 1917. After the War, the League of Nations handed Britain the Mandate to oversee the region of Palestine.

Time moved on, and an increasing number of Jews made aliyah to Palestine,[15] settling into both town and country, establishing settlements through the purchase of land, much of which was swamp or desert. Through much sweat and the hard toil of social collectives such as kibbutzim, these tracts of waste and empty land were transformed into fruitful, thriving communities which encouraged still more Jews to come. As the 1930's drew on, Nazi Germany began to stir. The British however, seeking to appease the Arabs, were reluctant to allow increased Jewish immigration from Europe. When war broke out in 1939, the Jews immediately supported the Allies and many signed up for the British Army. The Mufti of Jerusalem, Hajj Amin el-Husseini,[16] fell in with Hitler as their common purpose was to seek the eradication of the Jewish people. The war concluded and the work of Hitler's death camps was exposed to the world's shocked and guilty gaze. Ezekiel's valley of dry bones would take on a new and horrifying meaning as the oven doors were opened and mass graves uncovered.

> *Then He said to me, 'Son of man, these bones are the whole house of Israel. Behold, they say, 'Our bones are dried up and our hope has perished. We are completely cut off.' Therefore prophesy and say to them, 'Thus says the Lord God, 'Behold, I will open your graves and cause you to come up out of your graves, My people, and I will bring you into the land of Israel. Then you will know that I am the Lord, when I have opened your graves and caused you to come up out of your graves, My people. I will put My Spirit within you and you will come to life, and I*

---

15. For those looking for an introduction to the subject, I recommend Leon Uris' book *'Exodus'*. It is a fictionalised story set against the backdrop of the Birth of Israel, and a great read. To the best of my knowledge, it paints a reliable picture
16. The Islamic religious leader in Jerusalem. He wrote in his diary *'Our fundamental condition for cooperating with Nazi Germany (during WW2) was a free hand to eradicate every last Jew from Palestine and the Arab world. I asked Hitler for an explicit undertaking to allow us to solve the Jewish problem in a manner befitting our national and racial aspirations and according to the scientific methods innovated by Germany in the handling of its Jews. The answer I got was: 'The Jews are yours.'*

will place you on your own land.

"Then you will know that I, the Lord, have spoken and done it," declares the Lord.

Ezekiel 37.11-14

Europe didn't want the Jews and most Jews didn't want to stay in countries that had largely given them up to the concentration camps. Despite this moral pressure, the British now reduced permitted immigration levels still further, so blockade - running became the strategy for Jewish refugees to enter Palestine by evading Britain's Royal Navy. Again, during this time, the Jews bought land legally at extortionate prices from Arab landlords who were more than happy to do a deal. Again, the land was transformed. The numbers grew and with them, the tension increased between Arab and Jew. The British authorities, with a massive military presence, attempted to maintain order but generally (with some honourable exceptions, such as Orde Wingate) sided with the Arab cause.

The Jews had been campaigning for a state of their own, and in 1947, the UN granted their wish through a vote at the General Assembly. In May 1948 David Ben Gurion announced the new state, which would be called Israel. Despite Israel's pleas for a peaceful co-existence, on that same day, seven Arab states[17] declared war, committing themselves to Israel's annihilation. The Arabs told their people in Palestine to flee, promising that once a swift victory had been secured, they could return and seize the Jewish-owned territories and property. The Arabs left, many expecting a quick and profitable homecoming – they were to be disappointed. The fledgling State of Israel had been born in a day, but now faced a desperate fight for its survival. History records the result. Israel survived. More wars followed, including those of 1967 and 1973. On each occasion, Israel, vastly outnumbered, had been threatened with bloody annihilation but had been victorious, and on each occasion Israel got bigger. Some of this land was later traded for peace, such as the Sinai being given back to Egypt and Gaza being handed to the Palestinians. Gaza then became a terrorist enclave,[18] disproving the international community's assumption that the conflict was about land. This fact is routinely ignored by the international community and most of the media.

---

17. Egypt, Transjordan, Iraq, Syria, Lebanon, Saudi Arabia and Yemen
18. In the period 2001-12, over 12,000 rockets have been launched from Gaza at Israel. Over half of these launches took place after Israel left Gaza in 2005. Surely if land was the problem, the rockets should have stopped

CHAPTER SEVEN

It is a long and complex story and I'm sure I don't do it justice here. However, it is important that we have a basic appreciation of the political and military background before we progress. I recommend the reader to check out the bibliography for a more detailed study into this topic. I would also warn again against accepting the media's analysis and reporting regarding Israel and the Palestinians. You will almost always find that on deeper investigation, Israel has been misrepresented.[19] Take the time to establish the facts and challenge misreporting.

Figure 30. The Western Wall Plaza at night. The ashlar stones that formed the retaining wall of Herod's temple are the larger blocks that extend two-thirds of the way up the wall.

We should also note that Israel is tiny. Its heartland, from *Dan to Beersheba*[20] is only 150 miles long and 45 miles wide at its narrowest point. It is around one quarter

---
19. The Media, as typified by the UK's BBC, typically sides with the Palestinian cause. This is achieved by the relentless playing down or ignoring of organised Palestinian terrorism, whilst routinely exaggerating 'Israeli aggression', so making Israel into a Goliath, and the Palestinians into a David. Websites such as HonestReporting and BBCWatch do an excellent job in exposing this bias
20. The Old Testament uses this phrase eight times to describe the land of Israel

the size of Scotland, and those who seek to divide her would make it far smaller. The Palestinian Authority (Fatah) publicly claims 'Eastern' Jerusalem and the 'West Bank', although we should note that they have stated many times (in Arabic) that they will not rest until they possess the whole of Palestine 'from the river to the sea'.[21] More than twenty years of watching the Middle East situation has brought me to the opinion that this is not so much about the Palestinians wanting a homeland, but about denying Israel theirs. History provides ample evidence that the Arab states have no affection for the Palestinians, merely using them as a pawn to embarrass and pressure Israel into ceding territory.

The international Quartet (UN / EU / Russia and the US) also seek to divide Jerusalem, with the eastern city becoming the capital of a new Palestinian State. The Catholic Church too has an agenda. All have their own plans and Israel comes under tremendous political and media pressure to comply, whilst fighting a daily battle against Hamas from Gaza in the south, internally in the West Bank and against Hezbollah in the Lebanon to the north. It is interesting that most Israelis, including a majority of those in government, would actually settle for a Palestinian State if the 'two state solution'[22] were to bring peace. It has been said, and I would concur, that this is not a 'peace' process but a 'piece' process that seeks to dismantle Israel 'piece by piece'.

So these are the views of men, but our purpose here however is not to dwell too much on politics or human opinion. The Psalmist tells us:

*The Lord **nullifies the counsel of the nations**. He **frustrates the plans of the peoples**. The **counsel of the Lord stands forever, the plans of His heart from***

---

21. Fatah is painted as being Israel's 'moderate' partner for peace. Their Religious Affairs Minister Mahmoud Al-Habbish stated on PA TV in 2010 that '*throughout history, the capital of the Palestinian State*' was Jerusalem, despite the fact that only the Jews have ever had a capital city there. Their Mufti, Mohammed Hussein, stated '*there never was a temple in any period*' on the Al Aqsa Mosque site.

    Fatah's Charter is worth a look too: Article 12 calls for 'the complete liberation of Palestine, and eradication of Zionist economic, political, military and cultural existence through violence. Article 17 states that 'armed public revolution is inevitable'. Article 19 requires 'armed revolution is a decisive factor in the liberation fight and in uprooting the Zionist existence, and this struggle will not cease unless the Zionist state is demolished and Palestine completely liberated'

    Fatah continues to commemorate its terrorists, naming schools and streets after them, and refuses to recognise Israel as the Jewish State. Some peace partner.

22. There have been many conferences to mediate between Israel and the Palestinians, such as the Oslo and Madrid summits. Whilst Israel has generally honoured its commitments, the Palestinians have made little or no effort to fulfil their side of the bargain. This is routinely ignored by both the international community and the media

generation to generation. Blessed is the nation whose God is the Lord, the people whom He has chosen for His own inheritance.

Psalm 33.10-12

So what does the God of Israel have to say about the land of Israel?

Scriptural references – the land belongs to Israel

Who	Ref	Promise
Abram	Gen 12.7	The LORD appeared to Abram and said, 'To your descendants I will give this land'
	Gen 13.15	Now lift up your eyes and look from the place where you are, northward and southward and eastward and westward; for all the land which you see, I will give it to you and to **your descendants forever**
Abram	Gen 15.7	And He said to him, I am the LORD who brought you out of Ur of the Chaldeans, to give you this land to possess it
Abram	Gen 15.18	On that day the Lord made a covenant with Abram, saying, To your descendants I have given this land, From the river of Egypt as far as the great river, the river Euphrates
Abram	Gen 17.8	I will give to you and to **your descendants after you**, the land of your sojournings, all the land of Canaan, for **an everlasting possession**; and I will be their God
Abraham	Acts 7.4-5	Then he left the land of the Chaldeans and settled in Haran. From there, after his father died, *God* had him move to this country in which you are now living. But He gave him no inheritance in it, not even a foot of ground, and *yet*, even when he had no child, He promised that HE WOULD GIVE IT TO HIM AS A POSSESSION, AND TO HIS **DESCENDANTS AFTER HIM**
Abraham	2 Chron 20.7	Did You not, O our God, drive out the inhabitants of this land before Your people Israel and give it to the descendants of Abraham Your friend **forever**?
Isaac	Gen 26.3-4	Sojourn in this land and I will be with you and bless you, for to you and to **your descendants** I will give all these lands, and I will establish the oath which I swore to your father Abraham. I will multiply your descendants as the stars of heaven, and will give **your descendants** all these lands
Jacob	Gen 28.3-4	And behold, the LORD stood above it and said, I am the LORD, the God of your father Abraham and the God of Isaac; the land on which you lie, I will give it to you and to **your descendants**

Who	Ref	Promise
Jacob / Israel	Gen 35.10-12	God said to him, Your name is Jacob. You shall no longer be called Jacob, but Israel shall be your name. Thus He called him Israel. God also said to him, I am God Almighty. Be fruitful and multiply. A nation and a company of nations shall come from you, and kings shall come forth from you. The land which I gave to Abraham and Isaac, I will give it to you, and I will give the land to **your descendants** after you
Jacob / Joseph	Gen 48.3-4	Then Jacob said to Joseph, God Almighty appeared to me at Luz in the land of Canaan and blessed me, and He said to me, 'Behold, I will make you fruitful and numerous, and I will make you a company of peoples, and will give this land to your descendants after you for an **everlasting possession**
Joseph / brothers	Gen 50.24	Joseph said to his brothers, I am about to die, but God will surely take care of you and bring you up from this land to the land which He promised on oath to Abraham, to Isaac and to Jacob
Moses	Exodus 6.4+8	I also established My covenant with them, to give them the land of Canaan, the land in which they sojourned.... I will bring you to the land which I swore to give to Abraham, Isaac, and Jacob, and I will give it to you *for* a possession; I am the LORD
Moses	Exodus 32.13	Remember Abraham, Isaac, and Israel, Your servants to whom You swore by Yourself, and said to them, 'I will multiply your descendants as the stars of the heavens, and all this land of which I have spoken I will give to **your descendants**, and they shall **inherit** *it* **forever**
Joshua	Numbers 14.8	If the LORD is pleased with us, then He will bring us into this land and give it to us—a land which flows with milk and honey
Moses	Numbers 33.53	you shall take possession of the land and live in it, for I have given the land to you to possess it
Moses	Deut 3.18	The LORD your God has given you this land to possess it
Moses	Deut 4.22	For I will die in this land, I shall not cross the Jordan, but you shall cross and take possession of this good land
Moses	Deut 9.4-6	Do not say in your heart when the LORD your God has driven them out before you, 'Because of my righteousness the LORD has brought me in to possess this land,' but it *is* because of the wickedness of these nations *that* the LORD is dispossessing them before you. It is not for your righteousness or for the uprightness of your heart that you are going to possess their land, but *it is* because of the wickedness of these nations *that* the LORD your God is driving them out before you, in order to confirm the oath which the LORD swore to your fathers, to Abraham, Isaac and Jacob. Know, then, it *is not* because of your righteousness *that* the LORD your God is giving you this good land to possess, for you are a stubborn people

Chapter Seven

Who	Ref	Promise
Joshua	Josh 1.11	Pass through the midst of the camp and command the people, saying, 'Prepare provisions for yourselves, for within three days you are to cross this Jordan, to go in to possess the land which the LORD your God is giving you, to possess it'
Joshua	Josh.11.23	So Joshua took the whole land, according to all that the LORD had spoken to Moses, and Joshua gave it for an inheritance to Israel according to their divisions by their tribes
Joshua	Joshua 21.43	So the LORD gave Israel all the land which He had sworn to give to their fathers, and they possessed it and lived in it
Jehoshaphat	2 Chron 20.7	Did You not, O our God, drive out the inhabitants of this land before Your people Israel and give it to the descendants of Abraham Your friend **forever**?
Jeremiah	Jer 32.21-22	You brought Your people Israel out of the land of Egypt with signs and with wonders, and with a strong hand and with an outstretched arm and with great terror; and gave them this land, which You swore to their forefathers to give them, a land flowing with milk and honey
Jeremiah	Jer 32.41	I will rejoice over them to do them good and will faithfully plant them in this land with all My heart and with all My soul
Psalmist	Psalm 105.42-44	For He remembered His holy word *with* Abraham His servant. And He brought forth His people with joy, His chosen ones with a joyful shout. He gave them also the lands of the nations, that they might take possession of *the fruit of* the peoples' labor

This is not an exhaustive list. There are other verses that prove the point, but the reason I present as many as 27 references is to make the point emphatically that as far as God is concerned, He has given the land of Israel:

- to Abraham, through Isaac and Jacob **and their descendants after them**
- with **defined borders**
- **as an everlasting possession**
- **forever**

Moses made it abundantly clear that God didn't give the land to the people of Israel because of any righteous quality they might have possessed, but to fulfil His promise and keep His covenant. These passages utterly refute the argument of those who claim that Israel has forfeited the land either because they 'rejected Jesus', or because Israel is now 'the same as any other nation' and therefore the land belongs instead to anyone who has 'legal' claim to it. This view is widely held in the established Church today, vociferously champions a Palestinian State and is politically popular. Truth however is not decided by democracy but by the word of God, and those who have a problem with the State of Israel can take it up with Him. This is a solemn warning: Christians must be *very* careful taking sides against Israel, because the God of Israel is sworn to cursing those who curse her. I certainly do not condone everything that the State of Israel or the Jews do, but history shows that God will treat men and nations as they treat His people. He keeps His promises too.

So much for the opinion of men then.

But if Israel owns the land, why then has its people been uprooted from it throughout history? Israel has been conquered and exiled by Assyria, Babylon and Rome. Why would the Lord allow it? The Lord warned Moses from Mount Sinai:

> *Yet if in spite of this you do not obey Me, but act with hostility against Me, then I will act with wrathful hostility against you, and I, even I, will punish you seven times[23] for your sins. Further, you will eat the flesh of your sons and the flesh of your daughters you will eat. I then will destroy your high places, and cut down your incense altars, and heap your remains on the remains of your idols, for My soul shall abhor you.* ***I will lay waste your cities as well and will make your sanctuaries desolate,*** *and I will not smell your soothing aromas.* ***I will make the land desolate so that your enemies who settle in it will be appalled over it. You, however, I will scatter among the nations and will draw out a sword after you, as your land becomes desolate and your cities become waste.***

> *'Then the land will enjoy its Sabbaths[24] all the days of the desolation, while you are in your enemies' land; then the land will rest and enjoy its Sabbaths. All the days of its desolation it will observe the rest which it did not observe on your Sabbaths, while you were living on it. As for those of you who may be left, I will also bring weakness into their hearts in the lands of their enemies. And the sound of a driven leaf will chase them, and even when no one is pursuing they will flee as though from the sword, and they will fall. They will therefore stumble over each other as if running from the sword, although no one is pursuing; and you will have no strength to stand up before your enemies. But you will perish among the nations, and your enemies' land will consume you. So those of you who may be left will rot away because of their iniquity in the lands of your enemies; and also because of the iniquities of their forefathers they will rot away with them.*

Leviticus 26.27-39

---

23. Considered in Chapter 2
24. This prophecy was specifically fulfilled during the Babylonian exile of the Jewish people, but the principle was established

CHAPTER SEVEN

This powerful warning was given under the dispensation of Law[25], and it is clear that Israel's residency in the land was conditional upon them keeping the covenant and Laws. There are many such passages that describe the conditional nature of Israel's possession of its land.[26] Israel's persistent, wilful and deliberate disobedience and rebellion would result in the enactment of the curse. The warning described in Leviticus is chilling and describes with great accuracy the events of AD70, 135 and beyond. It is amazing that as far as Israel was concerned, their trouble maker was not the Romans, but the Lord God of Israel. The Romans might have been the instrument of that judgment, but it was the Lord who wielded it. Again, for the student of prophecy, it demonstrates the certainty of God's word. We should note this for the times to come, because, as the Lord says, 'I change not'.

There is also a warning from Obadiah concerning those nations that oppress Israel:

> *For the day of the Lord draws near on all the nations.* **As you have done, it will be done to you. Your dealings will return on your own head**
>
> Obadiah 15

For years I have followed the news feeds about Israel and witnessed nations that opposed her militarily, politically, or economically. In every case I saw God's judgment fall upon them through natural disaster, economic and political problems. He who touches her touches the apple of God's eye.[27] Next time you see someone criticise or act against Israel, keep your eye on the news. God will judge.

From Sinai to the Cross, Israel's relationship with and possession of the land was determined by their obedience to the Covenant and their rejection of the Kingdom. As we have already seen in previous chapters however, something began to stir in the late 19th century. By this time the nation of Israel had been in abeyance, almost deep hibernation, for over 1,800 years. It was now almost as if the Lord had said

---

25. The Mosaic Law comprised 613 commandments (according to Maimonides). James 2.10-11 tells us that *'if we stumble on one part, we are guilty of all'*. The children of Israel could thus not pick and choose what to obey, but were subject to its entirety, both as individuals and as a nation before God. In the Lord's grace he had provided remedies for their sin through sacrifices, but wilful, persistent and deliberate disobedience would trigger the curses described above. Christians are not under Law, but Grace (Romans 6.14, 7.5-6, & 10.4). Jesus 'abolished the Law of Commandments' (Ephesians 2.14-15) so the Jews too are no longer subject to it, but must now seek salvation through Christ
26. See also Joshua 23.15-16; Deuteronomy 28.63-66 and 29.28; 2 Chronicles 7.19-22
27. Zechariah 2.8

'enough!' What took place between 1897 and 1947 did not happen because of any repentance or change of heart amongst the Jews, but as the sovereign act of a God who remembered His covenant. Even since 1948, there has been little repentance from Israel. For the most part, the Jews have tried very hard to be a nation 'like any other' in their lifestyle and culture, and tried to forget their religious heritage.

However, the Jews are the chosen people and the Lord does not permit them adopting the behaviour of other nations – in fact, He detests it.

> ***What comes into your mind will not come about,*** *when you say:* '*We will be like the nations (Gentiles), like the tribes (families) of the lands,* *serving wood and stone.' 'As I live,' declares the Lord God, 'surely with a mighty hand and with an outstretched arm and with wrath poured out, I shall be king over you. I will bring you out from the peoples and gather you from the lands where you are scattered, with a mighty hand and with an outstretched arm and with wrath poured out; and* ***I will bring you into the wilderness of the peoples, and there I will enter into judgment with you face to face.*** *As I entered into judgment with your fathers in the wilderness of the land of Egypt, so I will enter into judgment with you,' declares the Lord God.*
>
> Ezekiel 20.32-36

Both Derek Prince and David Pawson have used this verse to show that God hates any assimilation on the part of His people, becoming *like families in other lands*. He will not tolerate any attempt by the Jews to be *like any other* in lifestyle, culture or religion. All should note that the Jews are not and will never be like any other people. Note too that the warning concerning Israel's desire for assimilation is given in the context of their return to the land; once she has returned, she is subjected to *'the wilderness of the peoples'*. I would suggest that this describes the present political alienation of Israel and it has been permitted by God. It is a refining process for modern Israel, designed to bring them back to Himself, and we read daily in the news about the pressures that she must endure.

There is a day coming when Israel will humble itself, accept its guilt, and look on the One whom they have pierced. Then the Lord will again remember His covenant to them. First however, they must be brought to a point of such desperation where this repentance can take place. We will look at this in later chapters:

Continuing the words of the Lord from Sinai:

> *If they confess their iniquity and the iniquity of their forefathers, in their unfaithfulness which*

Chapter Seven

*they committed against Me, and also in their acting with hostility against Me— I also was acting with hostility against them, to bring them into the land of their enemies—or **if their uncircumcised heart becomes humbled so that they then make amends for their iniquity, then I will remember My covenant with Jacob, and I will remember also My covenant with Isaac, and My covenant with Abraham as well, and I will remember the land.** For the land will be abandoned by them, and will make up for its Sabbaths while it is made desolate without them. They, meanwhile, will be making amends for their iniquity, because they rejected My ordinances and their soul abhorred My statutes.*

Yet in spite of this, when they are in the land of their enemies, **I will not reject them, nor will I so abhor them as to destroy them, breaking My covenant with them; for I am the Lord their God. But I will remember for them the covenant** *with their ancestors, whom I brought out of the land of Egypt in the sight of the nations, that I might be their God. I am the Lord.*

Leviticus 26.40-45

Restoration to the Land

In the above passage, the Lord promises to remember the land. What does He mean by this? Jeremiah is our guide here. We have several passages to pick from[28]...

Behold, I will gather them out of all the lands to which I have driven them in My anger, in My wrath and in great indignation; and I will bring them back to this place and make them dwell in safety.

They shall be My people, and I will be their God; and I will give them one heart and one way, that they may fear Me always, for their own good and for the good of their children after them. **I will make an everlasting covenant with them that I will not turn away from them, to do them good**; *and I will put the fear of Me in their hearts so that they will not turn away from Me. I will rejoice over them to do them good and* **will faithfully plant them in this land with all My heart and with all My soul.**

For thus says the Lord, 'Just as I brought all this great disaster on this people, so I am going to bring on them all the good that I am promising them. Fields will be bought in this land of which you say, 'It is a desolation, without man or beast; it is given into the hand of the Chaldeans.' Men will buy fields for money, sign and seal deeds, and call in witnesses in the land of Benjamin, in the environs of Jerusalem, in the cities of Judah, in the cities of the hill country, in the cities of the lowland and in the cities of the Negev; **for I will restore their**

---

28. See also Jeremiah 23.3, 30.3-9, 32.15, 32.41, & 42.10; and Ezekiel 36.35 & 47.14

fortunes (will bring their captives back home),' declares the Lord

Jer 32.37-44

So we have established from the Bible that as far as God is concerned, the land belongs to Israel. It is clear that certain aspects of the above passage have not yet been fulfilled. It would not be true for example to say that the people of Israel as a whole have either fulfilled the required conditions, or have experienced the full blessing and the new and better covenant promised. Clearly then, we have a partial fulfilment (i.e. Israel has returned to the land) but with more to come at some future time.[29] We will return to this theme in chapter 14.

Israel is resident in the land, albeit with hostile neighbours and the disapproval of the vast majority of nations and the established Church. The Law has been abolished, yet Israel has not, for the most part, tasted the age of Grace. So what then of Israel's relationship with the Church?

Part 4 – Israel and the Church

I committed my life to Christ as a 13 year old in 1973 and for as long as I can remember, the Church has helped itself generously both to Israel's Bible history and promises. Over the years I assumed this was the norm, but when the Holy Spirit illuminated my understanding about God's purpose for Israel in the late 1980's, my Bible suddenly made much more sense. Once I had made the decision to allow the Bible to speak for itself, I found myself questioning the teaching of many church leaders and the doctrine of some Christian movements, who had appropriated God's dealings for Israel as belonging to the Church.

This spiritualising of Biblical Israel (known as Replacement or Dominion Theology) resulting in their being ignored by the Church, bears an uncanny resemblance to 135AD, when, as we saw earlier, it was as if for the Roman Empire, Israel had never existed. Coincidence? I don't think so. Rather, I believe the same spirit is behind both, namely, to down-play, displace and belittle God's elect. What is of serious concern though here is that this anti-Israel spirit is operating in and through the Church. Interestingly, I noticed that whilst the Church was happy to help itself to the blessings due to Israel, it was less keen to adopt its curses!

---

29. This is an example of the 'depth of field' aspect of prophecy described in the preface

CHAPTER SEVEN

So am I saying that Christians can learn nothing and take nothing from the Old Testament, more than three-quarters of your Bible? Not at all. There are (at least) three legitimate means of applying Old Testament truth concerning Israel to our experience as Christians:

- Israel as an example

For I do not want you to be unaware, brethren, that our fathers were all under the cloud and all passed through the sea; and all were baptized into Moses in the cloud and in the sea; and all ate the same spiritual food; and all drank the same spiritual drink, for they were drinking from a spiritual rock which followed them; and the rock was Christ. Nevertheless, with most of them God was not well-pleased; for they were laid low in the wilderness.

*Now **these things happened as examples for us**, so that we would not crave evil things as they also craved. Do not be idolaters, as some of them were; as it is written, The people sat down to eat and drink, and stood up to play. Nor let us act immorally, as some of them did, and twenty-three thousand fell in one day. Nor let us try the Lord, as some of them did, and were destroyed by the serpents. Nor grumble, as some of them did, and were destroyed by the destroyer. **Now these things happened to them as an example, and they were written for our instruction, upon whom the ends of the ages have come***

1 Corinthians 10.1-11

- The Law of Moses as a shadow

*For the Law, since it **has only a shadow of the good things to come** and not the very form of things, can never, by the same sacrifices which they offer continually year by year, make perfect those who draw near*

Hebrews 10.1

- To foretell Christ

Then I said, 'Behold, I have come. (In the scroll of the book it is written of Me) to do Your will, O God.

Hebrew 10.7

So what of Israel in the New Testament? Is it mentioned, or has its relevance expired? Absolutely not! Of its 27 books, the words Israel or Israelite are used some 77 times. Never once are these used as a synonym for the Church.[30] So, it seems we can use Israel as a type, an example and a shadow of what is to come, but we have

---

30. See *The Destiny of Israel and the Church* by Dr Derek Prince for a full discussion

no scriptural basis for replacing 'Israel' with the 'Church'. Primarily then, in the New Testament the word 'Israel' means 'Israel'.

The Church's debt to Israel

The classic New Testament chapters regarding Israel's future are to be found in Romans 9-11. I suggest you read them all, but we will dip into them here to see what the Apostle Paul has to say on the matter:

> *But if some of the branches (Israel) were broken off, and you (the Church), being a wild olive, were grafted in among them and became partaker with them of the rich root of the olive tree, do not be arrogant toward the branches; but if you are arrogant, remember that* ***it is not you who supports the root (Israel), but the root supports you (the Church).***
>
> *You will say then, Branches were broken off so that I might be grafted in. Quite right, they were broken off for their unbelief, but you stand by your faith.* ***Do not be conceited, but fear; for if God did not spare the natural branches, He will not spare you, either.***
>
> *Behold then the kindness and severity of God; to those who fell, severity, but to you, God's kindness, if you continue in His kindness; otherwise you also will be cut off. And they also, if they do not continue in their unbelief, will be grafted in, for God is able to graft them in again. For if you were cut off from what is by nature a wild olive tree, and were grafted contrary to nature into a cultivated olive tree,* ***how much more will these who are the natural branches be grafted into their own olive tree?***
>
> Rom 11.17-25 (my comments in brackets)

Figure 31. Wild Olives trees in Israel

Remember that without Israel we Christians would have no Bible, no Apostles, no prophets and no Saviour. The Church owes a significant debt to Israel.

Many Christians hold the position that God has finished with Israel. How does Paul address this?

Chapter Seven

> *I say then, God has not rejected His people, has He? May it never be! For I too am an Israelite, a descendant of Abraham, of the tribe of Benjamin.*
>
> *God has not rejected His people whom He foreknew*
>
> Roman 11.1-2

I suggest that this could not be clearer.

However, according to 11.8,

> *God gave them a spirit of stupor, eyes to see not and ears to hear not, down to this very day.*

Part of God's judgment for disobeying His Laws and rejecting the Kingdom is a *partial* blindness and deafness, which can be clearly seen in the Jewish people today, both inside and outside of Israel. That this blindness is not total is evidenced by the many Messianic Fellowships springing up in Israel. But what worked *against* Israel, worked *for* the Church. Christians cannot be arrogant about their opportunity to gain access to the Kingdom of God, and there is coming a time when Israel will be restored. We should be grateful to God and respectful of Israel, for this opportunity to be grafted into the olive tree.

Are the Jews responsible for the death of Christ?

The tap-root of Jewish anti-Semitism is to be found in the notion that the Jews killed Christ. Peter, preaching in Jerusalem says in Acts:

> *But you disowned the Holy and Righteous One and asked for a murderer to be granted to you, but put to death the Prince of life, the one whom God raised from the dead, a fact to which we are witnesses*
>
> Acts 3.14-15

So Peter confirms that the Jews *did* Kill Jesus. However, we should also note that He was tried and convicted not just in a Jewish court, but a Roman one also. He was condemned by the Roman Prefect, Pilate, and finally crucified by (Gentile) Roman soldiers,[31] who could have been from any country (not just Italy), as the legions co-opted men from many lands that they conquered. Surely too, it was mine and

---

31. It has not been determined which soldiers performed the crucifixion, as there is no record of a particular legion being stationed in Judaea in this period. It seems that those who carried out the crucifixion were auxiliaries who were typically recruited from lands within the empire

your sin that resulted in Christ's death, that One should die for all. I would suggest that only he that is 'without sin' should be casting stones at the Jews here. Can any Christian say that it was not their own sin that sent Christ to the Cross? I suggest that every nation, every ethnic group has at some time been responsible for committing an atrocity. We shouldn't judge others, lest we be judged ourselves.

A final thought: not every Jew desired the death of Christ. Clearly neither His family, disciples, nor Jesus' other followers would not have wanted His death, so accusing the whole people of this act is mistaken.

Will every Jew be saved?

In Romans 11.25-27 Paul tells us:

> *For I do not want you, brethren, to be uninformed of this mystery—so that you will not be wise in your own estimation—that a partial hardening has happened to Israel until the fullness of the Gentiles has come in; and so* **all Israel will be saved;** *just as it is written, The Deliverer will come from Zion. He will remove ungodliness from Jacob. This is My covenant with them, when I take away their sins*

Unless the Lord had allowed this partial hardening of Israel (from Jesus' ministry up to the present day), then the Gentiles would have had no entrance into the Kingdom of God.

Earlier in the letter, Paul clarifies precisely what he means by Israel:

> *For they are* **not all Israel who are descended from Israel;** *nor are they all children because they are Abraham's descendants, but through Isaac your descendants will be named. That is, it is* **not the children of the flesh who are children of God, but the children of the promise are regarded as descendants**

Rom 9.6-8

It is clear therefore that only a remnant of Israel will be saved. A remnant was saved from the wilderness under Moses. A remnant of 42,000 returned from the Babylonian exile. A remnant escaped from the concentration camps after WW2. The principle of the remnant has a long and still incomplete association with the people of Israel. I am certainly not saying that those who died in the camps were rejected by God – He alone is judge and knows the hearts of men and He alone can determine eternal destiny.

Chapter Seven

We must also differentiate between those who are of Jewish descent,[32] and those Jews who live by faith. Throughout the history of Israel, there have been Jews who have followed the Lord by faith (See Hebrews 11). But there are also many who rebelled against and rejected Him. Since the Cross salvation is by faith in Jesus Christ alone. Examples of those who have rejected Him include the 3,000 that were killed by the Lord at Sinai, the rebellious rulers described in book of Kings, or those who perished in the wilderness. We cannot know and are in no position to judge.

Paul goes on to quote Isaiah:

> *Isaiah cries out concerning Israel, Though the number of the sons of Israel be like the sand of the sea,* ***it is the remnant that will be saved***
>
> Rom 9.27

Again, it is clear that only the remnant will be saved and this will be on the basis of their faith.

Ezekiel tells us:

> *For I will take you from the nations, gather you from all the lands and bring you into your own land.* ***Then I will sprinkle clean water on you, and you will be clean; I will cleanse you from all your filthiness and from all your idols.*** *Moreover, I will give you a new heart and put a new spirit within you; and I will remove the heart of stone from your flesh and give you a heart of flesh. I will put My Spirit within you and cause you to walk in My statutes, and you will be careful to observe My ordinances*
>
> Ezekiel 36.24-27

Notice the order here: the Lord first takes the Jews from among the nations, then returns them to their own land, and only *then* cleanses them. We are witnessing the return right now, but await the cleansing of Israel.

Don't be critical of the Jews – like us in the Church, God hasn't finished with them yet!

The remnant of Israel is growing:

- 3,000 were saved when Peter preached on the day of Pentecost (traditionally the day that the Law was given to Moses). Shortly after this, the Jews rejected

---

32. i.e. descended from Jacob

- the Kingdom of God
- Jews amongst the community in Asia were saved (see Acts)
- in modern-day Israel, Messianic fellowships are growing substantially
- the end of the age will see 144,000 Jews from every tribe sent out as evangelists
- on Jesus' return, all Israel (i.e. the Israel of faith) will be added

Does the Church have a responsibility to Israel?

I believe the answer here is a resounding yes. But what does this responsibility comprise? We have seen how we have been grafted in to the 'olive tree', so what can Christians do?

I would suggest that there are four areas of responsibility:

- Isaiah 40 commands someone to '**comfort** my people'. Who is the command addressed to, who can this 'someone' be? I believe the only logical choice is the Church. It is our duty as Christians to comfort the Jews in word (through encouragement) and practically through deed. Ask God what He wants you to do. There are many opportunities to be grasped: Holocaust survivors who live in poverty; young, lonely members of the IDF who have no families to visit during the feasts; those who have made aliyah and have few resources.[33]

- To **preach Christ** crucified. The Law is an obsolete system and faith in Christ is the only hope for salvation of the Jew. How will they hear unless they have a preacher? Have you ever shared your testimony with a Jew?

- To **pray for the peace of Jerusalem.** We are seeing in this book the pivotal role of this city in the future of the Kingdom. We can make a difference through our prayers and Jerusalem needs watchmen

- Jesus said that *'Truly I say to you, to the extent that you did it to one of **these brothers of Mine**, even the least of them, you did it to Me'*. (Matthew 25.31-44). This includes those who are hungry, thirsty, need clothing, are sick or in

---

33. If the reader would like to help I suggest a good place to start is by contacting the International Christian Embassy in Jerusalem via http://int.icej.org/

prison. Who were Jesus brothers? Strictly speaking - the Jew. More generally too, we may include Christians. I would also encourage you to lobby for Israel. Writing to the government and holding the media to account are two such strategies. How many letters have you written?

God loves Palestinian Arabs too, and there are many Christians in this community. Love for the Jew must not stop us from loving those of Arab descent.

Part 5 – Conclusion

There is not one explicit verse or passage in either Old or New Testament that states that:

- God has permanently finished with Israel
- the Church has replaced Israel
- the Church is now a substitute for Israel or that
- the Church has been given the right to judge Israel

There are however many verses we have seen that describe God's Covenant with Israel and His giving of the land as an everlasting possession to them. We see throughout history that God has warned His people Israel through His prophets. He has from time to time punished and temporarily rejected them (as in Hosea) but He then restores and regathers them. There is no doubt that the Lord was angry with Israel, but in the New Testament we have also seen how He warns the church too.

Both Israel and the Church share common ground in that:

- we are both a chosen people. Jesus told His disciples that *you did not choose Me, but I chose you* (John 15.16)
- neither are perfect, both are a work in progress
- both can be 'cut off' (see Romans 9-11; the story of Ananias and Sapphira also)

- both are to live by faith (Hebrews 11)
- both will be present and used by God during the Tribulation (see Chapter 10)
- both will be present in the Millennium (see Chapter 14)
- both will share in the New Jerusalem. Why else would the names of the twelve tribes be inscribed there?

For I am not ashamed of the gospel, for it is the power of God for salvation to everyone who believes, **to the Jew first and also to the Greek (Gentile)**

Rom 1.16

This is a Kingdom principle: God starts with the Jews, then the Gentiles. The gospel was taken first to the Jews, then the Gentiles. Judgment came first to the Jews during the pogroms and Holocaust, so what next for the Church? Events in Israel are often associated with activity of the Holy Spirit in the Church. Israel was fighting for survival in the Yom Kippur war of 1973. That same year, I became a Christian in the aftermath of the nationwide Festival of Light in the UK. It was no coincidence that I, like thousands of others, came to know Christ at that time, because the Spirit of God was moving in both Israel and the Church.

Today, many nations are openly hostile to the Jews. Some in the West hide behind a facade of political correctness, but are nevertheless anti-Semitic, directing their hatred at Israel, the collective Jew. Whilst there is still opportunity, Christians can and should do all they can to pray and take action to oppose this. The prophecies that we have examined so far show clearly that Israel will come under increasing pressure as time goes by, but the Lord of Hosts says in Jeremiah that those who touch Israel touch the 'apple of His eye' and that He will shake His hand against them.

Christians should stand with her. One day, we will share the New Jerusalem with Israel. Better start now to get know our new neighbours.

We will give the final words here to Isaiah and Jeremiah. The prophet Isaiah states (chapter 49):

- God will be **glorified in** Israel (v3)
- Israel will be a **light to the Gentiles** (v6)

- Israel is **chosen** by God (v7)
- the Lord will **comfort** Israel (v13)
- the Lord will **not forget** Israel (v15)
- Israel will **not be ashamed** (v23) and
- the Lord will **contend with those** who contend with Israel (v25)

Jeremiah too is emphatic:

> *Thus says the Lord, who gives the sun for light by day and the fixed order of the moon and the stars for light by night, who stirs up the sea so that its waves roar. The Lord of hosts is His name.*
>
> *If this fixed order departs from before Me, declares the Lord, Then the offspring of Israel also will cease from being a nation before Me forever.*
>
> *Thus says the Lord, If the heavens above can be measured and the foundations of the earth searched out below, then I will also cast off all the offspring of Israel. For all that they have done, declares the Lord.*
>
> Jeremiah 31.35-37

- Have the sun, moon, stars and sea departed? **No.**
- Can heaven above be measured, or the foundations of the earth be searched out? **No.**
- Has Israel ceased from being a nation before God? **No.**
- Has the Lord cast off the seed of Israel? **No.**

Chapter 8 The Temple rebuilt

And Jesus cried out again with a loud voice, and yielded up His spirit. And behold, the veil of the temple was torn in two from top to bottom.

Matthew 27.50-51

Figure 32. The 3rd Temple – showing speculative location between the Dome of the Rock and Mosque of Omar.

Part 1 – Introduction

When the cry *"it is finished"* sounded from the Cross, the veil of the Temple, some 20M high by 10M wide and as thick as a man's hand, was torn in two from top to bottom. With this declaration, Jesus brought the dispensation of Law to an end. From now on, within the age of Grace, there would be no more need for temple, blood sacrifice or priesthood. However, tradition would keep the Jews following

Chapter Eight

their religious routine until AD70, when, as we have described earlier, Herod's Temple was permanently and utterly destroyed.

Will the Temple ever be rebuilt, or is this just a dream for religious Jews? There are Biblical clues that strongly suggest that we will see another temple in Jerusalem at the end of the age and that it will have a part to play in the final events not just in Israel but of the whole world too. In Chapter 8, we will consider the basis for the rebuilding of the so-called '3rd Temple'. In order to understand this topic better, it will help if we first appreciate a little of the purpose and history of what preceded it and what will follow. Our investigation will take us back to the times of Abraham, Moses, Solomon and Herod and forward (in chapter 14) through the Millennium and into eternity future.

We will also consider the practicalities of reconstructing the 3rd Temple and what signs we might look for. It may surprise the reader that plans are already being drawn up for a new building. Some of its vessels have already been made and the project is part-funded. The problem however, is that sitting foursquare on the site is a mosque, the third holiest site in Islam, under the authority of the Muslim Waqf. As things currently stand, Jews may not pray nor participate in any religious activity on the Temple Mount. Meanwhile, the Waqf oversees the systematic destruction of its archaeology, in a vain attempt to remove any evidence that the Jews ever had a presence on the Mount. The Israeli government does little to stop this vandalism for fear of inflaming the situation. The location is undoubtedly the most politically tense square mile in the world today.

As we travel back into Bible history, we find a succession of physical structures where the children of Israel could approach their God to worship and sacrifice:

- The Tabernacle – Moses
- The First Temple – Solomon
- The Second Temple – Jeshua and Zerubbabel
- The Second Temple – Herod

Chapter Eight

Part 2 – The Tabernacle – Moses

Three months after[1] the children of Israel had escaped the bondage of Egypt, they came to the foot of Mount Sinai. It was here that the Lord commanded Moses:

> *Let them construct a sanctuary for Me, that I may dwell among them. According to all that I am going to show you, as the pattern of the tabernacle and the pattern of all its furniture, just so you shall construct it*
>
> Exodus 25.8-9

Before this Sanctuary or Tabernacle was built,[2] Moses would take his own tent outside the camp to meet the Lord face to face.

> *Now Moses used to take the tent and pitch it outside the camp, a good distance from the camp, and he called it the tent of meeting. And everyone who sought the LORD would go out to the tent of meeting which was outside the camp. And it came about, whenever Moses went out to the tent that all the people would arise and stand, each at the entrance of his tent, and gaze after Moses until he entered the tent. Whenever Moses entered the tent, the pillar of cloud would descend and stand at the entrance of the tent; and the LORD would speak with Moses. When all the people saw the pillar of cloud standing at the entrance of the tent, all the people would arise and worship, each at the entrance of his tent. Thus the LORD used to speak to Moses face to face, just as a man speaks to his friend.*
>
> Exodus 33.7-11

The Tabernacle was a temporary and portable dwelling for the Lord that would contain the Ten Commandments and Ark of the Covenant. It would serve as a place for sacrifices and allow the priests to minister to the Lord and mediate between Him and the people. It was utilised throughout the sojourn in the wilderness and the conquest of Canaan. It was to be fabricated from material offerings that had been given willingly by the people:

- gold, silver, bronze
- blue, purple and scarlet thread
- fine linen and goat's hair
- ram skins dyed red

---

1. Exodus 19.1
2. Exodus 36.8ff

Chapter Eight

- badger skins
- acacia wood
- oil for the light
- spices for the anointing oil and for the sweet incense
- onyx stones
- stones to set in the ephod and breastplate of the High Priest

The detailed pattern for the design of the Tabernacle is provided for us in Exodus 26. Hebrews 8 explains though how Jesus is our High Priest now and how the Tabernacle was a mere copy or a shadow of the better covenant that was to come after the Cross:

> *Now the main point in what has been said is this: we have such a high priest, who has taken His seat at the right hand of the throne of the Majesty in the heavens, a minister in the sanctuary and in the true tabernacle, which the Lord pitched, not man.*
>
> *For every high priest is appointed to offer both gifts and sacrifices; so it is necessary that this high priest also have something to offer. Now if He were on earth, He would not be a priest at all, since there are those who offer the gifts according to the Law;* **who serve a copy and shadow of the heavenly things, just as Moses was warned by God when he was about to erect the tabernacle; for, See, He says, that you make all things according to the pattern which was shown you on the mountain.** *But now He has obtained a more excellent ministry, by as much as He is also the mediator of a better covenant, which has been enacted on better promises. For if that first covenant had been faultless, there would have been no occasion sought for a second. For finding fault with them, He says:*
>
> *Behold, days are coming, says the Lord, when I will effect a new covenant with the house of Israel and with the house of Judah. Not like the covenant which I made with their fathers on the day when I took them by the hand to lead them out of the land of Egypt. For they did not continue in My covenant, and I did not care for them, says the Lord. For this is the covenant that I will make with the house of Israel: After those days, says the Lord, I will put My laws into their minds, and I will write them on their hearts, and I will be their God, and they shall be My people, and they shall not teach everyone his fellow citizen, and everyone his brother,*

saying, 'Know the Lord,' for all will know Me, from the least to the greatest of them.

For I will be merciful to their iniquities, and I will remember their sins no more.

When He said, A new covenant, **He has made the first obsolete. But whatever is becoming obsolete and growing old is ready to disappear**

Hebrews 8.1-13

In Chapter 7 we discussed how the Law of Moses could legitimately be interpreted as a type, copy, or shadow of what was to come. Hebrews makes it clear that there is a deeper meaning here and that the Tabernacle was built to a heavenly pattern. This more excellent pattern is clearly linked to Israel receiving a better covenant and better promises through Christ's ministry. We also have here another reference to the old covenant (the Law) passing away and becoming obsolete to make room for a better one. Hold that thought until chapter 14.

So the Tabernacle provides a type or shadow of the Lord's relationship first with the Jews, but also by inference to the Church.

The floor plan for the Tabernacle would become a template for all subsequent temples.

CHAPTER EIGHT

Figure 33. Model of the Tabernacle, as seen in Israel, Timna Park.

After Canaan had been conquered the Tabernacle was positioned at Shiloh, where it remained for the 300 year period of the Judges. It was finally brought to Jerusalem by King Solomon.[3]

Part 3 – The First Temple – Solomon

The temples of Jerusalem define the city's archaeological periods. The first temple period spans around 1000BC to 586BC, at which time Solomon's temple was destroyed by the Babylonian ruler Nebuchadnezzar II. A thousand years before Christ, King David had bought a parcel of land[4] on Mount Moriah from Araunah the Jebusite and built an altar there.[5] David was not permitted by the Lord to build

---

3. 1 Kings 8.1-5
4. This was a threshing floor, typically a bowl shaped area, set out of the prevailing breeze, that was used to separate wheat from its stalk. Most Bible scholars believe that this site was the place where Abraham had offered his son Isaac as a sacrifice to the Lord 1000 years before (Gen 22). Abraham had earlier erected an Altar to the Lord 'who would provide'. In 29AD, the Lord did indeed provide a sacrifice, His own Son Jesus on this same mountain
5. 2 Samuel 24.25

the temple as he had shed innocent blood, so the duty fell to his son Solomon. This was the first time that the Lord would dwell in a permanent house amongst His covenant people, Israel.

So around the mid 10th century BC:

> *It came about in the four hundred and eightieth year after the sons of Israel came out of the land of Egypt, in the fourth year of Solomon's reign over Israel, in the month of Ziv which is the second month, that he began to build the house of the LORD... In the eleventh year, in the month of Bul, which is the eighth month, the house was finished throughout all its parts and according to all its plans. So he was seven years in building it.*
>
> 1 Kings 6.1 and 37-38

The First Temple was based on the same proportions as the Tabernacle, though twice its size and far more ornate. It would have been a magnificent sight, fitted out in the local limestone, cedar from Lebanon and gold. When it was dedicated, the glory of the Lord descended and filled the Temple.

Some 400 years later, after a period of persistent sin and rebellion by Israel, the temple was destroyed.

> *Now on the seventh day of the fifth month, which was the nineteenth year of King Nebuchadnezzar, king of Babylon, Nebuzaradan the captain of the guard, a servant of the king of Babylon, came to Jerusalem.* **He burned the house of the LORD,** *the king's house, and all the houses of Jerusalem; even every great house he burned with fire*
>
> 2 Kings 25.8-9

The passage then describes how the temple's artefacts that had been made by Solomon were removed by Jerusalem's conquerors. Solomon's magnificent temple, that had once contained the Ten Commandments and Ark of the Covenant, now lay as an empty and broken shell. The children of Israel were exiled into Babylonian captivity.

> *By the rivers of Babylon, there we sat down and wept, when we remembered Zion. Upon the willows in the midst of it we hung our harps. For there our captors demanded of us songs, and our tormentors mirth, saying, Sing us one of the songs of Zion. How can we sing the Lord's song in a foreign land?*

> *If I forget you, O Jerusalem, may my right hand forget her skill. May my tongue cling to the roof of my mouth if I do not remember you, if I do not exalt Jerusalem above my chief joy*
>
> Psalm 137.1-6

CHAPTER EIGHT

Little evidence remains today of the first Temple. The Babylonians made a complete destruction, and then Herod the Great, who had later built deep foundations for his majestic buildings, had scoured away its walls, courts and footings. All that was left of the Temple from this period were artefacts and small finds.[6] Modern archaeologists base their understanding of the plan of the first Temple on the Bible and topographical analysis of Jerusalem's landscape.

Part 4 – The Second Temple - Herod

In 538 Cyrus, the Persian King, (who had since conquered Babylon) issued a decree for the Jewish captives to return to Jerusalem and granted them permission to restore their Temple. Jeshua, the high priest, and Zerubbabel the king led this work.[7] Some 22 years later (5th Adar, 516BC) the Second Temple was completed, but Jerusalem itself remained broken down. Ezra's arrival in 457BC was to teach the people the Law, strengthen their faith and begin to re-establish the Temple rituals. When Nehemiah came to the city in 445 he oversaw the rebuilding of Jerusalem's walls. So Jerusalem was re-established. The Second Temple was not as large or ornate as the first. You can follow the account in Ezra, Nehemiah and Haggai.

In 167BC, Antiochus Epiphanes (more of whom in Chapter 9) captured Jerusalem. He desecrated the Temple by bringing pig's flesh into the Holy place and offering sacrifices to himself. This was an abomination of desolation, but not the one that Jesus had foretold, as that was yet future. The Jews retook Jerusalem in 164BC under Judah Maccabee, and rededicated their Temple.[8]

Around 20BC, Herod the Great embarked on his great project to modernise Jerusalem. As we mentioned earlier, this was not because he was a godly man, the opposite in fact. Rather, he sought to appease the Jews to gain political popularity. With a force of 10,000 men he embarked on a number of projects, the most ambitious of which was the Temple. In effect, he demolished the earlier edifice rebuilt by Zerubbabel and Jeshua and dug deep foundations that eradicated the

---

6. It is possible, likely even, that David's Palace, from the same period, has been located in Jerusalem (2 Samuel 5.11), discovered in 2005
7. Ezra 3.2
8. This is remembered in the Jewish festival of Hanukkah, the Festival of Lights, or Feast of Dedication. It falls in late November or early December, and is celebrated with the lighting of a menorah, a seven-branched candlestick

work of the returnees from Babylon. Herod extended and enlarged the Temple Mount platform in order to create a larger space for his new structure. We know from recent archaeological evidence that construction was still ongoing at the time of Christ. Because sacrifice had continued uninterrupted since the time of the return from Babylon, the Temple was still known as the Second Temple, even though it had effectively replaced that built by Jeshua and Zerubbabel.

An interesting footnote to the First and Second Temples is that they were both destroyed on the same day of the fifth Hebrew month, 9th Ab.[9]

The destruction of the second temple in AD70 was discussed at length in Chapter 2.

So much for the past then. But what about the future?

Part 5 – The Third Temple

Any project manager will tell you that the technical challenges of projects are always demanding but relatively straightforward. With time, perseverance and a little ingenuity they can be overcome. The political aspects of projects are a  different matter altogether. In changing the status quo of any situation, the essential problem is that different people want different things. Often, those with conflicting or opposing views have significant influence over project outcomes. I would suggest that the political opposition to the building of the 3rd Temple is unprecedented for any project in world history. The Palestinians,[10] liberal Jews, the UN and the EU are all at odds with religious Jews. So how can a new Temple come into existence when all the world wants one thing (a divided Jerusalem and Palestinian State) and a few in Israel want something else?

---

9. This day, which occurs during July / August, is when Jews remember the tragedies that have befallen them. The fast 'Tisha B'Av' is a day of mourning, which concludes three weeks of remembrance. Traditionally Jews will not marry or celebrate during this time. The book of Lamentations will be read in their Synagogues, and the cabinet in which their scriptures are held is draped with a black cloth.

    9th Ab has also been associated with the day when Moses shattered the stone tablets of the ten commandments; the Roman army's victory over Bar Kochba in AD135; and the expulsion of Jews from England in (1290) and Spain (1492)

10. The Waqf today denies the Jewish Temple ever existed in spite of clear, unequivocal archaeological evidence. *The PA Mufti Muhammad Hussein stated on PA TV News in January 2012: 'They [the Jews] want to say or suggest that this place (the Temple Mount) was once, according to their claim, a Temple. However, in truth, there never was a Temple in any period, nor was there, at any time, any place of worship for the Jews or others at the Al-Aqsa Mosque site'*

CHAPTER EIGHT

Political Assessment – current status

A decision to commit to the building of the 3rd Temple will require the most 'hawkish' Israeli government ever, way beyond those of Netanyahu and Shamir. It will probably mean that every attempt to secure a 'two State solution' will  have failed, the so-called 'peace process' will have been exhausted, that a majority of the Israeli people want a temple and that Israel has reached the point where it has ceased to care what the United Nations thinks. It might also suggest a diminishing of the power of the Palestinians to shape Middle-eastern politics (through the media) to such a point that there is insufficient resistance to challenge its construction. This could possibly be because events elsewhere in the world have shifted the focus of the nations temporarily away from Jerusalem. It could also have something to do with the decline in the power of the Islamic Leopard as postulated in chapter 5. It may even require something that changes the facts on the ground (i.e. the reality of an Islamic holy site on the Temple Mount) such that there is a perceived window of opportunity to be grasped by Israel (in particular, the religious right wing).[11] It is unlikely that Israeli bulldozers would unilaterally demolish the Dome of the Rock or Al Aqsa mosque, so we must assume that some unforeseen event triggers this action. Whether this is a natural phenomenon (such as an earthquake) or human intervention (war or act of terror) we do not know and cannot guess.

When we consider also that the Talmud[12] suggests that the Messiah will lay the cornerstone[13] of the 3rd Temple, we might possibly suggest that the Jews may mistakenly identify Antichrist, the new ultra-politician, as Messiah. It is probable that he will have given his assent to provide Israel with a mandate to proceed with construction and be perceived as a peacemaker. There is no doubt that Israelis are growing weary of seeking to appease America, the UN and world's press corp. The growing tide of world-wide anti-Semitism may provoke a defiant reaction from

---

11. Members of the 'Habayit Hayehudi', or Jewish Home party, have expressed their desire for the 3rd temple
12. The Talmud is the body of Jewish law and legend, and is comprised of the Mishnah (the text) dating from c200AD and Gemara (the commentary) dating from c 500AD. Over 6000 pages long, it contains the opinions of many rabbis on many subjects
13. This appears to be a misinterpretation of Psalm 118.22 *'the stone the builders rejected has become the chief cornerstone'*. This is a classic example of reading a truth into the wrong dispensation, as its eventual fulfilment by the Messiah will take place in the Millennium not the present age. Vv23-24 then continue *'this is the day that the Lord has made, we will rejoice and be glad in it'*. A day to rejoice indeed !

the Jews. The State of Israel already possesses the economic might and military capability to be able to ignore the objections of its immediate neighbours. Should Israel decide to build the 3rd Temple, there is probably little in reality that the Islamists could do about it. It would undoubtedly result in a surge of religious nationalistic fervour throughout Israel. If America and the EU were so weakened by their worsening economic problems and the anti-Israeli UN were ignored, who could oppose the plan?

We are speculating, clearly. But at some point, scripturally, there must come a time when there is sufficient political power to shift the status quo to allow the building of the 3rd Temple. We don't know when or how this will come about, but come about it must. What justification do we have for being so bold in this assertion?

Religious Perspective

Up to the Cross, the Jews were a people under the Law of Moses. Their righteousness and relationship with God was based on obeying a set of laws. If they sinned or fell short then they could make an appropriate sacrifice to atone for their sin and make themselves right again with Him. Their religion required priests, a Temple and the shedding of blood through sacrifices. We have considered above how the Lord abode in a temple made with hands in the Tabernacle and Temples of Solomon and Herod. Once Herod's Temple had been destroyed in AD70, the Jews were bereft and have sought to re-establish it ever since. It is something almost programmed into the soul of every Jew. At Passover they would say 'next year in Jerusalem', but grieve that the Temple Mount was trampled by Gentile Muslims. At Jewish wedding feasts, the bride and groom crush a wine glass underfoot to remember the broken Temple. It would be an understatement to say that the Temple is in engraved on the hearts of those Jews who fear their God.[14]

Some Jews hope the 3rd Temple will usher in the return of the Messiah, and the

---

14. Traditional Jews pray three times daily for the restoration of their temple with the prayer *'Because of our sins we were exiled from our country and banished from our land. We cannot go up as pilgrims to worship Thee, to perform our duties in Thy chosen house, the great and Holy Temple which was called by Thy name, on account of the hand that was let loose on Thy sanctuary. May it be Thy will, Lord our God and God of our fathers, merciful King, in Thy abundant love again to have mercy on us and on Thy sanctuary; rebuild it speedily and magnify its glory'*. Wherever they are in the world, they face towards Jerusalem (specifically the Western Wall) when praying

start of the Millennial age in which Israel will experience both blessing and the much yearned-for peace. Believe me when I say I wish this were true. However, we have demonstrated in earlier chapters that our reading of the end-time schedule is different. Scripturally, the Tribulation must be endured before Christ's return. We will examine the detail around this view over the next chapters.

Many evangelical Christians visit Jerusalem to celebrate the feasts of Israel, such as Sukkot, the Feast of Tabernacles[15] with the Jews. It is wonderful that this action blesses both Jew and Christian. However, Christians must be careful that they do not start to bring themselves under the Law of Moses. We are not under Law but Grace. The only way of salvation is through faith in Jesus Christ, to the Jew first, but also to the Gentiles. Jews will not be saved unless they repent and believe in Him. There is therefore now no need for a temple, priests or sacrifices to obtain salvation and I don't believe that it is right for Christians to contribute to this project. The fact that the Bible foretells the building of a 3rd Temple is not based on the Lord's agreement, but instead concerns His foreknowledge of what will actually happen. It isn't what God wants, but He knows that the Jews of Israel will do it as they continue to follow the obsolete Law. In so doing, they will instigate the wrath of the Antichrist and ultimately, the return of Messiah, Jesus Christ.

So what does the Bible say regarding the 3rd Temple? I know that some Christians have 'spiritualised' this area, believing that the rebuilt temple is Christ's body and not a physical structure. Let us consider five scriptures to show that this 'spiritualisation' view is incorrect.

Scriptural basis for 3rd Temple

In Matthew 24 Jesus refers to two verses from the prophet Daniel:

> *Forces from him will arise,* **desecrate the sanctuary fortress**, *and do away with the* **regular (daily) sacrifice**. *And they will set up the* **abomination of desolation**
>
> Dan 11.31

> *From the time that the regular* **(daily) sacrifice** *is abolished and the* **abomination of desolation** *is set up, there will be 1,290 days*
>
> Dan 12.11

---

15. The Feast of Tabernacles is also known as the Feast of Booths (or tents). It is one of the three great pilgrimage festivals of the Jewish year. It derives from Leviticus 23.42, when all Israelites had to dwell in tents for seven days to remember their 40 year sojourn in the wilderness. Zechariah 14.16-17 makes it clear that Gentiles can and should participate in this feast

Chapter Eight

*....and then the end will come. Therefore when you see the **abomination of desolation** which was spoken of through Daniel the prophet, **standing in the holy place** (let the reader understand), then those who are in Judea must flee to the mountains*

Matthew 24. 14b-16a

As we saw in chapter 2, Jesus' context here is to do with the Temple and the end-times. He clearly foresaw a future Temple. In chapter 2 we discussed how this was a separate event (and therefore a different temple) from the activities of 70AD. Daniel also spoke of a daily sacrifice, and a sanctuary. Clearly, in order for someone to desolate the sanctuary and interrupt sacrifice, then a sanctuary must exist at that time.

Paul too, when writing to the Church at Thessalonica, warned that Antichrist would sit in the Temple. Again, if he is to sit in the Temple then it must exist. This did not happen before it was destroyed in AD70 and again must relate to a future temple.

*Let no one in any way deceive you, for it will not come unless the apostasy comes first, and the man of lawlessness is revealed, the son of destruction, who opposes and exalts himself above every so-called god or object of worship, so that **he takes his seat in the temple of God, displaying himself as being God***

2 Thess 2.3-4

Finally, we turn to John and the Revelation. He describes how the Gentiles will tread underfoot the outer court of the Temple and holy city for 42 months.

*Then there was given me a measuring rod like a staff; and someone said, Get up and measure **the temple of God and the altar, and those who worship in it.** Leave out the court which is outside the temple and do not measure it, for it has been given to the nations (Gentiles)[16]; and they will tread underfoot the holy city for forty-two months*

Rev 11.1-2

The 42 month (3 ½ year) period is located within the Tribulation and clearly end-time. There can be no doubt then from scripture that a rebuilt temple will exist at the time of the end and that it will be desolated by the Antichrist. It is probable that

---

16. This suggests that the 3rd Temple will actually share the Temple Mount with the Muslim shrines that presently occupy that location. It is possible that Antichrist will negotiate an agreement between Muslim and Jew, so allowing construction, and thereby being perceived as a peacemaker. There is another possibility too: the Muslims may be persuaded to allow the 3rd Temple because it might be perceived to be necessary for the return of their prophet. These two possibilities seem to compliment each other

CHAPTER EIGHT

this Temple will be destroyed by the great earthquake that will split Jerusalem into three when Jesus returns. We will return to this in Chapter 11.

3rd Temple as a project

Before we leave the subject of the 3rd Temple, we should consider what is involved at a practical level. The Temple won't just drop down out of the sky, but will involve detailed planning and a lot of hard work. There will be cranes and concrete; stonecutters and weavers and a real sense of zeal. An example of this activity is the ceremonial robes worn by the high priest, which use a particular shade of bluish-purple. A 2,000 year old scrap of cloth recovered from Masada has been analysed and it was found that the dye came from a particular snail. This dye is now being recreated to allow the robes to be fabricated.

The diagram below identifies a number of related conditions that must all be fulfilled before temple worship can be restored. In order to read it you should start from left to right, saying "in order to restore temple worship, we must secure Israeli governmental consent, identify the correct location, fabricate the artefacts" and so on. And then "in order to secure government consent, we must (either) make a unilateral decision, or agree a solution...". This is an exercise in sufficiency logic. Every condition must exist in reality to allow the next level to progress.

Let us look briefly at each area:

- **secure government consent** – this is discussed above

- **Identify correct location** – there have been a number of studies over the years seeking to determine the exact location of the Holy of Holies,[17] which could only be entered by the High Priest once a year. Orthodox Jews today will not step on the Temple Mount for fear of walking over the Holy place. The general consensus is that it is positioned under the Dome of the Rock. However, Tuvia Segiv, an Israeli architect has suggested that the Temple was actually placed south of the Dome but north of Al Aqsa and that there is ample room to build the Temple between the two structures without demolishing the Muslim shrines. The Jewish Temple could conceivably co-exist with them and this idea

---

17. See *'The Quest'* by Dr Leen Ritmeyer for an authoritative explanation of the archaeology of the Temple Mount, and location of the temples

is inferred by the 'court of the Gentiles' being 'outside the Temple' discussed above.

- **fabricate the artefacts** – The Temple Institute is dedicated to rebuilding the Temple and has already completed the High Priest's uniform, including the breastplate and ephod. To date, they advise over 60 vessels have been restored. These can be viewed by visitors in Jerusalem or via their website.[18]

- **build the structure** – again here the Temple Institute has created a modern architectural plan for the 3rd Temple, combining the latest building standards with research from Biblical, Talmudic and other historical sources

- **prepare qualified priesthood** – the Mishnah contains detailed information regarding the activities of the priesthood. However, in order to qualify them for Temple service the ashes of a red heifer[19] are required for ritual purification. Without this cleansing, they cannot progress

- **commence sacrifice** – the act of commencing sacrifice in the Temple is a key milestone and one we should watch for. It may be the sign that begins the seven years of the tribulation

---

18. Their website can be visited at http://www.templeinstitute.org
19. Numbers 19 requires that the children of Israel bring the ashes of a red heifer, 'without spot, or blemish', that had never been 'under the yoke'. It must not have hairs of any other colour, and should be in perfect health. The significance is that this was the only sacrifice that was permitted to take place 'outside the camp' (i.e. it did not need a functioning tabernacle or temple). Its purpose was to ritually cleanse those who had become unclean. In so doing, the sacrifice would qualify the modern-day priesthood for temple service. A number of candidates for the extremely rare red heifer have recently been identified, but these were subsequently rejected as being imperfect, so the search goes on

Chapter Eight

The 3rd Temple – a project overview

- **Restore Temple Worship**
  - Secure Israeli Government assent
    - either Make unilateral decision
    - or Agree solution with the Waqf
    - or Agree solution at the UN
  - Identify the correct location
  - Fabricate Temple artefacts
    - Menorah, bowls, utensils etc
  - Build the structure
    - Secure necessary funding
    - Assemble skilled workforce
    - establish the design
    - Gather appropriate materials
    - Prepare the ground
  - prepare suitably qualified Priesthood
    - Confirm priestly line
    - provide training
  - Commence sacrifiices
    - breed red heifer

(Red boxes indicate the need for political agreement)

Chapter Eight

Speculation concerning the Temple Vessels

Some believe that artefacts, including the Ark of the Covenant, are stored in chambers under the Temple Mount. However, Revelation states:

> *the temple of God which is in heaven was opened; and the ark of His covenant appeared in His temple, and there were flashes of lightning and sounds and peals of thunder and an earthquake and a great hailstorm*
>
> Rev 11.19

The Ark therefore currently resides in the heavenly temple, and will only be revealed at the last trumpet.

Others speculate that the Vatican possesses certain artefacts and vessels such as the Menorah (the seven-branched candlestick). These are said to be stored in vast, underground treasure caves in Rome and were inherited from the Roman Empire by the early Church. The Vatican has denied this is the case. In 1996, Israeli Religious Affairs Minister Shimon Shetreet formally requested the Pope for an official enquiry to investigate the matter.[20]

The rebuilding of the 3rd Temple is a definite candidate for the signs of the times that Jesus told us to watch for. It is here that Antichrist will sit in the *Naos*, the Holy Place, and declare himself to be god, triggering the 3 ½ year Great Tribulation. As we have said, the Christian perspective is that there is no need for it, but despite this it will still be built.

This won't be the last Temple though. We will consider the 4th Temple in Chapter 14.

---

20. Described by the Jerusalem Post January 27, 1996

Chapter Eight

Chapter 9   The Antichrist – man of sin

I kept looking, and that horn was waging war with the saints and overpowering them.

Daniel 7.21

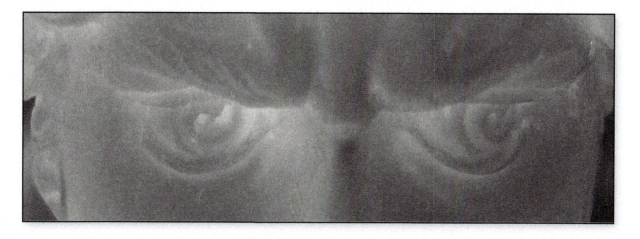

Part 1 – Introduction

The existence of Antichrist has been foretold since the time of Daniel and is a major theme of scripture. We are therefore required to study and understand him. Analysis of scriptural names reveals characteristics about the individual, so we will therefore begin our study by looking at the different names that describe Antichrist. We may also turn to the lesson of history: forerunners or types of Antichrist in both the Bible and through the ages provide valuable insights. These will build together into a comprehensive picture of his nature and activity at the end of the age.

We will complete our study by looking at the role of the False Prophet.

Let us start by considering for a moment where the world finds itself right now:

Chapter Nine

- the nation of Israel, battle-weary after decades of war, terrorism and international pressure seeks a peacemaker

- religious Jews look for Messiah to establish their Temple, deliver them from oppression and establish the kingdom of God

- the nations of the world, having endured economic turmoil and global instability look for one who can bring order and prosperity

- Muslims look for the return of their prophet (known as the 12th Imam or Mahdi) to usher in a global Islamic caliphate based on Sharia Law

- large multi-national corporations need economic stability and a secure business environment in their relentless pursuit of shareholder value and profit

- secular humanists want an 'ultimate man' to worship and revere, as well as to eradicate every vestige of religion from society

- homosexuals will appreciate a man who 'does not desire women'[1]

- occultists and practitioners of New Age practices or mysticism will follow a man who is able to display supernatural power and signs

As we discussed in chapter 6, the western media has over the last 10 years been sensationalising the cult of celebrity. Many of today's 'stars' have little talent or integrity, yet their fans worship them as gods, basking in the reflection of their counterfeit glory. These people often lead tragic lives. The present generation has been fed on this phenomenon, with a resulting erosion of discernment between good and evil. Generations gone by, which were under God-fearing governments and education systems did possess a certain discernment in this area, but this has now been largely displaced. An example of this occurred 10 years ago with the death of Diana, Princess of Wales. On the same day, Mother Teresa of Calcutta also died, famous for dedicating her life to outcasts, yet her death was virtually ignored by the media. Celebrity is all to this generation, and those who are godly are disdained.

---

1. Daniel 11.37

I sincerely believe that Satan is behind this culture of celebrity and that it is merely one of many strategies whose purpose is to prepare the ground for Antichrist to step onto the world stage.

Part 2 – Names of Antichrist

Antichrist is described in scripture by various names. We will examine each below:

Antichrist (Greek: *antichristos*) is used only in John's epistles and means one who is *against* or *instead* of Christ. It can also mean one who comes in the *guise* of, or one who opposes Christ, the anointed One. Any religion, human agent or agency that denies Jesus Christ and His relationship with the Father is therefore under the spirit of antichrist.

Ultimately, the Antichrist will seek to replace and oppose Jesus and come strongly and ferociously against those who worship Him.

> *Children, it is the last hour and just as you heard that antichrist is coming, even now **many antichrists have appeared**. From this we know that it is the last hour.*
>
> 1 John 2.18

> *Who is the liar but the one who denies that Jesus is the Christ? This is the antichrist, the one who **denies the Father and the Son***
>
> 1 John 2.22

> *...every spirit that **does not confess Jesus is not from God**; this is the **spirit of the antichrist**, of which you have heard that it is coming, and now it is already in the world*
>
> 1 John 4.3

> *For many deceivers have gone out into the world, those who **do not acknowledge Jesus Christ as coming in the flesh**. This is the deceiver and the antichrist.*
>
> 2 John 7

We may learn much by meditating on the above verses, particularly with reference to other religions and pseudo-Christian cults. Jehovah's Witnesses, Mormons, and

Chapter Nine

liberal Christians for example do not believe in the deity of Christ.

1 John 4.3 above also describes the spirit of antichrist which is at work in the world. This spirit, operating behind governments, media and corporate entities is relentlessly preparing the ground for Antichrist. It is this spirit which is behind (for example) today's equality, diversity and inclusivity policies, which actively promote homosexual rights and oppose Christian principles. It is important to note that whilst humans are involved in this activity, they are not the authors or instigators, merely the puppets through which these policies are enacted. We know from Ephesians that we don't wage war with flesh and blood, but with spiritual forces in heavenly places.[2] So too here:

> **The Beast** (Greek: *therion*) is used in Revelation 13 and means a wild beast. The term is used to describe both Antichrist (the first beast) and the False Prophet (the second beast). We would do well to compare those who exhibit the spirit of the Lamb with those of the Beast: the former is gentle, meek, self-sacrificial; the latter cruel, domineering and violent. Jesus advised us that *by their fruits shall you know them.*
>
> The next three names are taken from 2 Thessalonians 2.1-12, which we will explore in detail under the next section.
>
> **Man of Sin** – it is his nature to sin, and to promulgate sin. Sin is not just about breaking God's laws, but also concerns those who seek independence from Him. Many humanist intellectuals take the position that their own wisdom and understanding know best and they scorn those who follow any religion. The man of sin will take this view to the extreme.
>
> **Son of Perdition (or destruction)** – his end is destined in destruction.
>
> **Lawless One** – he will recognise no law, no boundaries, no traditions. He will have no respect for what has gone before and will take many by surprise when his true nature is revealed.

In summary therefore, we can see that antichrist is manifested in three forms:

---

2. Ephesians 6.12

- **The Antichrist**, an individual being who will be incarnated in human flesh at the time of the end.

- **many antichrists**, lesser beings who also take human form and exhibit certain characteristic traits of the one who is to follow them. These are forerunners and prototypes of the Antichrist, and throughout history have attacked and persecuted God's people, whether Christian or Jew.

- the **spirit of antichrist** which is at work now in the world in its systems, organisations and processes, as well as through the ungodly. It is preparing the ground for the entrance of the Antichrist, and working relentlessly against both the Church and the true Israel.

Part 3 – Types and Forerunners of Antichrist

Our primary source for these role models is the Bible. However, history is littered with those who manifest the same hallmark characteristics of our adversary. We will consider below a number of examples of the many antichrists foretold by John that have already come and are still to come.

Space does not permit more than an introductory précis, so I would ask that you consider these thumbnail sketches as a primer, with a view to performing some personal research on your own part. As you read, make a mental checklist of the characteristics.

The dates indicate the duration of the reign.

Nimrod

(Hebrew: *marad* = to rebel). Nimrod was the founder of Babylon, the centre of godless, human-based pleasure, endeavour and independence from God. He was a rebel, who chose to set himself against God and His people (see Gen 10.8-10 and 1Chron 1.10).

Prince of Tyre

Ezekiel 28 describes two rulers, one a king and the other a prince.

The King of Tyre was in Eden, an anointed cherub. He had access to the mountain of God and was 'perfect in his ways' until iniquity was found in him. His heart was lifted up, his wisdom was corrupted and he was cast down and is to become 'no more forever'. This is clearly a picture of the origin and end of Satan.

The Prince of Tyre is a man who proclaimed himself a god. He lifted up his heart in pride and sat in the seat of gods. He is described as being wiser than Daniel and no secret can be hidden from him. His wisdom has made him very wealthy. He will ultimately die the death of the slain and be thrown down into the Pit. It is interesting to note that he *'will die the death of the uncircumcised'*, a broad hint that he may be a Gentile.

Whether this prince is a specific description of the Antichrist, or merely a forerunner we cannot tell, but it is most informative of his character and work.

Antiochus Epiphanes IV (175-164BC)

The conquests of Alexander the Great created the Seleucid Empire. When Antiochus Epiphanes came to power, he, like any ruler of this age liked to set out to conquer, but was suspicious of events in his own country whilst on campaign. At this time Jerusalem was under Greek dominion, so came under Antiochus' power. He demanded that the Jews should accept Greek culture and broke promises that he had made in respect of their religion. This resulted in him robbing and desecrating their Temple. He integrated all the Gods with Zeus as their head and made the Jewish Temple into the Temple of Zeus or Dionysus whom he equated with the God of Israel.

He forbade the worship of God and forced the Jews to sacrifice to other gods. At this point he set himself up as god, and commanded them to worship him. It was to this act that Jesus referred to illustrate the future 'Abomination that makes desolate' that would occur at the end of the age.

Herod the Great (73-4BC)

Herod was an amoral monster. He was a master manipulator who used the patronage of Mark Anthony (after whom he built and named the Antonia Fortress to the North of the Temple) and Octavian (later to become Augustus Caesar) to secure his Kingdom over the province of Judaea.

His rule was typified by assassination, intrigue, insecurity and magnificent building projects, including the 2nd Temple that Jesus knew and taught in. As we saw in chapter 2, the Temple had been built to secure favour with the Jewish people. However, they still treated Herod as an impostor, being half Arab, half Jew, and thought of him as a Roman 'stooge'. Herod was outwardly and publicly religious, but inwardly corrupt.

He was insecure and dealt ruthlessly with any perceived threat to his throne, including the massacre of the infants in Bethlehem[3] to ensure that Jesus, the Son of David could not take his throne. However, the wise men warned Mary and Joseph to escape into Egypt. Herod's action is typical of the spirit of Antichrist, which comes fiercely and violently against those who are anointed by the Spirit of God and seeks to kill and destroy them.

Hadrian (117-138AD)

Hadrian's uncle Trajan sought to destroy Israel completely. He commanded that Jews be killed across the whole of today's Middle East. Tacitus the historian wrote at the time that *'the Jews were seen as hostile to the Roman Empire, regarding as profane everything we hold sacred, whilst permitting what we abhor'*. On Trajan's death, Hadrian became Caesar.

He visited Jerusalem in 130AD and decided to annihilate the city. He ordered its destruction and the building of the new Roman city of Aelia Capitolina[4] in its place. The city was to house shrines to Greek, Roman and Egyptian gods. He built a temple to Jupiter[5] on the Temple Mount and set an equestrian statue to himself over the site of the Jewish Temple's Holy Place.

---

3. Matthew 2.16-18
4. After his own name Aelius, and the Roman god Jupiter
5. Jupiter was the Roman equivalent of the Greek god Zeus, the chief of the Olympian gods. He was said to control the phenomena of the heavenly realm, including the thunderbolt (seen not only on the collars of Nazi SS, but also Harry Potter's forehead!). As chief of the gods, Jupiter is a clear parallel for Satan. The siting of his temple on the Temple Mount shows how he tried to displace the true God. This parallel is confirmed by Revelation 2.13, where we are told that Satan's seat was then at Pergamum. The Great Altar of Zeus which sat on the hill there was dismantled and later rebuilt at the Staatliche Museum in Berlin, where it may be seen today. This took place between 1901 and 1930, and its influence may relate to the rise of the Kaiser and Nazism

Chapter Nine

Figure 34. Altar to Zeus in the Pergamonmuseum, Berlin.

It is interesting to note that the next building to occupy this site would be the Islamic Dome of the Rock. Following Antiochus Epiphenes' dedication of the Jewish Temple to Zeus and Hadrian's Temple to Jupiter, came this building on which is inscribed 'God has no son'. This activity of displacement, denial and opposition is typical antichrist behaviour. Whilst less overt, it is gaining prevalence in society today as the world becomes rapidly less tolerant of Judaeo-Christian precepts, resulting in their systematic erosion.

Hadrian is remembered in history as a restless traveller who efficiently reorganised his Empire, consolidating Rome under Greek culture. He was a homosexual, suffered fits of rage and was capable of acts of extreme violence.

His most enduring legacy was to rename Judaea as 'Palestine' (Latin: Philistia).[6] In seeking to erase completely the Jewish people, he used the name of the Philistines, a people who had ceased to exist some 600 years earlier. 'Hadrian's curse', as it has been called by some, has been an immense and ongoing source of trouble to Jewish people. The spirit of Antichrist even now seeks to remove the Jewish people from their God-given land and replace them with Islamists. Those who oppose Israel's right to the land are thus motivated by this spirit.

Adolf Hitler

What can we say about Adolf Hitler that has not already been said? There is no

---

6. In their report presented in 1938 to the League of Nations, the British made it clear that *'The name 'Palestine' is not a country but was considered a geographic region.'* The 1922 Times Atlas of the World reflects the view at that time that Palestine was a region, including not just Judaea and Samaria, but also Syria, the Lebanon, Transjordan, Iraq and northern Egypt. To confuse the modern State of Israel with a mythical pre-existent Palestinian State conflates Hadrian's 'curse' on Judaea with poor geo-political history

doubt that Satan sought through him to destroy the Jewish people in the ovens of Europe. But would Israel have come to exist as a state today if there had been no Holocaust? I doubt it. The genocide was highly organised, looking for the greatest efficiencies in the business of death. Will the Tribulation be less severe than this? Jesus said not.

Ezekiel's vision of the valley of dry bones is a stark picture of the camps. It is no coincidence that Ezekiel 37 and 38 prophesy not only that these bones would live, but that the Lord would bring the *whole house*[7] of Israel into the Land. The two events are clearly linked in the sight of God.

These are just a few examples of those who exhibit the spirit of Antichrist. More exist in history and the reader can probably imagine a number of today's national leaders (of such nations as North Korea or Iran) who exhibit at least some of these characteristics. I recommend you take time to prayerfully study them in more detail.

Part 4 – The Nature and Activity of Antichrist

Now we request you, brethren, with regard to the coming of our Lord Jesus Christ and our gathering together to Him, that you not be quickly shaken from your composure or be disturbed either by a spirit or a message or a letter as if from us, to the effect that the day of the Lord has come.

- *Let no one in any way deceive you, for it **(that day) will not come unless***
- ***the apostasy** (departure from revealed doctrine) comes first, and*
- ***the man of lawlessness** is revealed, the **son of destruction**, who*
  - ***opposes** and*
  - ***exalts himself above every so-called god or object of worship,***
  - *so that he takes his seat in the temple of God, displaying himself as being God.*

*Do you not remember that while I was still with you, I was telling you these things? And you know what restrains him now, so that in his time he will be revealed. For the mystery of lawlessness is already at work; only he who now restrains will do so until he is taken out of the way. Then that **lawless one** will be revealed whom the Lord will slay with the breath of His mouth and bring to an end by the appearance of His coming; that is, the one whose coming is in accord with the activity of Satan, with **all power and signs and false wonders,** and with*

---

7. This makes it clear that the whole of Israel will be brought back to the land, and suggests events will conspire to cause a yet-future and major aliyah from the US and Europe into Israel

Chapter Nine

> ***all the deception of wickedness*** *for those who perish, because they did not receive the love of the truth so as to be saved. For this reason God will send upon them a deluding influence so that they will believe what is false, in order that they all may be judged who did not believe the truth, but took pleasure in wickedness*
>
> 2 Thess 2.1-12 (my comments in brackets)

These words need little explanation. Note that Paul is clear that Jesus won't return, nor will we be gathered to Him, until Antichrist has been revealed. We are then given clear signposts for that day i.e. it cannot happen until …

- *the* apostasy comes first, a massive departure from sound doctrine far greater than we have currently seen. You might be surprised that it is God who sends the delusion to those who did not receive the love of the truth (this, incidentally, is why it is futile attempting to argue someone into the light of God. Pray for them instead).

- Antichrist sitting in the Temple (which must therefore have been rebuilt), portraying himself as god. This is the event that signals the beginning of the second phase of the Tribulation.

Note that he exalts himself against all that is called god or worshipped: at this point Antichrist will subordinate every earthly religion to himself, including Judaism, Christianity, Islam, Buddhism and so on.

Paul then adds that Antichrist will possess *all* power, signs, lying wonders and unrighteous deception. The word 'all' must be taken seriously. Our protection against that deception is to cultivate right now a strong love of the truth. **'The lie'** that Paul describes is one of the lies told to Eve by Satan in Gen 3.5 *'you will be like God'*. This deception, that 'god lies within us', has been evident through the New Age movement and its derivatives.

The 'one who restrains' is Christ's representative on earth, the Holy Spirit, showing yet again that it is God Almighty who determines and controls the pace of the end-time programme.

This is a powerful picture of what is to come, but we can more obtain yet more detail from Revelation 13:

Chapter Nine

Then I saw a beast coming up out of the sea, having ten horns and seven heads, and on his horns were ten diadems, and on his heads were blasphemous names.

And the beast which I saw was

- *like a **leopard**, and*
- *his feet were like those of a **bear**, and*
- *his mouth like the mouth of a **lion**.*

*And the dragon gave him his power and his throne and great authority. I saw one of his heads as if it had been slain, and his fatal wound was healed. And **the whole earth was amazed and followed** after the beast; they **worshiped the dragon** because he gave his authority to the beast; and they **worshiped the beast**, saying, Who is like the beast, and who is able to wage war with him?*

*There was given to him a mouth speaking arrogant words and blasphemies, and **authority to act for forty-two months** was given to him. And he opened his mouth in blasphemies against God, to blaspheme His name and His tabernacle, that is, those who dwell in heaven.*

Figure 35. The Beast.

*It was also given to him to **make war with the saints and to overcome them**, and authority **over every tribe and people and tongue and nation** was given to him.*

All who dwell on the earth will worship him, everyone whose name has not been written from the foundation of the world in the book of life of the Lamb who has been slain.

If anyone has an ear, let him hear. If anyone is destined for captivity, to captivity he goes; if anyone kills with the sword, with the sword he must be killed. Here is the perseverance and the faith of the saints

Note first that the Beast rises up from the sea, which tells us that he comes from the nations and is therefore Gentile. The leopard, bear and lion have been encountered before (see Chapter 5) and suggest he is of Muslim descent, arises from Eastern Europe and that he speaks English. Daniel 11.37 tells us that he will not recognise the god of his fathers, so he will abandon and play-down his Muslim heritage and adopt humanism. It is interesting that many world leaders today,

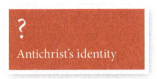

such as Barack Obama and David Cameron, are making similar moves from their religious roots.

It may be that he grabs the world's attention when he recovers from a fatal head-wound, presumably with pictures being beamed around the globe. Those with no discernment will be highly impressed and beguiled into worshipping him. Celebrity worshippers watch out!

The term 'Saints' (Greek: *hagios*) means those who are separated or set apart. It is used of both Christian and faithful Jews in the New Testament and these will endure war for 42 months (3 ½ years) during the second phase of the Tribulation. Antichrist will overcome them and they will either be slain or led into captivity. The Beast's authority will be all-encompassing, over every tribe, tongue and nation, including Israel, the USA, the EU and UK.

This will be the ultimate test of faith and patience and those who are alive at that time will be granted grace to endure or escape. Do you wonder why we encounter various problems now and it seems prayers go unanswered? It is because we are being trained in many trials *now* so that we will triumph *then*. This ultimate separation will then take place between those whose names are in the Book of Life and those who aren't. There is and can be no middle ground. Remember that God sees the beginning from the end and is more interested in how you finish than how you start. He has committed Himself to watch over you and complete in you the work He started.

Daniel sheds further light on Antichrist's nature:

> *The fourth beast will be a fourth kingdom on the earth, which will be **different from all the other kingdoms and will devour the whole earth and tread it down and crush it** (into pieces).*
>
> *As for the ten horns, out of this kingdom ten kings will arise; and another will arise after them, and he will be different from the previous ones and will subdue three kings. He will speak out against the Most High and wear down the saints of the Highest One, and he will intend to make alterations in times and in law;*
>
> *And they will be given into his hand for a time, times, and half a time. But the court will sit for judgment, and his dominion will be taken away, annihilated and destroyed forever*
>
> Dan 7.23-26

Chapter Nine

In the latter period of their rule, when the transgressors have run their course, a king will arise, insolent and skilled in intrigue.

His power will be mighty, but not by his own power, and he will destroy to an extraordinary degree and prosper and perform his will. He will destroy mighty men and the holy people. And through his shrewdness he will cause deceit to succeed by his influence. And he will magnify himself in his heart, and he will destroy many while they are at ease. He will even oppose the Prince of Princes, but he will be broken without human agency.

Dan 8.23-25

And he will make a firm covenant with the many for one week, but in the middle of the week he will put a stop to sacrifice and grain offering

And on the wing of abominations will come one who makes desolate, even until a complete destruction, one that is decreed, is poured out on the one who makes desolate

Daniel 9.27

Daniel confirms again that Antichrist will speak pompous words and will persecute the saints for 3 ½ years. Presumably it will offend him that the modern western calendar is based on Jesus' life, so he will attempt (but seemingly not succeed) in changing times. He will also attempt to change the law, some of which will even then be based on Judaeo-Christian principles.

He will make a covenant[8] with many for 7 years, but break it midway after 3 ½ years to begin the Great Tribulation. It is probable that the covenant will concern peace in the Middle East, probably between Israel and the Islamic nations. Remember that Israel still seeks her Messiah. What better man to broker this peace than a Muslim who has beaten death? It seems too good to be true and will be.

In summing up, it seems that Antichrist will initially be perceived as a peacemaker and will step onto a world stage that Satan has been preparing for him for centuries. A world whose senses have been dulled by celebrity worship will greet him with open arms. However, those who have true faith will have their senses trained by continual practice to discern good from evil.[9] He will combine the worst characteristics of every prototype antichrist from history as the Lord God of heaven and earth allows the refining pot to separate His chosen once and for all

---

8. A peace treaty, offered and guaranteed by himself. This covenant will be a satanic counterfeit of the New Covenant of Christ. Purporting to bring peace and order, it will bring chaos and every evil thing. Initially accepted by the Jews, it will seek to distract them from the New Covenant.
9. Hebrews 5.14

from this evil world.

This now brings us to the origin of the Antichrist:

> *The beast that you saw was, and is not, and is about to come up out of the abyss and go to destruction. And those who dwell on the earth, whose name has not been written in the book of life from the foundation of the world, will wonder when they see the beast, that he was and is not and will come*
>
> Rev 17.8

Antichrist, together with the False Prophet, is presently being held (restrained) in the Pit, from whence he will emerge at the appointed time, when the transgressors have reached their fullness. It seems he will be a fallen angel, who will take on bodily form, in his physical manifestation (much like Satan when he spoke through Judas) to play his part. He cannot be human as men are destined to die once, then comes judgment.[10] A mere man could not ascend from the Pit.

At the last, at the appointed hour, the court of Heaven will be seated and will decide that it is time for him to be broken without human means and he will be cast alive into the lake of Fire, where he will be tormented night and day forever. Hallelujah!

Part 5 – The False Prophet

> *Then I saw another beast coming up out of the earth; and he had two horns like a lamb and he spoke as a dragon.*
>
> *He exercises all the authority of the first beast in his presence. And he makes the earth and those who dwell in it to worship the first beast, whose fatal wound was healed.*
>
> *He performs great signs, so that he even makes fire come down out of heaven to the earth in the presence of men. And he deceives those who dwell on the earth because of the signs which it was given him to perform in the presence of the beast, telling those who dwell on the earth to make an image to the beast who had the wound of the sword and has come to life. And it was given to him to give breath to the image of the beast, so that the image of the beast would even speak and cause as many as do not worship the image of the beast to be killed.*
>
> *And he causes all, the small and the great, and the rich and the poor, and the free men and the slaves, to be given a mark on their right hand or on their forehead, and he provides that*

---

10. Hebrews 9.27

no one will be able to buy or to sell, except the one who has the mark, either the name of the beast or the number of his name. Here is wisdom. Let him who has understanding calculate the number of the beast, for the number is that of a man; and his number is six hundred and sixty-six

Rev 13.11-18

The False Prophet appears after the Antichrist and comes out of 'the earth', suggesting he is of Jewish descent. The above passage needs little explanation, but we should note that this prophet is the Antichrist's worship leader and possesses great supernatural power. It is good to remember that just because one manifests this power, does not mean it is necessarily of God. We are commanded to test the spirits, to see whether they are of God. Many in the Church today see signs and wonders and blithely assume that they are of God. This failure of discernment has blighted many churches and a number of revivals,[11] as gullible believers so confused demonic activity with the work of the Holy Spirit.

The Prophet will project an image of the Beast - whether it is of technological or supernatural media, we cannot tell.

The Beast's number is significant. We have already considered that 6 is the number of man. An enumeration of the Greek letters of Jesus' name for example gives us 888.[12]

	Greek Letters	Values
JESUS	Ι	10
	Η	8
	Σ	200
	Ο	70
	Υ	400
	Σ	200
	Total	**888**

Eight is associated with regeneration and resurrection, the beginning of a new order. For example Noah was the 8th person, circumcision was performed on the

---

11. Read *'War on the Saints'* (unabridged) by Jessie Penn Lewis for an account of how this phenomena affected the Welsh Revival
12. Certain languages such as Latin, Hebrew and Greek use letters as numbers, and therefore allow us to calculate the mathematical value of individual words. We may not however use English for this purpose, so should not attempt to calculate the value of words from this language

Chapter Nine

8th day and Christ was resurrected on the 8th day of the week. Christ's Kingdom will be the 8th described by Daniel (see 'Times of the Gentiles' charts in chapters 2 and 5)

In like manner we are told to 'calculate' the number of the Beast. This suggests it will not be obvious, but will require some insight. It may seem obscured now, but will be revealed to those who need to know at that time.

Should we fear him? No! Jesus told us rather *to fear Him who can cast our soul into hell.....not him who destroys the body.* A healthy and holy fear of God will protect us from the fear of man, even the Antichrist.

Having now established the nature of Antichrist, we will next consider the events of the Tribulation.

Chapter 10   'War on the Saints': The Great Tribulation

For momentary, light affliction is producing for us an eternal weight of glory far beyond all comparison, while we look not at the things which are seen, but at the things which are not seen; for the things which are seen are temporal, but the things which are not seen are eternal.

2 Corinthians 4.17-18

Figure 36. Lightning

Part 1 – Introduction

It is now time to consolidate what we have learned from the Spine, Revelation and other scriptural sources to build a comprehensive picture of the Tribulation. It is important we understand why the Tribulation will happen, as well as the various stages it comprises. This chapter will therefore address:

- the purpose of the Tribulation
- the four stages of the Tribulation

CHAPTER TEN

Part 2 – The purpose of the Tribulation

It is probably true to say that most evangelical Christians believe that they will escape the Tribulation.[1] This view emerged in the Church only a century ago[2] and is popular for the obvious reason that our escape is imminent. Many cannot conceive why a loving God would expose His chosen and beloved to such intense suffering. This is a serious issue and worthy of some consideration, but we shall see that the theology is very straightforward. In Paul's letter to his young disciple Timothy, he states:

> *If we endure, we will also reign with Him*
>
> 2 Tim 2.12

Paul makes our qualification to reign conditional upon our ability to endure – the big word in the above verse being '*if*'. God wants overcomers, those who have been tested but have not given up; those whose faith has been exposed and stretched in the hard places over many years, yet who still keep on believing. I once met Alex Buchanan, who led Intercessors for Britain. Alex bore his cross cheerfully. He had suffered a stroke, affecting his speech and his wife was disabled and wheelchair-bound. He told me with a twinkle in his eye that the 11th Commandment was '*thou shalt bash on*'. His prophetic ministry was possibly the most profound I have witnessed in the UK during my lifetime. This ability to keep on keeping on through suffering is demonstrated by the British SAS and US Special Forces, whose recruits keep going when others give up. This principle must become the X factor of our faith.

> *...fixing our eyes on Jesus, the author and perfecter of faith, who for the **joy set before Him endured the cross**, despising the shame, and has sat down at the right hand of the throne of God*
>
> Hebrews 12.2

---

1. We will not discuss the pre-Tribulation rapture in detail, as the position of this book is clear, but would mention that there is no single explicit verse in the Bible that supports this view. As we have seen though, there are many passages of scripture that make it clear the Church will endure trouble
2. Championed by J.N.Darby

Chapter Ten

If this kind of faith is good enough for Jesus, it should be good enough for us.

We should consider another scripture:

> *Therefore, since Christ has suffered in the flesh, arm yourselves also with the same purpose, because he who has suffered in the flesh has ceased from sin*
> 1 Peter 4.1

Godly suffering causes sin to cease and to be of no effect. Jesus is coming back for a pure bride, so those alive at the end of the age must be prepared to go through the refiner's fire. In the believer's life the cross *always* precedes resurrection: Jesus had to endure Calvary to reach the Father's right hand and send us the Holy Spirit; Abraham had to be prepared to yield up Isaac as a sacrifice on Mount Moriah before he received the great promise from God; Moses killed a man then fled; Peter had to experience the humiliation and despair of denying Christ before he was qualified to lead the 1st Century church. It fits then that the end-time elect will have to endure the Tribulation to get to the Marriage Supper of the Lamb.

In the life of every true believer, whether Old or New Testament, past or present, we will find the marks of the Cross. You should check out those you follow in your Christian walk: unless the personal cross has done its work in them, they are likely to be affected by self, soulishness and carnality. For some it is a health issue, for others, financial hardship. It can be a family problem, persecution, or issues in the workplace. The Apostle Paul for example patiently endured his thorn in the flesh. All these trials are permitted by God for the purpose of perfecting us. His power is always perfected in our weakness. The popular prosperity or faith teaching has been a blessing to many, myself included, but tends to assume that those who are suffering do not need to and that there is always a straightforward way out if we follow their formula. It is as if those who are afflicted are somehow believed to be living beneath their inheritance. This can bring a sense of condemnation for those who are patiently enduring trials. We need balance here and the scriptural principle is that testing precedes true power. Before Jesus' ministry commenced and immediately after His baptism, He entered the wilderness in the *fullness* of the Spirit, but emerged after 40 days of testing in the *power* of the Spirit. Suffering is heaven-sent training to prepare believers for powerful service. There are no short cuts. The seed has to die before it bears fruit.

This is not a popular message, but Jesus stated unequivocally that unless we took up our cross daily, denying ourselves, we were not worthy to be called His disciples. It was His way, and He is our example, so it must also be our way. A servant is not above his Master. We weren't promised a cushion but a cross, an instrument of death to self. Thus, one purpose for the Tribulation, the greatest test of all time, is to refine us, loose us from sin, pave the way for the resurrection and prepare us for the responsibility of managing God's Kingdom in the Millennium. We should always keep in mind that its primary purpose is the preparation and refining of His Church and the people of Israel.

Malachi prophesied to the house of Israel:

> *Behold, I am going to send My messenger, and he will clear the way before Me. And the Lord, whom you seek, will suddenly come to His temple; and the messenger of the covenant, in whom you delight, behold, He is coming, says the LORD of hosts. But who can endure the day of His coming? And who can stand when He appears? For* ***He is like a refiner's fire and like fullers' soap. He will sit as a smelter and purifier of silver, and He will purify the sons of Levi and refine them like gold and silver, so that they may present to the LORD offerings in righteousness***
>
> Malachi 3.1-3

This refining is addressed here specifically to the Sons of Levi, but it will affect both Israel and the Church – our Father in Heaven will not treat His sons differently, not show partiality. The Church cannot help itself to the promises due to Israel and ignore the conditions upon which they were given. Remember that *those whom the Lord loves He disciplines, and He scourges every son whom He receives.*[3]

Our studies in both the Spine and Revelation demonstrate beyond any reasonable doubt that the order is first the Tribulation, then Christ's Return, then the Millennium. There has been a school of thought in the modern Church that Christians will somehow 'take the land for Jesus' and the Church will go from strength to strength and usher in the Millennium. Over the years this has been given various names, including for example Dominion, or Kingdom Now Theology. I wish it was true. This thinking affects modern doctrine and worship, but unfortunately

---

3. Hebrews 12.6

is found nowhere in the Bible. We need to be careful what choruses and hymns we sing, as well as the teaching we bring ourselves under. As so often, this error is derived by a confusing of dispensations and in this case, reads Millennial truth into our present age of Grace.

National impact

There is another aspect of the Tribulation that we must consider, and that is in relation to unrighteous men and nations. God has a purpose for them too. At the end of Revelation we find:

> *Let the one who does wrong, still do wrong; and the one who is filthy, still be filthy; and let the one who is righteous, still practice righteousness; and the one who is holy, still keep himself holy*
>
> Rev 22.9

A separation or divergence is taking place, with the hearts of those who have rejected God becoming harder and yet more sinful in their independence and rebellion. There is a broad way that leads to destruction and a narrow way that leads to life. Few will find it. We see it in the present day. It is becoming gradually harder to be a believer in society, as the world grows less tolerant of us. As Proverbs 4.18 puts it, *But the path of the righteous is like the light of dawn, That shines brighter and brighter until the full day*

The Greek word **thlibō** which forms the root of the word for 'Tribulation' means to compress, squash (as grapes), to throng or trouble, afflict, or distress. Grapes must be pressed before the wine can be enjoyed, so it is with the Tribulation. A Roman Tribulum was a threshing sledge, a heavy implement dragged by cattle that had stones or flints embedded in its underside. It was dragged over the crops in order to separate the wheat from the chaff. As believers, we can appreciate the symbolism of wine and grain being prepared.

Tribulation past and present

History records many instances of tribulation, which serve as foreshadowings of the 'Great' Tribulation.

Chapter Ten

Major Persecutions through history

event	who principally affected	when	location	implemented by
Roman	Christians	c64-300AD	Roman Empire	Nero, Domitian, Trajan, Decius, Valerian, Diocletian, Galerius
The Inquisition	Jews Christians	1200 - 1500	Europe Britain	Apostate Christians
Pogroms (A Pogrom was a violent, organised riot, condoned by the authorities, and directed at local the Jewish population)	Jews	late 19th to early 20th Century	Eastern Europe	Russian Orthodox Church Communists
Holocaust	Jews Russians Poles	1930-45	Europe	Nazi Germany

In both the Inquisition and the pogroms, we saw an unholy alliance of apostate church and state persecuting God's chosen people. Even in the Holocaust Hitler was influenced by German theologians such as Martin Luther who believed that we must blame the Jews for the death of Christ. Whilst terrible, none of these persecutions could be considered as global events. The Great Tribulation will change this.

Modern-day Persecution

event	who principally affected	when	location	implemented by
Persecuted Church	Christians	now	Top 10* North Korea, Afghanistan, Saudi Arabia, Somalia, Iran, Maldives, Uzbekistan, Yemen, Iraq, Pakistan	Communism Islam
			* As defined by Open Doors World watch List (internet). In 2012 Open Doors listed 50 countries where Christians are persecuted. Their ranking is based on 1. Freedom of religion guaranteed by State 2. Attitude of State towards Christians 3. Can churches function freely ? 4. Can Christians express their faith freely ? 5. Incidence of persecution (killings, arrests, kidnappings & attacks	
General anti-Semitism	Jews	now	Global	Islamists Secular humanists Apostate Church

It is amazing how the Church is growing rapidly under persecution in countries like Saudi Arabia and China. Tertullian said in the 2nd Century that 'the blood of martyrs is the seed of the church', and so it has proved. Where there is no persecution, the Church generally declines.

I have not included in the above table the increasing trend of anti-Christian prejudice, evidenced by political correctness and changes in the law. It has resulted in Christians within Europe and the UK being prosecuted for upholding Bible values. For example, a Christian man and wife in Cornwall, UK were successfully sued for refusing to let a homosexual couple rent a room in their family Guest House. The State and judiciary now back homosexual rights above Christian values. The UK government started to introduce a law legalising homosexual marriage in 2013. Whilst they claim the rights of church ministers would be 'protected' if they chose to object, we know where this is leading.

We should also mention that whilst most Western countries publicly legislate against 'racism', this is rarely applied to prejudice against Israel and Israelis. The vast majority who oppose 'Zionism' are actually anti-Semitic, but dress it up in political terms. Israel has been described as the 'collective Jew' and many people and organisations feel it is a legitimate target and that this is somehow different from anti-Semitism. It is not and God is watching, taking note and missing nothing.

So 'Tribulation' is a process of being pressed and crushed for the purpose of preparation. In the free western nations we take our religious freedom for granted. However, in the majority of nations today Christians and Jews are under pressure from:

- Islam
- Communism
- Eastern Religions such as Hinduism or Buddhism
- Secular Humanism
- drug cartels
- tribal gangs

The persecuted Church, very much like anti-Semitism, goes largely unreported in the mainstream media. Silvano Tomasi, an Archbishop and Vatican permanent observer to US agencies in Geneva recently stated that as many as 100,000 Christians are killed every year for their faith.[4] If mentioned at all the truth is usually hidden in ambiguous language of 'warring factions', for example the ongoing organised jihad in Nigeria against the Church. Unless you subscribe to organisations like Open Doors (regarding the Persecuted Church) or HonestReporting (regarding Israel) then you are probably unaware of what is really happening. I would go further than that: if you rely upon the mainstream media for your information you are almost certainly being misinformed about the reality of the situation. The spirit of antichrist and secular humanism dominates these organisations and in any practical terms is unaccountable. An example of this is the 2004 Balen Report, a study commissioned by the BBC into their coverage of the Israel-Palestinian conflict. Despite numerous attempts under the UK's Freedom of Information Act, the BBC has defiantly refused to publish it, even to the degree of spending several hundreds of thousands of pounds in defending this position in the High Court. You might ask yourself what they have to hide.

The BBC further showed its disdain for Jewish blood when it failed to give attention to the massacre of a young Jewish family at Itamar in Israel. Two young Palestinian men broke into their home, stabbed the family members to death and decapitated the baby boy. The BBC later apologised, citing the fact that the day of the massacre had been a 'big news' day. Those who monitor their output remain unconvinced.

For some, it seems that the Tribulation has already started. Why does the Church in the west think it should be exempt from such suffering?

Part 3 – The Four Stages of the Tribulation

In 1815 the volcanic Mount Tambora off the coast of Indonesia exploded. This was the world's largest ever recorded eruption and its ash cloud surrounded the whole earth. It caused in 1816 what became known as 'the year without a summer' and resulted in famine and death on a world-wide scale, dimming sun, moon and stars. The Phobetron will make 1816 look like a July 4th firework party.

---

4. Catholic Herald 3rd June 2013

Chapter Ten

Let us remind ourselves of the scene immediately after the Phobetron and just before the Tribulation:

A third of all the earth's vegetation has been destroyed, including grass, trees and other plants. The followers of the Beast have been afflicted with painful sores. A third of the oceans have been turned into blood and a third of the sea creatures have died. A third of all ships were destroyed and all who were on the sea have been killed, suggestive of major global tsunamis. A third of the rivers and springs have become bitter and the rivers have turned to blood. The sun, moon and stars have lost a third of their light, possibly through atmospheric pollution and mankind has been sunburned causing them to blaspheme God.

This particular fading of celestial bodies is a preview of the full 'lights out' in sun, moon and stars that will occur at the end of the Tribulation, when none of these heavenly bodies will give their light. We don't know what the cause of these cataclysmic events will be, but volcanic activity must be a strong candidate. This, combined with extreme Sun-spot activity and solar flares, could explain many of the above phenomena. We mentioned earlier the potential effects of an increase in the South Atlantic Magnetic Anomaly which is also impairing the earth's ability to deflect solar radiation.

Think for a moment how this will affect your town, your home, your family, your job. What about the impact on food, water and commerce? How will your government react? What will the media be reporting? Who will they blame and what action will they take? The whole earth is being taken into unprecedented territory, and people will react either with fear or with faith. The authorities will be dismayed, with no viable fallback plans to cope. There will be wonderful opportunities for evangelism, as Christians will be the only people who will have an explanation.

These events are not science fiction, but Biblical fact, and are coming to a place near you in the not too distant future. And this is merely the warm-up act for the Tribulation.

In Chapter 5 we combined the events of the Spine with those from Revelation. We saw how the Tribulation comprises 4 stages:

Chapter Ten

- Part #1 – martyrs

- Part #2 – the abomination of desolation

- Part #3 – demonic outpouring & Beast's kingdom smitten

- Part #4 - Armageddon

Bible students understand that the Tribulation will last for seven years. However, we can glean more detailed information with careful study. The angel who appeared to the prophet Daniel informs us:

Seventy weeks have been decreed for your people and your holy city:

- *to finish the transgression,*

- *to make an end of sin,*

- *to make atonement for iniquity,*

- **to bring in everlasting righteousness,**

- **to seal up vision and prophecy and**

- **to anoint the most holy place.**

So you are to know and discern that from the issuing of a decree to restore and rebuild Jerusalem until Messiah the Prince there will be seven weeks and sixty-two weeks.[5]

It will be built again, with plaza and moat, even in times of distress. Then after the sixty-two weeks the Messiah will be cut off and have nothing.

*And the people of **the prince who is to come** will destroy the city and the sanctuary. And its end will come with a flood; even to the end there will be war; desolations are determined.*

*And **he will make a firm covenant with the many for one week, but in the middle of the week he will put a stop to sacrifice and grain offering; and on the wing of abominations will come one who makes desolate, even until a complete destruction, one that is decreed, is poured out on the one who makes desolate***

even until a complete destruction, one that is decreed, is poured out on the one who makes desolate.

(Daniel 9.24-28)

---

5. This 69 week (i.e. 69 sets of 7 years) period equates to 483 years or 173,880 days (Jewish years of 360 days). Nehemiah 2.1-8 provides us with the date of the decree to rebuild Jerusalem of 454BC. Using this date as the starting point brings us to AD29, the date of Messiah being 'cut off'

The passages highlighted in bold relate to the end of the age. We know that Messiah was cut off in 29AD. He had made an end of transgression and sins, and made reconciliation for iniquity through His finished work on the Cross. However we have not yet seen everlasting righteousness come in, nor vision and prophecy sealed[6] up, or the most holy place anointed. These remain as yet in the future. Also in the future is an intriguing reference to a final 'week', or seven year period where the 'prince who is to come' will 'make a peace treaty with many'. The 69 sevens plus the final seven provide us with a total of 70 sevens of years in God's dealing with Israel.

This seven year period is the key to the Tribulation. A Jewish year, on which this prophecy was based, comprised 360 days, so seven years would be 2,520 days. The treaty is broken in 'the middle of the week' i.e. after 1,260 days or 3 ½ years. For such specific timings to be given is quite unusual in scripture. Normally prophecy is linked to a description of certain events and durations are not normally provided, but this is an extraordinary time and God's people have been given specific information upon which they can act.

Within Daniel there are six references to this period that we should consider, each providing information about activity and duration.

---

6. These 'seals' are surely a reference to the seven seals of Revelation, opened by Jesus Himself

Chapter Ten

The seven years of Tribulation in Daniel

Ref	Daniel	Years of Tribulation 1-7 / Christ's Return (8)	Comments
9.27	He will make a firm **covenant** with the many for **one week**, but in the **middle of the week** he will put a **stop to sacrifice and grain offering**; and on the wing of abominations *will come* one who makes desolate, even until a complete destruction, one that is decreed, is poured out on the one who makes desolate	Abomination of Desolation (mid-year 4)	The seven year covenant established then broken
7.25	He will speak out against the Most High and wear down the saints of the Highest One, and he will intend to make alterations in times and in law; and **they will be given into his hand for a time, times, and half a time**.		Saints given into hands of Antichrist. 'Saints' is a generic term in scripture including both Christians and believing Jews
12.6-7	How long *will it be* until the end of *these* wonders?... that it would be for **a time, times, and half a time**; and as soon as they finish shattering the power of the holy people, all these events will be completed		The power of the holy people shattered and all things finished
8.13-14	How long will the vision *about the* **regular sacrifice** apply, while the transgression causes horror, so as to allow both the holy place and the host to be trampled? He said to me, **For 2,300 evenings and mornings; then the holy place will be properly restored**	2220 days / 2,300 days	Working backwards from the cleansing of the sanctuary at the end of year 7 takes us to 220 days into year1. A likely point for the prophecy of Daniel 8.24-25 of Antichrist's dealing with other world rulers
12.11	From the time that **the regular sacrifice is abolished and the abomination of desolation is set up,** *there will be 1,290 days*		
12.12	How blessed is he who keeps waiting and attains to the 1,335 days		There is less certainty over the purpose of these 'extensions' beyond the end of the 7 year period. They probably include the judgments, cleansing and restoration of the Sanctuary, various 'tidying up' activities (see Ezekiel 39.12), and celebration including the Marriage Supper of the Lamb. This will be considered in Chapters 11 and 14

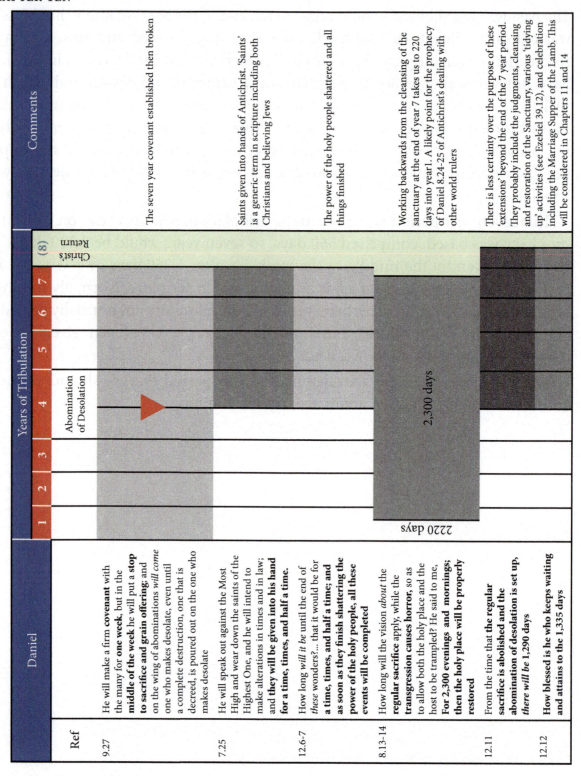

Chapter Ten

Figure 37. The Phobetron: lightning, fire and smoke.

Chapter Ten

Having now looked at the overview of the seven years, let us now return to the four sections of the Tribulation.

Part#1 – Martyrs

These martyrs come from *every* tribe, tongue, people and nation, so we must assume that this group includes Christians. This is a sobering confirmation that Christians must endure the Tribulation.

We are not given a specific date or event for the commencement of the seven years other than that they will follow hot on the heels of the Phobetron. Some overlap between Phobetron and Tribulation may be possible however and I suggest both these 'phases' follow soon after the transitionary period postulated earlier. The transitionary period may well exhibit isolated but ever more frequent incidences of Phobetronic happenings. These may possibly include extreme weather events, earthquakes, tsunamis, signs in the skies, disease, famine, political turmoil and economic problems.

We know that at an early stage Antichrist will make his peace treaty or covenant 'with the many'. Most believe this concerns Israel and peace is certainly something that Israel seeks desperately. This treaty will initially seem good news to the people and government of Israel, however things will rapidly deteriorate when the Antichrist reveals his true nature.

As we have previously discussed, it is possible that this treaty could pave the way for the rebuilding of the Jewish Temple, but this is speculation. My view is that the Temple will have been built prior to this, as there is insufficient time for a project of this scope and complexity to be completed in the 220 days inferred by Daniel 8.13-14. Whatever the cause or date of its construction, a functioning Temple (including priests and offerings) must exist by now as it is required for the coming abomination in Part #2.

We should also consider the emergence of the 4 horns / 10 horns here. Whilst it is not possible to be specific about timings, this confederation of global leaders will have been subordinated either during or before Part #1, but certainly before Part#2 of the Tribulation. The Beast will have devoured, broken in pieces and (if we accept the speculation from Chapter 5) stamped on and crushed the UK / USA, Russia and Islamic / Arabic nations by this stage. This gives him the freedom and licence to 'devour the whole Earth' without significant opposition, leading up to the abomination of desolation.

It also makes sense that the Mark of the Beast (666) will by now have come into operation. People must receive this mark on their forehead or hand to allow them to buy or sell. A very recent development is a flexible tattoo, containing a chip that may be worn on the arm to carry passwords for mobile phone and internet. The majority of goods sold today already bear a laser mark revealing this sinister connection.

Figure 38. Bar Code.

The binary form of '6', which is 110,[7] can be seen on the right, left and centre of this mark. Three of these 110's give us 666.

When we combine this with 'chip' technology implanted in our pets, the ability to perform financial transactions becomes possible. With electronic fraud a real problem in the banking system, the pressure will be on to comply. If you resist, you will be asked what you have to hide, so you will have to make a personal stand to resist this. Anyone whose money is held electronically will be required to use their mark to make transactions or move their money around. If your money is confiscated, you will be totally reliant on God to provide your needs. He won't let you down.

Some supermarkets are also currently using your mobile phone to track your movements in and around their stores, so the technology can be combined and developed to locate you and monitor your behaviour. Manufacturers are now installing global positioning systems in vehicles that send information about speed and location to a centralised monitoring agency. The possibilities for big government control are therefore almost limitless.

For believers, whether Christian or Jew, taking the Mark is not an option. Let me be absolutely clear about this: **don't take the Mark**. It is likely that the Mark of the Beast will occur around the same time as the covenant or peace treaty. This treaty will demonstrate the Beast's credentials and the globalised population will find it hard to

---

7. In binary 6 = 1x4, 1x2, and 0x1 i.e. 110, depicted by two long lines and a space

Chapter Ten

resist, so bringing themselves under the control and scrutiny of Antichrist's world government.

It is worth mentioning that the Mark probably won't affect the African bushman, or the man on the Russian Steppe, the Amazonian tribesman, or those in the 'wilderness', out in the 'sticks'. Generally speaking, sin is concentrated in urban areas.[8] Rural situations tend to observe more traditional values and are harder to subvert.

There is in this period a step-change in hatred towards Christians from all nations where, historically, it has been acceptable to be a believer. This now includes the US, the UK and all western nations. Their governments will by now have been totally subordinated to Antichrist's world rule. There will also be an increase in false prophets and resultant deception. Lawlessness will be rife and some evangelical Christians will begin to betray one another. Jesus tells us in Matthew 24 that the love (agape[9]) of many (most) will grow cold. This will be as a result of the cycle of offence, betrayal, hatred, deception and lawlessness.

Jesus goes on to say that it is the one who goes on enduring to the end who will be saved. He also states that:

> *This gospel of the kingdom shall be preached in the whole world as a testimony to all the nations, and then the end will come*
>
> Matthew 24.14

So this isn't just about the Antichrist. The true Christ is ensuring that even to the last moment, men and women will have an opportunity to repent and be saved. This verse also tells us that the end is conditional upon the Gospel reaching all nations, so is very much within our influence! When the full number of the Gentiles has been brought into the Kingdom, then all Israel will be saved too.[10] Every penny donated to missions, every tract handed out and every time you share your testimony, brings Jesus' return closer. My own father was saved a few minutes before he died. It is truly never too late, as the thief on the cross discovered. We should pray for those whose lives are near the

---

8. This principle started with Nimrod's city of Babylon
9. Only born-again Christians are capable of expressing agape
10. Romans 11.25

end, trusting that the Lord will be merciful.

Part #1 of the Tribulation will last for 3 ½ years. We now enter Part #2.

Part #2 – the Abomination of Desolation

The second period of 3 ½ years is described as the 'Great' Tribulation.

The Bible contains many references to events in the heavens that affect matters on Earth. We know from Revelation that there is to be a war in heaven. Satan and a third of his angels will be cast down to the earth. He is angry and knows his time is short. On a positive note, there should be less interference with our prayers,[11] so we can expect spectacular and miraculous answers to godly prayer. Up to this point the 'prince of the power of the air' had free access to heaven where he could accuse believers before God night and day, as he did with Job. He can now no longer do this. This shift in the heavens will affect life on earth. We will see more hostility, but greater prayer power and a dramatic increase in miracles – these will become the norm at that time.

It is likely that Satan's fall coincides with the Abomination of Desolation. Antichrist will desolate the Temple and declare himself as god. He will bring an end to sacrifice and offering. This event will herald a time of unprecedented trouble and persecution greater than anything ever experienced by mankind, whether ethnic cleansing, pogrom, Inquisition or the gas ovens of the Holocaust. Another final step-up in deception now occurs, with both false christs *and* false prophets performing supernatural signs and wonders. These will be so subtle and spectacular that even the elect (chosen) may be deceived. Don't be deceived: because something is supernatural it doesn't always mean it is *of* or *from* God. Start to train your discernment now, because your eternal future depends upon it. Ask God for discernment, cry out for wisdom!

The woman of Revelation 12 now flees to the wilderness, away from towns and cities, where she will be looked after. My interpretation is that she might represent a portion of God's end-time people, both Jew and Christian. They will

---

11. In Daniel 10 we read how the Prince of Persia withstood the angel who was bringing a message from the Lord. These principalities inhabit the heavenly realm and seek to obstruct and hinder our prayers. The casting down should make things easier !

be supernaturally empowered, with amazing signs and wonders and powerfully dramatic answers to prayer. Thousands of years ago Moses was in a wilderness, leading God's people to deliverance, and they received manna, quails and water from the rock. Should we expect that 'end-timers' will receive any less than they?

Part #3 – Demonic Outpouring and Beast's kingdom smitten

The casting down of Satan not only empowers Antichrist but also causes a frenzy of demonic activity. The events of the 5th Trumpet and Joel described in Chapter 4 are now upon us. The demons are released to torment and destroy. Darkness covers the earth. The Beast's followers gnaw their tongues in pain but still do not repent. As Daniel tells us,[12] *the wicked will act wickedly; and none of the wicked will understand.*

I would suggest that by now Israel has realised that a huge mistake has been made in trusting the Antichrist. Once the Abomination of Desolation happens, a wave of shock must pervade Jewish society. The 144,000 Jewish witnesses will have been active in spreading the Gospel, proclaiming the Kingdom of God. But how many will turn to God? This is a question that will be addressed in Chapter 11, where we consider Christ's return. If you can't wait until then, take a look at the last three chapters of Zechariah.

Leading up to Armageddon, a third of the earth's people will have been killed by fire, smoke and brimstone. This is not difficult to believe with today's nuclear, biological, chemical or conventional weapons, and strongly suggests that Antichrist does not go unopposed by the nations. The weapons of Pakistan, Syria and North Korea are almost in the grasp of Islamic terrorists now, so it is difficult to predict who might have access to them in the future. At the present time, stockpiles of such weapons are sufficient to destroy the earth's population many times over. Some commentators have stated that the world will not end in nuclear annihilation. I agree, but believe they will be used and we will come close.

---

12. Daniel 12.10

CHAPTER TEN

Part #4 – Armageddon

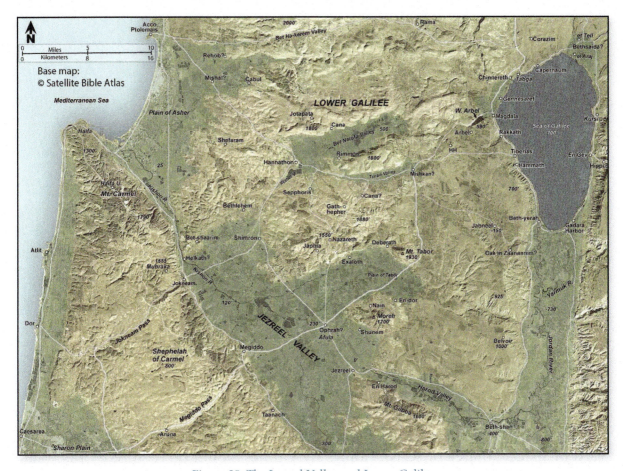

Figure 39. The Jezreel Valley and Lower Galilee.

It would be a mistake to think of Armageddon as a single and swift event. In the first Iraq war when the USA and her allies decided to remove Saddam Hussein, many months were required to plan, mobilise, then implement the invasion. Operation Overlord, the allied invasion of Normandy in 1944 saw 160,000 troops embarked on the first day on 6th June, and 3 Million in place by August. Planning had been going on for at least a year. I have stood in the Map Room of Southwick House on Portsdown Hill in southern England, where Eisenhower uttered the command "OK, let's go" to launch the D-Day campaign. The effort in planning was immense, complex and well-organised.

Chapter Ten

Figure 40. Looking north-east from Har Megiddo across Highway 66 and over the plain of Jezreel.
Nazareth, Jesus' home is ten miles away on the left horizon.
The Hill of Moreh is right of centre, with Tabor to its left.
This vast plain will be the battlefield for Armageddon

Armageddon requires the gathering of 200 Million[13] soldiers. Simple calculation shows that were such an army to be assembled, with each soldier having one square yard of space, an area of some 9 miles by 9 miles would be required. This rough indication does not account for military vehicles, facilities, infrastructure or the logistic support required by modern armies. The mustering ground could well occupy the whole of the Jezreel valley. This is a triangular plain between the hills of Galilee in the north and those of Samaria to the south. On the east is Mount Tabor, Moreh and Gilboa and to the west is Carmel. This defines an area of some 20 by 15 miles. With other valleys leading into Jezreel the available area is considerably larger.

The army will congregate around the Hill of Megiddo, 'Har Megiddon' in northern Israel. Winston Churchill described this place as the 'cockpit of the nations', as it makes an ideal battlefield. Geographically it is on the road that joins Africa, Asia

---

13. Some have challenged the translation of this number and believe it is 1,200,000, which seems a more realistic figure

and Europe, allowing access from those nations.

We are told that the Euphrates will have been dried up to allow passage to the armies from the east. We are not told whether this is a man-made, natural or supernatural event. This is a distance of some 550 miles from Israel and would involve travelling via Iraq, Syria and northern Jordan into the Jezreel. Assuming this route, an army would be moving west potentially from Pakistan, India or even further East, from China. We also know that armies will be drawn from Russia and the Caucasus in the north, from Turkey in the west, and Libya and Ethiopia in the south.

We are provided with a detailed preview of the battle. Ezekiel chapters 38-39 make interesting reading (I have highlighted the identity of the modern nations in bold and placed the ancient names in brackets):

> *And the word of the Lord came to me saying, Son of man, set your face toward Gog of the land of Magog, the prince of **Russia** (Rosh), **Georgia** and **Causcasus** (Meshech and Tubal), and prophesy against him and say, 'Thus says the Lord God, Behold, I am against you, O Gog, prince of Rosh, Meshech and Tubal. I will turn you about and put hooks into your jaws, and I will bring you out, and all your army, horses and horsemen, all of them splendidly attired, a great company with buckler and shield, all of them wielding swords; **Iran** (**Pakistan and India ?**) (Persia), **Ethiopia** and **Libya** (Put) with them, all of them with shield and helmet; **Turkey** (Gomer) with all its troops; **Armenia** (Beth-togarmah) from the remote parts of the north with all its troops—many peoples with you.*
>
> *Be prepared, and prepare yourself, you and all your companies that are assembled about you, and be a guard for them. After many days you will be summoned; in the latter years you will come into the land that is restored from the sword, whose inhabitants have been gathered from many nations to the mountains of Israel which had been a continual waste; but its people were brought out from the nations, and they are living securely, all of them. You will go up, you will come like a storm; you will be like a cloud covering the land, you and all your troops, and many peoples with you.*
>
> *'Thus says the Lord God, It will come about on that day that thoughts will come into your mind and you will devise an evil plan, and you will say, 'I will go up against the land of unwalled villages. I will go against those who are at rest, that live securely, all of them living without walls and having no bars or gates, to capture spoil and to seize plunder, to turn your hand against the waste places which are now inhabited, and against the people who are gathered from the nations, who have acquired cattle and goods, who live at the center of the world.' Sheba and Dedan and the merchants of Tarshish with all its villages will say to you,*

Chapter Ten

'Have you come to capture spoil? Have you assembled your company to seize plunder, to carry away silver and gold, to take away cattle and goods, to capture great spoil?"

Therefore prophesy, son of man, and say to Gog, 'Thus says the Lord God, On that day when My people Israel are living securely, will you not know it? You will come from your place out of the remote parts of the north, you and many peoples with you, all of them riding on horses, a great assembly and a mighty army; and you will come up against My people Israel like a cloud to cover the land. It shall come about in the last days that I will bring you against My land, so that the nations may know Me when I am sanctified through you before their eyes, O Gog.

'Thus says the Lord God, Are you the one of whom I spoke in former days through My servants the prophets of Israel, who prophesied in those days for many years that I would bring you against them?

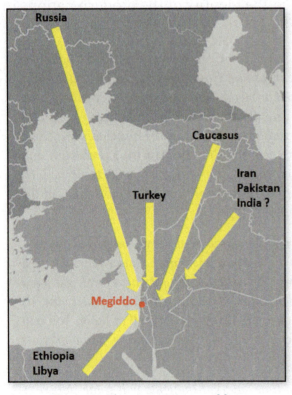

Figure 41. The route to Armageddon

The correlation between this account and that in Revelation is remarkable. We are not short of detail here, and the account speaks for itself. We can make a number of observations however:

- the army from the north comes from the area we earlier identified as the possible origin of Antichrist

- the army of Gog doesn't come of its own volition, but is drawn down by the Lord to its destruction. Again we see that the Lord is in command. Gog seems to be collective term for an alliance of nations that come against the Lord and His elect. Magog may be their abode. These entities will emerge again at the end of the Millennium (see chapter 14), so there are clearly nations that will rebel even then

- Saudi Arabia, Sardinia and Yemen pass comment on the action, but it is not immediately clear that they take part in the onslaught

Zechariah too provides us with a detailed account of how this battle will unfold. We will investigate this in chapter 11.

I'm sure most readers will be aware of that moment in watching a movie when it seems that the situation is hopeless, all is lost, and there is no way out. Well, this is it. However, we have had the advantage of reading the end of the book, so we know how it finishes. If you are still around, now is the time to take Jesus' advice and look up to witness the greatest sight you will ever see. If you are already with the Lord, you will soon be arriving so can look down as you approach from the east, looking down through the clouds onto the battleground.

Enjoy the view!

Chapter Ten

Chapter 11 — The Return of Jesus Christ – Thy Kingdom come

But who can endure the day of His coming? And who can stand when He appears? For He is like a refiner's fire and like fullers' soap.

He will sit as a smelter and purifier of silver, and He will purify the sons of Levi and refine them like gold and silver, so that they may present to the LORD offerings in righteousness.

Malachi 3.2-3

Figure 42. Sun through the trees at Galilee

Part 1 – The Incomparable Christ

The Word became flesh at the end of the 1st Century BC, but this was not the first time He had visited earth in physical form. As we discussed in Chapter 4, He had

Chapter Eleven

been here before.

At that time, He had come in disguise as the son of a carpenter, born in a stable, and His glory was for the most part veiled. There were a few glimpses of His splendour, however: on the Mount of Transfiguration with Moses and Elijah; again when He stated that before Moses was, '**I am**'; and later in Gethsemane when the soldiers came to take Him, He said '**I am He**', and they fell to the ground, stunned by this brief revelation of His glory.

As a young Christian back in the 1970's, I remember being given a leaflet entitled 'The Incomparable Christ'. The words made a great impression on my mind, and have always stayed with me:

More than nineteen hundred years ago, there was a Man born contrary to the laws of life. This Man lived in poverty and was reared in obscurity. He did not travel extensively. Only once did He cross the boundary of the country in which He lived; that was during His exile in childhood.

He possessed neither wealth nor influence. His relatives were inconspicuous and had neither training nor formal education.

In infancy He startled a king; in childhood He puzzled doctors; in manhood He ruled the course of nature, walked upon the waves as pavement, and hushed the sea to sleep.

He healed the multitudes without medicine and made no charge for His service.

He never wrote a book, and yet perhaps all the libraries of the world could not hold the books that have been written about Him.

He never wrote a song, and yet He has furnished the theme for more songs than all the songwriters combined.

He never founded a college, but all the schools put together cannot boast of having as many students.

He never marshalled an army, nor drafted a soldier, nor fired a gun; and yet no leader ever had more volunteers who have, under His orders, made more rebels stack arms and surrender without a shot fired.

He never practiced psychiatry, and yet He has healed more broken hearts than all the doctors far and near.

Once each week multitudes congregate at worshiping assemblies to pay homage and respect to Him.

The names of the past, proud statesmen of Greece and Rome have come and gone. The names of the past scientists, philosophers, and theologians have come and gone. But the name of this Man multiplies more and more. Though time has spread nineteen hundred years between the people of this generation and the mockers at His crucifixion, He still lives. His enemies could not destroy Him, and the grave could not hold Him.

He stands forth upon the highest pinnacle of heavenly glory, proclaimed of God, acknowledged by angels, adored by saints, and feared by devils, as the risen, personal Christ, our Lord and Saviour.

We are either going to be forever with Him, or forever without Him

(Author unknown)

Many are puzzled that Jesus didn't establish the Kingdom of God on this visit. That was not His purpose. He did however come to proclaim it to the House of Israel, foreknowing that it would be rejected. His return, which we will consider here, will be quite different, when we will see Him revealed in His full power and glory, as King of Kings and Lord of Lords. There are those who say, "if there is a God, why doesn't He stop all the trouble?" One day soon, when His plan of salvation is complete and He has placed all things under His feet, He will.

Part 2 – Rationale

In building our picture of Christ's return, we will be drawing on a number of sources. We have already considered the Spine and its relationship to the seals, trumpets and bowls of Revelation. Throughout this book they have been helping us construct our frame of reference. Now is the time to introduce the happy ending, for those whose names are written in His book. Clearly, the ending will not be a happy one for those who have chosen to reject Him.

In building the picture, we will weave together the accounts from Zechariah, Ezekiel, Revelation and Daniel, along with various other references from both Old and New Testament. These will provide additional detail and insight.

To ensure reliability, we need to establish both the *horizontal* and the *vertical* alignment of our schedule. **Horizontal alignment** will ensure events follow a sound chronological pattern from first to the last. This approach will be applied within

CHAPTER ELEVEN

a particular source, for example within the events of the Spine. This horizontal chronology was presented in chapter 5. We will add details here from the prophet Ezekiel.

Vertical alignment requires us to accurately 'peg-down' events *across* apparently miscellaneous sources, allowing us to combine descriptions of the same event from different passages of scripture. We have performed this approach already to the earthquakes between the Spine and Revelation, and could also apply it to the description of the Sun turning to blood as referenced in both the Spine and Zechariah, or the events at Megiddo from Ezekiel, Zechariah and Revelation.

This horizontal and vertical 'mesh' will then provide us with a robust grid to which we can append those prophecies where we have not been given a specific timescale.

Part 3 – Armageddon: Zechariah & Ezekiel's preview

Revelation provides us with the headlines for Armageddon, but we need to turn to Ezekiel and Zechariah to see the detailed picture of the battle. In chapter 10 we saw how Antichrist had mobilised his vast army in the Jezreel valley, and that all seemed hopeless for Israel. Here, we will see the response from heaven.

Let us start with Zechariah:

The burden of the word of the Lord concerning Israel:

Thus declares the Lord who stretches out the heavens, lays the foundation of the earth, and forms the spirit of man within him,

*Behold, I am going to make Jerusalem a cup that causes reeling[1] to all the peoples around; and when the siege is against Jerusalem, it will also be against Judah. It will come about **in that day** that I will make Jerusalem a heavy stone for all the peoples; all who lift it will be severely injured.[2] And all the nations of the earth will be gathered against it.*

***In that day**, declares the Lord, I will strike every horse with bewilderment and his rider with*

---

1. Even now Jerusalem is making nations act irrationally. For example, both the UK and US governments issued strong condemnations against Israel in 2012 for declaring its intention to build homes in an uncontested area. The nations will become further intoxicated by this 'cup', and their judgment will become increasingly impaired and irrational
2. We have already indicated in previous chapters how those nations and empires that have meddled with Jerusalem have been severely bruised, including the Ottoman, British, Soviet/Russian and US

Chapter Eleven

madness. But I will watch over the house of Judah, while I strike every horse of the peoples with blindness. Then the clans of Judah will say in their hearts, 'A strong support for us are the inhabitants of Jerusalem through the Lord of hosts, their God.' **In that day** *I will make the clans of Judah like a firepot among pieces of wood and a flaming torch among sheaves, so they will consume on the right hand and on the left all the surrounding peoples, while the inhabitants of Jerusalem again dwell on their own sites in Jerusalem.*

The Lord also will save the tents of Judah first, so that the glory of the house of David and the glory of the inhabitants of Jerusalem will not be magnified above Judah. **In that day** *the Lord will defend the inhabitants of Jerusalem, and the one who is feeble among them* **in that day** *will be like David, and the house of David will be like God, like the angel of the Lord before them. And* **in that day** *I will set about to destroy all the nations that come against Jerusalem.*

I will pour out on the house of David and on the inhabitants of Jerusalem, the Spirit of grace and of supplication, so that they will look on Me whom they have pierced; and they will mourn for Him, as one mourns for an only son, and they will weep bitterly over Him like the bitter weeping over a firstborn. **In that day** *there will be great mourning in Jerusalem, like the mourning of Hadadrimmon in the plain of Megiddo. The land will mourn, every family by itself; the family of the house of David by itself and their wives by themselves; the family of the house of Nathan by itself and their wives by themselves; the family of the house of Levi by itself and their wives by themselves; the family of the Shimeites by itself and their wives by themselves; all the families that remain, every family by itself and their wives by themselves.*

In that day *a fountain will be opened for the house of David and for the inhabitants of Jerusalem, for sin and for impurity. It will come about* **in that day**, *declares the Lord of hosts, that I will cut off the names of the idols from the land, and they will no longer be remembered; and I will also remove the prophets and the unclean spirit from the land. And if anyone still prophesies, then his father and mother who gave birth to him will say to him, 'You shall not live, for you have spoken falsely in the name of the Lord'; and his father and mother who gave birth to him will pierce him through when he prophesies. Also it will come about* **in that day** *that the prophets will each be ashamed of his vision when he prophesies, and they will not put on a hairy robe in order to deceive; but he will say, 'I am not a prophet; I am a tiller of the ground, for a man sold me as a slave in my youth.' And one will say to him, 'What are these wounds between your arms?' Then he will say, 'Those with which I was wounded in the house of my friends.'*

Awake, O sword, against My Shepherd, And against the man, My Associate, Declares the Lord of hosts. Strike the Shepherd that the sheep may be scattered; And I will turn My hand against the little ones.

It will come about in all the land, declares the Lord, That two parts in it will be cut off and

Chapter Eleven

perish, but the third will be left in it. And I will bring the third part through the fire, refine them as silver is refined, and test them as gold is tested. They will call on My name, and I will answer them. I will say, 'They are My people,' And they will say, 'The Lord is my God.'

Behold, a day is coming for the Lord when the spoil taken from you will be divided among you. For I will gather all the nations[3] against Jerusalem to battle, and the city will be captured, the houses plundered, the women ravished and half of the city exiled, but the rest of the people will not be cut off from the city.

Then the Lord will go forth and fight against those nations, as when He fights on a day of battle. **In that day** *His feet will stand on the Mount of Olives, which is in front of Jerusalem on the east; and the Mount of Olives will be split in its middle from east to west by a very large valley, so that half of the mountain will move toward the north and the other half toward the south.*

You will flee by the valley of My mountains, for the valley of the mountains will reach to Azel; yes, you will flee just as you fled before the earthquake in the days of Uzziah king of Judah.

Then the Lord, my God, will come, and all the holy ones with Him!

In that day *there will be no light; the luminaries will dwindle. For it will be a unique day which is known to the Lord, neither day nor night, but it will come about that at evening time there will be light.*

And **in that day** *living waters will flow out of Jerusalem, half of them toward the eastern sea and the other half toward the western sea; it will be in summer as well as in winter. And the Lord will be king over all the earth; in that day the Lord will be the only one, and His name the only one.*

All the land will be changed into a plain from Geba to Rimmon[4] south of Jerusalem; but Jerusalem will rise and remain on its site from Benjamin's Gate as far as the place of the First Gate to the Corner Gate, and from the Tower of Hananel to the king's wine presses. People will live in it, and there will no longer be a curse, for Jerusalem will dwell in security.

Now this will be the plague with which the Lord will strike all the peoples who have gone to war against Jerusalem; their flesh will rot while they stand on their feet, and their eyes will rot in their sockets, and their tongue will rot in their mouth. It will come about **in that day** *that a great panic from the Lord will fall on them; and they will seize one another's hand, and the*

---

3. This informs us that whilst we have identified the principle forces that come against Israel (see chapter 10), there are representatives from 'all the nations' in this great army
4. Geba is probably modern-day Jeba, 5 miles north of Jerusalem. Rimmon is probably the Tel-Halif, some 35 miles SSE of Jerusalem. This speaks of a massive geological rearrangement of Judaea, and is entirely consistent with Ezekiel's prophecy. We will consider this in chapter 14

hand of one will be lifted against the hand of another.

Judah also will fight at Jerusalem, and the wealth of all the surrounding nations will be gathered, gold and silver and garments in great abundance. So also like this plague will be the plague on the horse, the mule, the camel, the donkey and all the cattle that will be in those camps

Zechariah 12-14.15

The above passage is marked by two recurring themes:

- **Jerusalem** (which occurs some 37 times in the whole of Zechariah) so there can be no doubt that Jerusalem is very much part of God's end-time plan.
- **in that day** (which occurs 20 times in the whole of Zechariah). Clearly then these last few chapters describe Jesus' return and the events at that time.

The 20 mentions of 'in that day' are significant: the number 20 is generally associated with expectation e.g. Jacob waited 20 years to take possession of his wives; Israel waited for 20 years for a deliverer from Jabin. Both Israel and the Church share an expectation, particularly having just endured the Tribulation.

20 is a product of 10 and 2. The number 10 begins a new series of numbers (11, 12, 13...) so signifies the introduction of a new order (the 10 Commandments brought in the Law; Jesus made 10 'I am' statements; 10 kinds of animals in Eden). In the same way Jesus' return 'in that day' heralds a new order concerning the end of the Dispensation of Grace and beginning of the Millennium. The number 2 is generally used to emphasise or repeat something of importance. Therefore this day is the beginning of a new order for God's end-time government. It is interesting that the current hostility towards Israel's possession of Jerusalem and the desire to see it under Islamist, Papal or Humanist government is intensifying. They all have an agenda for Jerusalem, but thankfully, so does our God.

The final chapters of Zechariah use the words 'when' and 'then' rarely; hence we are not being presented with a sequential schedule of events in chronological order (as we saw in the Spine for example). The context here is clearly to do with the last days and Messiah's return. We may thus interpret these events as a series of individual *glimpses* into the final acts of the Tribulation and the return of Christ, rather like a news broadcast.

Chapter Eleven

Now we will continue the account of that awesome day from Ezekiel:

*It will come about **on that day**, when Gog comes against the land of Israel, declares the Lord God, that My fury will mount up in My anger. In My zeal and in My blazing wrath I declare that on that day there will surely be a great earthquake in the land of Israel. The fish of the sea, the birds of the heavens, the beasts of the field, all the creeping things that creep on the earth, and all the men who are on the face of the earth will shake at My presence*

The mountains also will be thrown down, the steep pathways will collapse and every wall will fall to the ground.[5] I will call for a sword against him on all My mountains, declares the Lord God. Every man's sword will be against his brother. With pestilence and with blood I will enter into judgment with him; and I will rain on him and on his troops, and on the many peoples who are with him, a torrential rain, with hailstones, fire and brimstone. I will magnify Myself, sanctify Myself, and make Myself known in the sight of many nations; and they will know that I am the Lord.'

And you, son of man, prophesy against Gog and say, 'Thus says the Lord God, Behold, I am against you, O Gog, prince of Rosh, Meshech and Tubal; and I will turn you around, drive you on, take you up from the remotest parts of the north[6] and bring you against the mountains of Israel. I will strike your bow from your left hand and dash down your arrows from your right hand. You will fall on the mountains of Israel, you and all your troops and the peoples who are with you; I will give you as food to every kind of predatory bird and beast of the field. You will fall on the open field; for it is I who have spoken, declares the Lord God. And I will send fire upon Magog and those who inhabit the coastlands in safety; and they will know that I am the Lord.

My holy name I will make known in the midst of My people Israel; and I will not let My holy name be profaned anymore. And the nations will know that I am the Lord, the Holy One in Israel. Behold, it is coming and it shall be done, declares the Lord God. That is the day of which I have spoken

Ezekiel 38.18-39.8

So Ezekiel confirms Zechariah, but also tells us that it is the Lord who draws the great army down from the north. Again we see how He commands, not men, and not Satan or his emissaries. The end-time agenda is wholly His. Concerning Magog, we are speculating. However it possibly describes the homeland of Gog. Those who dwell there, presumably looking on via the media, will have fire rained upon them. By this stage global society will have been totally polarised by the events of the

---

5. Including the walls of the 3rd temple
6. Moscow is directly north of Israel

Tribulation: there are two distinctly opposing camps, so we will either be for the Lord or against Him.

The great earthquake that has shaken every wall to the ground is assumed to be the same one as caused the major geological and geographical changes to Jerusalem and its surrounds.

Figure 43. The Plain of Jezreel from the mountains of Gilboa.

Part 4 – The Return of Christ: one event yet many

For many years I assumed that Christ's return was a single event, occurring in the twinkling of an eye. There is no doubt that His appearance will be instantaneous, but we will demonstrate that approximately 40 groups of activity are associated with the return.

We will also factor in here Revelation chapters 17-20.3, which provide a different perspective. Again, this passage does not provide us with a strict chronology, but glimpses of end-time events. In order to weave these sources into our schedule, we

Chapter Eleven

will use the solid framework of the Spine and the seals / bowls / trumpets to derive the order.

Before we examine Christ's return in detail, let us consider some of the characteristics of these events:

- they occur in rapid succession with some taking place 'within one hour', '30 minutes', or 'suddenly'. So having waited approximately 2000 years since Jesus' ascension from Olivet, and endured the seven hard years of the tribulation, the culmination of the age happens quickly. Zechariah's use of the phrase *'in that day'* surely refers to a literal day

- events occur both in the *invisible* realm of heaven and the *visible* realm of earth and sky, including the geological, meteorological, nautical or astronomical domains.

- the climax occurs when these two realms collide, as heaven comes to earth with spectacular consequences

- the focus is very much on Israel and Jerusalem

- it is a day of reckoning

In rapid succession, we will see the siege of Jerusalem lifted, Israel redeemed, retribution on Satan, the Beast, False Prophet, the Kings of the earth and the godless, and our mortal bodies transformed 'in the twinkling of an eye'. You will also receive an invitation to a celebratory supper!

A notional timetable for the activities associated with the return of Christ is presented below. I have shown separately those events instigated in the invisible realm from those that are manifested in the visible. The reader may also wish to refer back to the overall chronology provided in chapter 5 to appreciate the context of these events.

CHAPTER ELEVEN

Schedule of Christ's Return

Theme	Instigated in the Invisible Realm (The Throne Room, Heaven)	Manifested in the Visible Realm (National, geographical, geological, nautical, meteorological, celestial arenas)	Basis	Comments
■ Babylon destroyed		God visits His wrath on Babylon, which is destroyed in one hour by the 10 'horns'	Revelation 17-19.4	We are told that Antichrist's confederation (including the 10 rulers) perpetrates this onslaught on Babylon. Therefore it must happen late in the Tribulation before they are destroyed at Armageddon on Christ's return
(Neither the destruction of Babylon nor the Marriage Supper of the Lamb (marked ■) are straightforward to schedule from the facts available, however it seems reasonable to place Babylon first, and the Supper last)				
	'Time no longer'		6th Trumpet	The Dispensation of Grace ends
		Great earthquake	6th Seal	
'Immediately after the Tribulation…'		Sun darkened, Moon becomes as blood, stars fall (but it will be light at evening time)	Spine, 6th Seal, Zechariah	An unprecedented celestial event. Gen 1.14-15 tells us that these heavenly bodies were provided to indicate signs and seasons.
		Nations distressed, the sea and waves roaring, men's hearts failing	Spine	
	Powers of the heavens shaken		Spine	The 2/3 of stars (spiritual beings inc principalities & powers) that were not swept down by the Dragon's tail
	Heaven departed as a scroll when rolled up		6th Seal	Is heaven still required, being about to be emptied of its inhabitants who are to return to earth with Jesus?
		Every mountain & island moved out of its place	6th Seal	This is the beginning of the earth's 'geomorphing', and is probably linked to the great earthquake and roaring seas mentioned above
		Kings, great men, rich men, chiefs, captains, mighty men, bondmen & freemen hide from the great day of His wrath	6th Seal	These are those powerful and influential individuals who prospered under the Antichrist, colluding against Israel & the Church
Interlude	Silence in heaven for 30 minutes		7th Seal	
	Angel before God is given the 7 trumpets; another angel having a golden censer & much incense, offers it with the prayers of all the saints on the golden altar before the throne. He takes fire from the altar and casts it upon the earth		7th Seal	The final chapter of the end of the age is instigated by the prayers of the remnant Church on earth, whilst heaven waits expectantly

311

Chapter Eleven

Theme	Instigated in the Invisible Realm (The Throne Room, Heaven)	Manifested in the Visible Realm (National, geographical, geological, nautical, meteorological, celestial arenas)	Basis	Comments
The end announced: He shall reign, 'it is done!'	Voices in heaven; kingdoms of the world become the Kingdom of our Lord		7th Trumpet	
	'He shall reign forever'; the 24 elders worship God		7th Trumpet	The Alleluia chorus
	God destroys those that destroy the earth		7th Trumpet	
	Temple of God opened, the Ark is revealed		7th Trumpet	The Ark is currently in heaven (not in a museum or under the Temple Mount as some might believe !)
	A great voice from the throne 'it is done!'		7th Bowl	The Father's voice, last heard on earth at the Mount of Transfiguration. At Calvary Jesus cried 'it is finished' to bring the age of Law to a close. This cry now brings the Dispensation of Grace to an end
	Voices, thunder, lightning	earthquake	7th Seal, 7th Trumpet, 7th Bowl	A distinctive event that helps us to align events. This assumes that the 7th Seal, Trumpet & Bowl are synchronous and not separate events, and helps us to lock into our timeline
The sign of the Son of Man: Christ's appearing in the clouds		The day of the Lord comes as a thief in the night. When they say 'peace and safety' sudden destruction comes on them. The Sign of the Son of Man appears in heaven as He comes in clouds with great power & glory, and as 'the lightning flashes from the east to the west' The earth mourns	Spine 1 Thess 5.2-3	I would suggest this coming is visible worldwide. His 'Parousia' means an arrival or presence
		We are not in darkness such that this day would overtake us as like a thief…. so let us watch and be sober	1 Thess 5.4-6	Christian believers (who have been watchful and know their Bibles) will not be surprised, and will know the immediate season of His return at *that* future time (but not *yet*)
		'When these things start to happen, look up!'	Spine	
		The Lord descends from heaven with a shout, the voice of an archangel, and the trumpet of God The angels gather the elect from the 4 winds, and the farthest part of earth and heaven, including…..	Spine 1 Thess 4.16	This is the 7th trumpet, and is assumed to be co-incident with the voices, thunder and earthquake above

Chapter Eleven

Theme	Instigated in the Invisible Realm (The Throne Room, Heaven)	Manifested in the Visible Realm (National, geographical, geological, nautical, meteorological, celestial arenas)	Basis	Comments
		The return of the righteous dead: the saints who are 'asleep' with Christ come with Him	Zechariah 14.5 1 Thess 4.14	Christian believers who have died 'in Christ' and Jewish believers who died in faith (such as Abraham) who are currently in heaven / Paradise. This possibly includes also those 'of good conscience' (from Romans 2) who never heard the Gospel (See chapter 12 Judgment)
		The first resurrection: we 'won't all sleep', but we shall be changed, immediately, in the twinkling of an eye, and at the sounding of the last trumpet. The dead raised incorruptible. When we see Him, we shall be like Him	1 Cor 15. 51-52 1 John 3.2-3	There have been resurrections before (in the Gospels) but on this occasion those raised will be given new bodies formed of the dust of their old bodies. This physical matter will be transformed & reunited with their spirit (There will be a later resurrection of the *unrighteous* dead for judgment)
		Those who are alive and remain shall be caught up together with the 'dead' to meet the Lord in the air, thus we shall always be with the Lord	1 Thess 4.17	Christian believers on earth at the time of the end who have come through the Tribulation. These too will be changed in the twinkling of an eye
		Christ appears in the clouds on a white horse, followed by armies on white horses	Revelation 17-20.3	Christ will now be visible to everyone on earth
		He strikes the nations, and the birds are called to supper	Ezekiel 37.17-20	Retribution begins on the nations
Christ returns to Jerusalem		Jesus returns to Jerusalem 'in the same way' as the disciples saw Him go into heaven	Acts 1	He ascended from Olivet with the angels and will return in the same way
		The Lord's feet stand on the Mount of Olives, which is split North / South into two. The besieged remnant (of the Jews) flees from Jerusalem towards the east through this new valley. As part of these geological activities Jerusalem is raised up above all. The Great City is divided into three, and the cities of the nations fall	Zechariah 14.4 7th Bowl	The division into 2 and 3 is not contradictory. If Olivet is divided and moves north / south, then the main city would be left as a third western portion to be elevated

Chapter Eleven

Theme	Instigated in the Invisible Realm (The Throne Room, Heaven)	Manifested in the Visible Realm (National, geographical, geological, nautical, meteorological, celestial arenas)	Basis	Comments
The realisation and redemption of Israel		The remaining 1/3rd of the Jews in Israel who have been brought through the fire gaze upon Him who they pierced, repent and believe	Zechariah 13.8	Zechariah informs us that half of the inhabitants of Jerusalem will have been 'taken away' by this time, and that 2/3 of Israel has been 'cut-off' and killed by the invading armies. It is interesting that Jesus comes to Jerusalem and meets those surviving Jews there, not in the air. In effect, He is here completing the purpose of His earlier visit to establish the Kingdom of God
Jerusalem delivered		A plague falls on those who fought against Jerusalem	Zechariah 14.12 Ezekiel 38.22	Jesus delivers Jerusalem, 'gathering her under His wings', as was His desire
Massive topographical transformation of the earth		Every island fled away, and the mountains were not found	7th Bowl Ezekiel 38.20	Actual or figurative? But maybe the final process of geomorphing of the earth's surface in preparation for the Millennium
Hailstorm		Great hailstones fall out of heaven, and men blaspheme because of the weather	7th Bowl, 7th Trumpet	
Retribution on the Beast & False Prophet		The Lamb now makes war on the Beast and the kings of the earth; the Beast and False Prophet are taken and cast alive into the Lake of Fire; the rest are killed with the sword	Revelation 17-20.3 Ezekiel 39.1-8	Battle of Armageddon
Satan bound		Satan is bound and locked up in the bottomless pit for 1,000 years	Revelation 17-20.3	This event signals the beginning of the Millennium
Jerusalem restored		Jerusalem is restored; the Sanctuary is 'cleansed'	Daniel 8.14 Ezekiel Ch40-48	This will take time, care and attention to detail. Is this the meaning of the 1,290 days and 1,335 days? This will be discussed in chapter 14
■ Marriage Supper		The Marriage Supper of the Lamb	Revelation 17-20.3	

Whilst it is not possible to establish an exact schedule from these events, we can be reasonably sure of the general order of earthly activity following the final days of the Tribulation during which:

- Babylon is destroyed

- Sun, moon and stars are affected

- Christ appears in the clouds with the saints who were in heaven (their bodies resurrected from the earth)

- the rapture (or 'catching up') of Christian believers from the earth, whose bodies are instantly changed
- Christ comes to the Mount of Olives in Jerusalem
- Satan, the Antichrist and the False Prophet are cast down
- the army at Armageddon is destroyed

Chapter 12 of Zechariah is introduced as *'The burden of the word of the Lord concerning (or against) Israel'*. We are seeing the final crescendo of satanic activity against Israel that has been permitted by the Lord. But why does he allow it?

For two millennia Israel has rejected Jesus Christ and suffered tremendously in consequence. The Tribulation and revelation of Antichrist have brought them to the point where the remnant of Israel is now ready to acknowledge Jesus Christ. They will now *'look upon Him whom they have pierced'* and *'mourn for Him as an only Son'*. Israel has had to endure much trouble to get to this point, but it is God's eternal purpose which is paramount. During the Millennium there will be a thousand years for healing and restoration, and this testing and preparation is 'but for a moment', relatively speaking. This is the Refiner's Fire at full heat, where He 'purges the sons of Levi'.

The prophecies of Zechariah and Ezekiel speak for themselves, but let us draw out the key events, adding from Spine and Revelation where appropriate. In Chapter 10 we left the world under the sway of Antichrist. The Beast dominates world government and is persecuting and killing believers. His vast army is camped at Megiddo in the Jezreel valley. He is at the apogee of his unholy powers and all seems lost. The world has been devastated by cataclysmic events, natural, demonic and man-made. Babylon has recently been destroyed by the confederation of the 10 'horns' or Kings.

By this time, we understand from Zechariah that half of the population of Jerusalem will have been 'taken away' and two-thirds of Israel has been 'cut off' and killed. It seems that many nations of the world are represented in this onslaught against the Holy Land, which has been led by the ultimate humanist.

Chapter Eleven

At this point, there is a cry from heaven: 'It is done'. Remember that at Calvary Jesus cried from the cross 'it is finished' to end the dispensation of Law. This end-time cry will bring the Age of Grace to an end. We now have lightning, thunder, voices and another earthquake described in the seals, trumpets and bowls of Revelation.

Next comes a 30 minute silence, almost as if heaven is waiting in expectation. This is to allow the prayers of the saints to make full measure and be poured upon the altar, causing God to unleash the final act on the earth. It is astonishing and humbling that the Lord God, who up to now has dictated the pace of events, would now allow His saints to instigate this final chapter.

> *But we do not want you to be uninformed, brethren, about those who are asleep, so that you will not grieve as do the rest who have no hope. For if we believe that Jesus died and rose again, even so God will bring with Him those who have fallen asleep in Jesus. For this we say to you by the word of the Lord, that we who are alive and remain until the coming of the Lord, will not precede those who have fallen asleep. For the Lord Himself will descend from heaven with a shout, with the voice of the archangel and with the trumpet of God, and the dead in Christ will rise first. Then we who are alive and remain will be caught up together with them in the clouds to meet the Lord in the air, and so we shall always be with the Lord. Therefore comfort one another with these words*
>
> (1 Thess 4.13-18)

It is now time for the Rapture:[7] the dead in Christ will rise first, followed by the saints on earth, who will be caught up into the sky above Jerusalem to meet Jesus in the air. He will come with the saints from heaven, who will have been united with their transformed bodies. We are also told that when we see Jesus, we shall be just like He is.

Jesus' return will be first visible in the clouds above the earth, and travelling from east to west, with His final destination Jerusalem:

> *Just as the lightning comes from the east and flashes even to the west, so will the coming of the Son of Man be*
>
> Matthew 24.27

We know from the angel at His ascension that 'this same Jesus' will come in just

---

[7]. To believe Christ could return 'any time now' requires a major 'cut and paste' exercise on the logical order of both Spine and Revelation, our two primary sources for end-time prophecy

the same way as He left the Mount of Olives. We presume this means that He will descend now just like He ascended then, in bodily form, and that His angels will be present. Jerusalem will then be divided into three sections, and instantly the cities of every nation will fall.

Now is the time for great hailstones the size of boulders to fall on unrighteous men, at which they blaspheme, ending their lives as so many of the ungodly do, by cursing God. It is ironic that fallen man's final words on this earth will be to complain about the weather. This violent storm softens up the army of Antichrist at Armageddon. War ensues between him and the Lamb, and the Beast and his False Prophet are the first beings to be cast alive into the Lake of fire, where they will be tormented day and night forever and ever. The army is killed by plague and sword, and birds feast on the dead.

At this point, Satan, who has been wreaking havoc on earth for the last 3 ½ years is seized, bound in chains by the angel and cast into the bottomless pit. Here he will remain for 1000 years, until released.

Zechariah tells us that the Lord is now King over all the earth, and that Jerusalem may be safely inhabited.

מרן ואתא[8]

Marana-tha - The Lord has come!

---

8. A two word Aramaic expression from 1 Corinthians 16.22. Aramaic was the language that Jesus spoke

Chapter Eleven

Chapter 12 Judgment – days of reckoning

Therefore there is now no condemnation for those who are in Christ Jesus. For the law of the Spirit of life in Christ Jesus has set you free from the law of sin and of death.

Romans 8.1-2

Figure 44. Michelangelo – extract from the Last Judgment

Part 1 – Introduction

'How can a God of love send people to Hell?'
'Why do bad people always seem to get away with it?'
'Why is life so unfair?'

Chapter Twelve

'What about the man on the desert island who has never heard the Gospel – how can God condemn him?'

I guess every Christian has heard these and other questions that challenge God's judgment. This chapter will address these questions in the wider context of God's judgments. Many decide to reject God on the basis that 'they know better than Him' over these issues. This is merely an excuse for their independent and rebellious behaviour, typically seeking to elevate their own humanistic values, scientific knowledge or some other religious system over that of the Almighty God. They are, quite literally, putting themselves in judgment over God Almighty.

As usual, our first step here is to zoom right out to allow us to establish some relevant context. Before we look at judgment, we need to understand the Judge. We will therefore consider the nature of God, and we will do this by looking at some of the names by which He chooses to reveal Himself in His Word.

Part 2 – The Nature of the Judge

God has many names in the Bible. Rather than define Him according to our own imagination or understanding, it is important to meditate on how He has chosen to reveal Himself to us. In Romans, Paul advises us to be *'be transformed by the renewing of your mind, so that you may prove what the will of God is, that which is good and acceptable and perfect'.[1]* This renewing or reprogramming of our thinking, allows us to understand why the Lord does what He does. It serves to clear out thinking which is contrary to His will, leading to confusion. If we are not being regularly challenged to rearrange our theology and thinking, then we are probably not reading our Bibles properly. This is one aspect of working out our salvation…

Most Bible translations use a consistent convention to show these names, and a small selection of these is shown below:

---

1. Romans 12.1-2

CHAPTER TWELVE

Names of God

Hebrew Name	Conventional English Translation
Elohim	God
Jehovah (YHWH)	LORD (Caps)
El Shaddai	God Almighty
El Elyon	Most High God
Adonai	Lord
El Olam	Everlasting God
Jehovah Sabaoth	LORD of Hosts

We will consider two of these names to assist our understanding of His judgments, but I recommend you study all of them.[2]

Elohim, or **God**, is the One who stands in a covenant[3] relationship with His people. This name is in the plural form (i.e. 'Gods') and is first used in Gen 1.1 *'In the beginning God(s) created the heavens and the earth'*. Whilst Elohim is a plural noun, it is often used with singular verbs or adjectives (e.g. the verb 'to create' here is singular) which demonstrate He is three yet one.

This name is used some 2,700 times in the Old Testament, and (by the Law of first mentions) is to do with creation, and therefore reveals His primary nature. God the Creator (as revealed in Gen 1.1) can create something from nothing by the word of His mouth, or transform what already exists into something else e.g. the world spoken into being; eyes made from mud; loaves and fishes multiplied. Nothing is too difficult for Him!

Elohim is later mentioned in relation to covenant,[4] so also concerns the covenant with His chosen people, both Jew and Christian. By His nature, Elohim, as the covenant keeper, cannot rest until He has restored or recreated His creation and creature to make them good again. Elohim is in the restoration business.

---

2. See *'The Names of God'* by Andrew Jukes
3. A covenant is a formally sealed and mutually binding agreement between two parties
4. See Noah in Genesis 6.13, Joseph in Genesis 50.24. See *'By God, I will: The Biblical Covenants'* by David Pawson

Chapter Twelve

The nature of Elohim is also revealed in Jesus Christ in the New Testament. For example:

the Son of Man has come to seek and to save that which was lost

Luke 19.10

Jehovah, or **LORD**, is translated as *I am that I am*, and is a form of the Hebrew verb meaning 'to be'; One who 'is what He is'. It could also be translated as 'the existing One, or the unchanging and eternal One'.

Jehovah is used over 5,500 times in the Old Testament, and the primary quality revealed here is holiness and truth. In Exodus 3.4 for example, Jehovah made Moses remove his shoes at the burning bush because the place where he stood was holy ground. Study of the occurrences of Jehovah show that the thrice holy One looks for and requires holiness and truth in His subjects. By His nature He must without exception judge all that is false, sinful and evil. In Exodus 32.9-10 the Lord sought to consume the children of Israel for building a golden calf. It was only the intercession of Moses that stayed His hand.

Even the relationship between Jesus and His Father was interrupted at the Cross, when Jesus had taken upon Himself the sins of the world. He cried *'Father, why hast Thou forsaken Me?'* and the earth became dark for three hours. Sin separates us from the Father.

When Jesus revealed Himself as 'I am the Way, **the Truth**, and the Life', this too was a glimpse of Jehovah.

Jehovah looks for and rewards righteousness in His subjects, but enacts judgment when man disobeys. It is interesting that when He pronounces judgment, He also suffers.[5] He requires sacrifice, the shedding of blood[6] for the atonement of sin, and looks for His own likeness in His people, both Israel[7] and the Church. As Christians, we are 'in Christ', so when God looks at us He sees His Son's righteousness. When we add this to Paul's statement to the Romans that *'Therefore there is now no*

---

5. Genesis 6.3-7
6. Genesis 8.20
7. Deuteronomy 6.4-5

condemnation for those who are in Christ Jesus,[8] we can rejoice that Christians will not experience the judgments of condemnation, *provided* that we remain in Him and do not stray.

Jehovah's righteousness is not fully declared until He has made His own people righteous with His own righteousness. In His human incarnation, Jesus Christ we see that:

> *He made Him who knew no sin to be sin on our behalf, so that we might become the righteousness of God in Him*
>
> 2 Cor.5.21

Jehovah takes no pleasure in the death of wicked people.

> *Do I have any pleasure in the death of the wicked, declares the Lord God, rather than that he should turn from his ways and live?*
>
> Ezekiel 18.23

So a brief study of two of the names of God shows us much of His nature. God is revealed by many hundreds of names in His Word. The same Bible that reveals Him as *'God is love'* and *'He Himself is our peace'* also reveals Him as judge, One who is completely intolerant of sin, and One who can send man to Hell. We cannot pick and choose – all are true and there is complete consistency between the Hebrew names of God in the Old Testament and those revealed and manifested in Jesus in the New. He is the same yesterday, today and forever.[9]

We should also ask ourselves 'what kind of God do I believe in?' The only basis upon which we can know that He is a God of Love is that His word has revealed it. But the same word also reveals Him as a Holy God who by His nature cannot and will not tolerate sin, and must enact judgment. He is a consuming fire, as well as our loving Saviour and Shepherd. So within these two names we have the beautiful paradox: Jehovah is a consuming fire, wholly intolerant of sin, yet as Elohim He has made a way back into a new covenant through the blood of His own Son.

Now we have considered the Judge, let us look at how he divides humanity for judgment.

---

8. Romans 8.1
9. Hebrews 13.8

Chapter Twelve

Part 3 – Three Groups of People

In his first letter to the Church at Corinth, Paul identifies how God has grouped mankind into three categories:

*Give no offense either to **Jews** or to **Greeks** (Gentiles) or to the **church** of God*

1 Cor 10.32

In God's sight the world therefore comprises:

- **Jews** i.e. the descendants of Abraham through Isaac and Jacob. These were placed under the Law through God's covenant at Sinai. When Jesus came to Israel He presented them with the Kingdom of God, which as a nation they rejected. From that time therefore, God's dealings with Israel were interrupted and held in abeyance. However, as we saw in chapter 7, they have never ceased to be His chosen people, and we know that He watches over them and will restore Israel at the end of the age.

- 'Greeks' or **Gentiles** who comprise all other nations except Israel. We read in the Book of Acts that it was through Paul that the Gospel was preached to the Gentiles from the 1st Century AD onwards.

- the true **Church** i.e. those who have repented of their sins, and confessed Jesus Christ as Lord and Saviour. It goes without saying that the Church we are describing here is not your local denomination or a building. It is the collective body of Christ. There is a sense that Christians are part of a new and holy nation that now transcends and replaces their original nationality.[10] We should also mention here that there is a *false* church. The Gospels and Epistles contain many references to false believers, wolves in sheep's clothing, and deceivers. We will see a little later how the Devil has sowed these 'tares' in amongst the true Church to frustrate and hinder the work of God and misrepresent God's plan of salvation.

God will judge mankind according to these different groups, and His dealings between them differ. For example He gave laws to the children of Israel at Sinai.

---

10. See 1 Peter 2.9

These laws were not meant for the Gentiles, or for Christians,[11] but were given solely to Israel under the dispensation of Law. We must be careful to rightly divide the word of truth if we are to avoid any confusion.

Part 4 – Three types of Judgment

The Bible reveals three types of judgment:

- Judgments on Israel
- Summary Interim Judgments
- Eternal Judgment.

Let's take a look at each.

Judgments on Israel

Because the people of Israel are God's special possession they have been subjected to different judgments to either Christians or Gentiles throughout history, and to some degree, still are. Within this book we have considered many examples of how Israel has suffered. But why should this happen? We will briefly revisit our thinking from chapter 7 so that we may compare these judgments collectively.

We know that God is in covenant relationship to Israel, and both parties are subject to the requirements of that covenant, just as in a marriage. In Chapter 2 we considered seven punishments of God described in Leviticus 26. What else can we glean from this passage?

> *Yet if in spite of this you* **do not obey Me, but act with hostility against Me**, *then I will act with wrathful hostility against you, and I, even I, will punish you seven times for your sins. Further, you will eat the flesh of your sons and the flesh of your daughters you will eat. I then will destroy your high places, and cut down your incense altars, and heap your remains on the remains of your idols, for My soul shall abhor you. I will lay waste your cities as well and will make your sanctuaries desolate, and I will not smell your soothing aromas. I will make*

---

11. We should remember however that Jesus told His disciples that if they loved Him they would obey His Commandments. We cannot earn our righteousness by following laws, but He did re-iterate 9 of the 10 Commandments that still define God's way of living, and they should be the aim of every believer. We cannot 'earn' our righteousness by following them, but the Holy Spirit within us will help us to follow them

> *the land desolate so that your enemies who settle in it will be appalled over it. You, however, I will scatter among the nations and will draw out a sword after you, as your land becomes desolate and your cities become waste.*
>
> Lev 26.27-33

This is a perfect description of the judgment that came upon Israel for its lack of obedience to God's laws, and its continual, wilful rebellion against Him. It is a picture of devastation, typified by many invasions of Israel but culminating in the Roman siege of Jerusalem under Titus in AD70.

We saw in chapter 7 how God judges Israel on the basis of the Covenant He made with them. In that sense, the Jews are on a different page to the Gentiles. He treats them differently, and will do so until His return.

We also saw how Israel's attempts to be a nation 'like any other' are always met with God's chastisement. He has called them to be a separate people, holy and set apart to Him. Some believe that the pogroms and Holocaust resulted from Jewish attempts at assimilation into European society. If God cannot use 'fishermen' to gently and persuasively lure Israel to Himself, then he will use 'hunters' to violently drive them back into the land where He will deal with them.[12] I do wonder if increasing anti-Semitism is being allowed by the Lord to bring His people back to Israel. It is hard to be God's chosen people, but the end will make it worthwhile.

This judgment and refining will reach a crescendo as we draw near to the end of the age, particularly during the Tribulation. At that stage, Israel will be totally isolated, with only their God to turn to. Those who make up the true 'Israel of God' will then repent, return to Him and be saved. He has never forgotten His covenant with them and yearns that they would turn back to Him, as an errant wife to her husband.

There is coming a time however when *all* will be one in Christ Jesus, both Jew and Christian, so we will see a convergence of judgment at the end of the age.

Summary Interim Judgment

The second type of judgment we will consider is summary or interim judgments. Many times in scripture we see God performing such acts. Examples would include

---
12. Jeremiah 16.16

how Adam and Eve were expelled from Eden; the flood at the time of Noah; the judgment on Sodom for perverted sexual activity; and the judgment on Egypt when Pharaoh would not release the children of Israel.

Each of these judgments was a response to a significant sinful or rebellious act against God, or when a level of persistent iniquity had built up, as was the case at the time of the Flood. Another example is found in Gen 15.16, where there is reference to the *'iniquity of the Amorites not yet being full'*.

These interim judgments impact the immediate status of those who receive them, but their eternal status is pending. For example, when Nebuchadnezzar exalted himself, he was immediately judged and became like a beast in the field.

> *Is this not Babylon the great, which I myself have built as a royal residence by the might of my power and for the glory of my majesty?' While the word was in the king's mouth, a voice came from heaven, saying, 'King Nebuchadnezzar, to you it is declared: sovereignty has been removed from you*
>
> Daniel 4.30-31

However, he later repented and his honour and splendour were returned to him and he worshipped God. So despite receiving this interim judgment, this may well mean he is now within the Kingdom of God for eternity. You might meet him one day!

These judgments take place throughout history and in modern times. As mentioned earlier, I sincerely believe that the demise of the British Empire was due to its persistent opposition to the rebirth of Israel. Some believe also that Hurricane Katrina was God's judgment on New Orleans for its culture of drugs, voodoo, homosexuality and party spirit. Has there been repentance? Only God can judge, and He will. I confidently predict that America will experience greater and more frequent natural disasters than this, as she flouts the Lord's commandments. I would like to make it absolutely clear though that we must not equate every natural disaster with an act of judgment. Jesus was clear that the Tower of Siloam[13] did not collapse on and kill eighteen men because they were more sinful than any others. Jesus said those killed were no more sinful than *'**all** other men'* who lived in Jerusalem. The point is that all deserve to die, but the way of escape is via the Cross

---

13. Luke 13.4-5

Chapter Twelve

of Calvary and the salvation provided by Jesus' sacrificial death.

America is not alone. We will see these interventions in other countries too, because God does not change and yet mankind grows ever more rebellious and sinful as the age draws on and the harvest ripens. We should read our newspapers prayerfully. Our God is real and will not be mocked.

Eternal Judgment

The third type of judgment is Eternal Judgment. Hebrews 6.1 lists it as is one of the foundational doctrines, the basics of the Christian faith. If you are not familiar with them, you should be!

Eternal judgment takes place after the end of this present (Church) age. These judgments are also eternal in the sense that they will affect man's eternal destiny, status, punishment and rewards. You won't need me to tell you that it is therefore vital that every believer has an appreciation of their importance...

Before we examine them it would be helpful to have some understanding of spiritual 'geography'. The Bible gives us the names of various destinations where man's spirit may proceed when he dies. Popular thinking has it that heaven is a boring, staid existence inhabited by harp-playing angels, where the saints sit on clouds, wistfully longing for the mischief of their old lives. Hell is some kind of Las Vegas under the ground, a sort of eternal night club party for those who have rejected what they see as the 'hypocrisy' of religious belief. Over the years, unbelievers who have experienced suffering have said to me that Hell 'cannot be any worse than this life'. The reality of course couldn't be more different.

Let us see what the Bible actually says about these places:

Part 5 – Spiritual Geography

Paradise (Greek: *Paradeisos*) – whilst on the cross, one of the thieves turned to Christ and asked in faith if Christ would remember him when He came into His kingdom. Jesus answered and promised he would join Him today in Paradise. Paradise is a garden, a park, a place of comfort, happiness and rest. Up to the Cross, the end of the Dispensation of Law, Paradise was the destination of the righteous dead. It was also known as 'Abraham's bosom'. Abraham, as the father of faith and head of the family of Israel, had a special role here. Those with faith in God would qualify for entry at their life's end.

We know that Paul was caught up into Paradise in his experience with his thorn in the flesh.[14] It is possible that since the Cross, Paradise and Heaven may be different names for the same place. The Church at Ephesus was promised in Revelation that

> *To him who overcomes, I will grant to eat of the tree of life which is in the Paradise of God*

It seems therefore that there are particular rewards in Paradise for overcomers.

Heaven (Hebrew: *shamayim*; Greek: *ouranos*) – the word 'heavens' is used in a number of ways in scripture. It is clear that there are a number of 'heavens', so we are not just talking about one location. Paul describes how he was caught up to the third heaven,[15] leading some scholars to speculate that:

- the highest heaven is the abode of God (the third heaven)
- the 'heavens' display His glory,[16] and comprise the sun, moon and stars (the second heaven)
- however, we also know that Satan is the prince of the power of the air, or the atmosphere (the first heaven)

We are concerned here though with the destination of the Christian at the moment of death. When Stephen was martyred,[17] he looked into Heaven (not Paradise) and saw God's glory, and Jesus standing at His right hand'.

Heaven is certainly the present abode of the Godhead but clearly, Jesus has access to Paradise. Paradise may therefore have been the destination of the righteous dead before the Cross; whereas Heaven may now be the destination since the Cross. We do not know but may speculate that when Christ went from the Cross down into the earth He took the keys of Heaven and earth to lead those in Paradise in triumph

---

14. 2 Corinthians 12.4
15. 2 Corinthians 12.2
16. Psalm 19.1
17. Acts 7.54

CHAPTER TWELVE

into Heaven.

Sheol (Heb : *shehole*) Hades (Greek: *hades*) - these words are used synonymously as the interim destination or holding place of the unrighteous dead, with the Old Testament *Sheol* being used in identical fashion to the New Testament *Hades*. It is usually translated in most Bibles as the *Pit* or the *Grave*. There is a case to be made that prior to the Cross Hades comprised two areas, one for the unrighteous dead and Paradise, for the righteous dead.

A study of the use and context of both words reveals a place of mourning, sorrow, terror, silence, thirst, corruption, lack of knowledge, overwhelming regret (because it is too late for repentance) and punishment. Furthermore, there is a total loss of liberty and benefit. We have two clues as to its location: firstly, Jesus went *down* to proclaim His work to the spirits in prison;[18] secondly, as Lazarus[19] was being comforted in *'Abraham's bosom'*, the rich man looked up, tormented, to see Lazarus a long way away. So the realm of Hades was both below and distanced from Paradise.

The spirits of the unrighteous dead remain there to this day, awaiting bodily resurrection and judgment at the end of the Millennium.

Hell (Greek: *Gehenna*) – the word for Hell is used 12 times in the New Testament but never once used or revealed in the Old Testament.[20] There are those who say 'how can a God of love send people to Hell?', but it is the same Jesus who is responsible for 11 of these mentions of Hell. In effect, just about everything we know about Hell, we know from Jesus. As the physical incarnation of Jehovah, it was right that He should warn us of the consequences of sin.

The word Gehenna describes (and is transliterated from) the valley of Hinnom, which was some 500 yards to the south and steeply downhill from the Temple Mount. In ancient times it was where the worship of the God Molech took place, including child sacrifice in the fire. In Jesus' day, Hinnom was a rubbish tip, where refuse and human excrement were taken, and again was a place of burning and

---

18. 1 Peter 3.19
19. There is no suggestion that this story is a parable, but an account of a man who Jesus knew and recognised from His time in Jerusalem
20. Where the word 'hell' does appear in the Old Testament, it is a mistranslation of Sheol, which is elsewhere translated as grave or pit

smoke. The Gate on Jerusalem's southern wall was known as the Dung Gate, as it was through this route that human waste was carried away.

At present, there is nobody in Hell. It was created by God as the final destination for the Devil and his angels. Satan, who is called the prince of the power of the air,[21] and god of this world,[22] currently has the ability to rove about the earth[23] and access to Heaven to accuse believers.[24] We saw in the previous chapter how he will be cast down to earth in the Tribulation. Taking all this into account, Hell is not Satan's home. Yet.

God does not desire that any people go there and takes no pleasure in the death of the wicked (neither should we, by the way). However His holiness and their rejection of Him and His salvation mean that Hell is where many will go at the final judgment. We assume that this is the same location as the Lake of Fire described in Revelation.

Hell will be the final, permanent and eternal destination for all unrighteous dead, including humans, fallen angels and demons. Humans will remain in their physical body (into which they were resurrected at the end of the Millennium) conscious and in a permanent state of torment forever.[25] How shall we escape if we neglect so great a salvation?

Tartarus – 2Peter2.4-5 & 9-10 states:

> *For if God did not spare angels when they sinned, but cast them into hell (Tartarus) and committed them to pits of darkness, reserved for judgment, ... then the Lord knows how to rescue the godly from temptation, and to keep the unrighteous under punishment for the day of judgment, and especially those who indulge the flesh in its corrupt desires and despise authority*

The word Tartarus is used only here, and seems to describe a prison for certain angels that have been reserved for judgment. It may refer to those angels who had relations[26] with human women, seeking to corrupt the whole earth and thus affect the line of the seed of Eve, through which Messiah would come. There is an

---

21. Ephesians 2.2
22. 2 Corintians 4.4
23. Job 2.2
24. Job 2.3-4 and Revelation 12.10
25. Revelation 20.10
26. See Genesis 6.2-4

intriguing possibility that the *'heroes of old and men of renown'*[27], describe the gods of Greek mythology and were the offspring from these angelic-human liaisons.

Outer darkness – there is one final destination that we must consider. The realm of outer darkness is mentioned three times by Jesus, all in Matthew, and all in relation to those who had opportunity to inherit the Kingdom of God but who missed out through their actions. It is always used with the phrase *weeping and gnashing of teeth*, showing a sense of tremendous regret, and opportunity missed.

Matthew 8.12 shows how some of the children of Israel will exclude themselves from the Kingdom through their unbelief, but that some Gentiles will have faith and thus be included. Matthew 22.1-14 describes the Marriage Supper of the King: the invitations went out but those on the guest list chose to reject the offer. They too found themselves in outer darkness. Matthew 25.30 is the parable of the talents, describing how the Lord rewards those who have worked diligently to bring Him a return on His investment in them. However, the worthless servant who made no effort, no attempt, was cast into outer darkness. We should invest our talents wisely and work hard on the business of the kingdom.

Is outer darkness the same as Hell? We cannot say for certain but might speculate that it may be a lesser punishment. So near, yet so far away.

I hope this basic introduction to these locations will help the reader's understanding of judgment. It is a sombre topic and certainly one subject to speculation. However, eternal judgment is one of the foundational doctrines of the Christian faith. It may surprise the reader that there is not one but five eternal judgments, each having a specific purpose. They are summarised in the table below:

---

27. Genesis 6.4

Chapter Twelve

Eternal Judgment

Judgment	Ref	Who	Purpose	When	Consequences
Wheat and tares	Matt 13.24-30 and 36-43	Hypocrites and false brethren, 'sown' by the Devil amongst the true Church. They will be alive on the earth when Jesus returns	To allow the angels to remove or filter out impostors who had the external form of Christianity, but were not born again with true repentance and faith in Jesus Christ	On Christ's return at the end of the Tribulation	These will be cast into the lake of Fire, where there will be wailing and gnashing of teeth
Dragnet	Matt 13.47-50				We assume that they will meet the same end as the tares above
The 'Bema': The Judgment Seat of Christ	1Peter4.17-18 Rom 14.10+12 2Cor 5.10	True believers, the 'household of God', inc Jew and Christian, both those resurrected at Christ's return and those alive when He comes	An assessment of the quality and efforts of our individual work and service for the Kingdom. Our acts and behaviour, both good and bad, will be tested by fire, resulting in reward or loss. 1Cor 3.11-15	On Christ's return at the end of the Tribulation (but after the sifting of wheat/tares and the dragnet). Possibly during Daniel's 1,290 or 1,335 days	This is not a judgment of condemnation for the believer (see John 3.18, 5.24, Rom 8.1, Is 43.25). However, the unfaithful servant who made no attempt to build the kingdom was cast into outer darkness. Rewards may include money or stewardship over cities in the Millennium
The Throne of Christ's Glory	Matt 25.31-46 Joel 3.1-2	Those Gentile peoples from every nation who are alive and remain on earth on Christ's return (i.e. no Christians or Jews)	A separation of sheep and goat nations based on the criteria of how that individual or nation treated the 'least important of Jesus' brethren' i.e. Jews and (probably) Christians. This includes those nations who 'scattered My people' and have 'divided up My land' (of Israel) according to Joel	On Christ's return at the end of the Tribulation. Possibly during Daniel's 1,290 or 1,335 days	Those rejected are despatched immediately into the Lake of Fire prepared for the devil and his angels. Those accepted are given eternal life to inherit the Kingdom prepared for them from the world's founding. This judgment fittingly takes place in the Valley of Jehosophat to the east of Jerusalem, which has been enlarged by massive geological upheaval in the area around the Kidron valley
The Great White Throne	Rev 20.11-15	The dead (i.e. excluding Christians, Jews who survived the Tribulation, and Jewish 'Saints' who returned with Christ) of every previous age, including those who have never heard the Gospel	The final court of judgment against all sin and rebellion. These dead will have been resurrected and reunited with their bodies, and must face up to the consequences of their actions and choices. None will get away with anything	At the close of the Millennium	The unrighteous dead will be cast into the Lake of Fire. There is the probability also that some throughout history have never heard the Gospel or been exposed to God. Those of 'good conscience'(Rom 2) whose names were found in the Book of Life, will escape condemnation and be rewarded accordingly

CHAPTER TWELVE

The **Throne of Christ's Glory** addresses how the Gentile nations and their inhabitants treated the 'least of Jesus' brethren', a term which we may probably apply to both Jew and Christian. Matthew 25.31-32 explains how when Jesus returns, the living people from all nations will be gathered and separated as sheep and goats, depending upon how they treated the 'brethren'. The Law of Christ is that we should do to others as we would have them do to us, and just as the 'goats' have treated believers, so they also will be treated in an act of perfect justice. Just as the 'sheep' have blessed the 'stranger' (Jesus in the believer) then they too will be blessed.

We should never miss an opportunity to bless and assist our brothers and sisters in Christ, or the Jewish people, because it has eternal consequences.

If one country above all needs to show repentance it is my own nation of Britain. Britain possibly had more opportunity to bless Israel than any nation. However it has done more to frustrate, oppose and undermine her than any other: breaking the promise of the Balfour Declaration; denying immigration to Jewish refugees after World War 2; abstaining from voting for the creation of Israel in the UN vote in 1947, and refusing military assistance to the IDF during the modern Israeli/Arab wars are just some examples, the list is literally damning. The irony is that in the 19th century British church leaders and politicians supported the idea of establishing a homeland for the Jewish people. Today, there are still many British Christian 'Zionists' who actively lobby and pray for Israel.

Britain is not alone in its anti-Israeli stance however. Almost every nation is now pressing for the division of Israel and creation of a Palestinian State. Some States boycott Israeli goods, services, athletes, musicians and artists. Others turn a blind eye to or actively promote anti-Semitic activity. The God of Israel neither slumbers nor sleeps, misses nothing and keeps an accurate record.

The first two judgments listed above are the **wheat and tares**, and the **dragnet**. These are performed by the angels and their purpose is to filter out and remove false brethren who are alive when Jesus returns. The basic facts of the matter are stated in the table above but we certainly know that through the ages the Church has been infested with those who appear 'religious' but show no good fruit. These false believers might include:

- those who have persecuted or betrayed Jew or Christian
- those whose lifestyle and behaviour demonstrates that their love for God has grown lukewarm[28] or cold.[29]
- those who deny the fundamental doctrines of the Bible e.g. the virgin birth, resurrection, deity of Christ, and authority of scripture
- those belonging to pseudo-Christian cults, who have followed 'another Jesus'[30]
- those who may be outwardly 'religious', but who have not experienced the new birth[31] and have no personal relationship with Jesus Christ

The true Church exhibits the spirit of the Lamb. The false church exhibits the spirit of the Beast, which by its antichrist nature persecutes those of the Lamb spirit.

Now that the ungodly and false believers have been removed, all that remains on the Millennial earth are the 'completed' Jews and Christians, which Paul calls collectively the 'House of God'. All are now one in Christ Jesus, so subject to the same judgment. Romans 14.10-12 is written in the context of Romans 9-11, where Paul has made it clear that God has two peoples, the Israel and the Church. The **Judgment Seat of Christ** must therefore apply to both groups. It is not a judgment for condemnation, but is concerned with the rewarding of believers' service. We will be clothed in fine linen, according to the righteous acts that we have committed.[32] We know too that our works will be tested in the fire, to see what is gold, silver or precious stones, and what is of wood, hay and stubble. The only exception to this however is the believer who produced no 'talents' or 'minas' for his master. He was cast into outer darkness.

Rewards include both wealth and governmental authority over cities. We are presently being prepared for service in Christ's earthly Kingdom, so our faithfulness, skills and dedication in the little things right now will be translated into great responsibilities and blessing in the Millennium, which we will consider in detail in chapter 14.

---

28. Revelation 3.14-16 states that Jesus will vomit these out of His mouth
29. Matthew 24.12
30. 2 Corinthians 11.4
31. In John 3.3, Jesus advises Nicodemus, one of the most senior and religious Jews in the whole of Israel, that he cannot see the Kingdom of heaven unless he is born again, of water (baptism) and the spirit (baptism in the Holy Spirit)
32. Revelation 19.8

Chapter Twelve

The **Great White Throne** is the final judgment. Unlike the previous judgments, it occurs right at the end of the Millennium. At that time, whether they want to or not the dead will be resurrected in bodily form to face their God. Every knee shall bow and every tongue will confess that Jesus Christ is Lord. Every atheist and humanist; every Satanist and jihadist; every liberal theologian; every president and politician; every dictator; all the ungodly must now stand before Him who sits on the Throne and make this confession. It may well be their final utterance on earth before they are consigned to Hell. It is a fearsome thought.

If you are reading this now, there is still time and opportunity to repent. As long as you have breath and faith, it is never too late, as the thief on the cross next to Jesus discovered.

We should also consider that nobody gets away with their sins, crimes, or evil deeds. Everything has been recorded, and the punishment will be entirely just. Those who say 'life's not fair!' now, will have to agree that in the end, it was absolutely fair, and they ultimately reaped what they sowed in life. Justice will be done. As always with our Lord, He sees the beginning from the end of a matter, so neither the suicide bomber, nor the Nazi concentration camp guard who died unrepentant in old age in South America will evade justice. Jehovah said *'vengeance is Mine; I will repay'*[33], and He would have to deny His very nature if He did not.

Whilst it seems that the vast majority of those before the Great White Throne are consigned to Hell, there are possibly some whose names at this late stage will be found in the Lamb's Book of Life. This allows leeway for children who died in a state of innocence, those who had never heard the Gospel such as 'the man on the desert island' or those who lived before the Cross and outside of the nation of Israel. These are alluded to in Romans 2 as being judged based on being of *'good conscience'*, and who have diligently followed the Law written in their hearts. Creation has spoken to them and conscience has guided them into righteous choices and living, and we can be confident that the God of the whole world will 'do right'.

I would make mention of one final judgment. This will be performed by believers in the judging of both the world and angels.

---

33. Romans 12.19

Chapter Twelve

Does any one of you, when he has a case against his neighbor, dare to go to law before the unrighteous and not before the saints? Or do you not know that the saints will judge the world? If the world is judged by you, are you not competent to constitute the smallest law courts? Do you not know that we will judge angels? How much more matters of this life?

1 Cor 6.1-3

We presume that this takes place in the Millennium and is one of a number of responsibilities that we are currently being prepared for.

So then, here we have the eternal judgments of God. All His ways are just. Who are we to question His judgments? Who are we to question Him?

The work of the Holy Spirit described in John 16.8 is to *convict the world concerning sin, and righteousness, and judgment*. This judgment begins with the household of God, including Jews and Christians.

How can we begin to prepare for judgment? A good place to start is to *forgive those who trespass against us*, that our trespasses (sins) might be forgiven. We are told to *'judge not in case we are judged'*. We are also warned that the way we judge others is the way that we ourselves will be judged. No matter how serious or trivial the trespass against you, it is time to forgive, and tear up that 'IOU' that another has never given you. Let it go and let the Lord in to flood your soul with His grace, peace and healing.

It is also a time to get busy, because the harvest is plentiful but the workers are few. It is time to seek out the 'least of Jesus' brethren', the Jew and Christian, and bless them as we are able.

In closing, let us briefly reconsider why God judges:

- His nature requires it

- His holiness demands it

- He has warned us, whether by His word or through our conscience. We all have a choice of life and death

- He said He would, and cannot deny His word

- He has been very patient

- If He judged His own Son at Calvary *'He made Him who knew no sin to be sin on our behalf, so that we might become the righteousness of God in Him'*, then how can He ignore our sin? There is no partiality in God

- He sent *'His only begotten Son, that whoever **continually goes on believing** in Him shall not perish, but have eternal life.'*[34] All are invited.

A final warning: those branches who abide in the true Vine and bear fruit will be saved. Those branches which do not abide and have not borne fruit will be cast into the fire and burnt. The salvation of the believer is **conditional upon being in Christ at His return**. If we depart from Him we risk our salvation.[35]

---

34. John 3.16
35. See *'Once saved, always saved: A study in Perseverance and Inheritance'* by David Pawson

Chapter 13 End-Time Survivor – get ready, get set, go

Therefore we do not lose heart, but though our outer man is decaying, yet our inner man is being renewed day by day. For momentary, light affliction is producing for us an eternal weight of glory far beyond all comparison while we look not at the things which are seen, but at the things which are not seen. For the things which are seen are temporal, but the things which are not seen are eternal.

2 Cor 4.16-18

Figure 45. End Time Survivor.

Part 1 – Introduction

So how are you feeling? If you have stayed with us so far, well done! You have now come a long way in your understanding of the road ahead, and seen the grand plan

Chapter Thirteen

nearly to its end. You may have found that your theology has been rearranged. You may be concerned for yourself or your family. You may be a church leader. But how are we to respond?

We have a choice: we can react with fear or with faith. You may feel that you want to somehow escape beyond the reach of these events. I must be honest that was my reaction until I saw beyond that. However, escape is not an option. We have seen that the whole world will be beset by Antichrist and his spirit, and unprecedented natural events. These will pervade every aspect of life on earth.

I suggest that there are two stages we should consider:

- what to do right now in the lead-up to the end and
- what to do in the final Tribulation

The first stage is about getting prepared; the second is about endurance and supernatural provision. We will not stand *then* unless we get ready *now*. The Lord does nothing unless He first reveals it first to His prophets,[1] and we have seen throughout this volume many warnings about the days to come. These prophetic insights are specifically given to trigger a spiritual and practical response from us – in fact, both are interlinked. People generally have two reactions to change: the first is emotional, the second, logical. As you have read the previous chapters I have no doubt that your emotions have been affected, and it would be perfectly normal to feel anxious. This also triggers our spirit into making a response: this could drive us more into the Bible, deepen our prayer life, or spur on our evangelism. When Noah found out a flood was coming, he built the Ark. When Lot heard that the Lord would destroy Sodom, he got his family out. Faith has legs, and acts on what it believes. As you read this chapter, I want to challenge you: what are you going to do differently?

In terms of what we must do in the Tribulation, Jesus has already given us detailed instructions, and we will consider these below.

We know for a fact the global situation is deteriorating; moreover that it will then rapidly become much worse still. Things will then very suddenly become a whole lot better. We have also seen that these events are necessary. Simply stated,

---

1. Amos 3.7

there comes a time in human history where God says 'enough!', and where His righteousness and justice must collide with Satan, his rebellious angels and ungodly men, and He must deliver the Kingdom He promised.

Whether we like it or not, we are living in those times and that dispensation. God knows this, and in His foreknowledge He has chosen you to be part of what He will do. There is absolutely no way that the God-fearing Christian or 'completed' Jew can overcome these end-time events through their own power or wisdom. However, the Bible is full of examples written down to encourage us.

> *Let us run with **endurance** the race that is set before us, fixing our eyes on Jesus, the author and perfecter of faith, who for the joy set before Him **endured the cross, despising the shame**, and has sat down at the right hand of the throne of God.*
>
> Heb 12.1b-2

Jesus is our example and like Him, we must joyfully choose the way of the Cross. As His followers we are not above our Master, and must always do as He did. Jesus never promised to take us *out* of our troubles, but He did promise that He would be with us *through* them, and would never leave us.

> *These things I have spoken to you, so that in Me you may have peace. In the world you have **tribulation**, but take courage; I have overcome the world*
>
> John 20.31-33

We may have to reshape some of our theology because tribulation will have to be endured. However, as we are weakened, our strength increases:

> *My grace is sufficient for you, for **(My) power is perfected in weakness**. Most gladly, therefore, I will rather boast about my **weaknesses**, so that the power of Christ may dwell in me. Therefore I am well content with **weaknesses**, with **insults**, with **distresses**, with **persecutions**, with difficulties, for Christ's sake; for **when I am weak, then I am strong**.*
>
> 2 Cor 12.9-10

Christ's power is perfected when we are at our weakest. Joseph, for example, had to endure the humiliation of Pharaoh's dungeons before he was elevated to become the prime minister of Egypt. He bore his cross, and it performed a work in him, preparing him for service. We need to understand that the cross has two aspects:

Chapter Thirteen

- the first is that *Christ was crucified for me,* and took upon Himself all my sin and infirmity. As Dr Derek Prince has taught, at the Cross He took all the evil due to me, and exchanged it for all the good due to Him

- the second is that *I have been crucified with Christ, and that it is no longer I who live but Christ who lives in me.*[2]

Modern-day Christians tend to rejoice in the first aspect, but neglect the second. In effect, when I became a Christian and was baptised, the person that I was ceased to exist. It was crucified, died and buried. Because of this principle in his life, Paul was able to say that *death works in us, but life in you.*[3] Once you have understood that the person that you were is *dead,* your new life will begin to take on a different meaning.

We should also remember that the seven years of the Tribulation will be relatively brief. For the majority of believers around the world, their trouble started long ago, with the loss of freedoms, property, family members and their lives. We in the west have got off lightly up to now, but not for much longer.

We are told that:

> *All discipline (chastening) for the moment seems not to be joyful, but sorrowful; yet to those who have been trained by it, afterwards it yields the peaceful fruit of righteousness*
>
> Heb 12.11

Fix this in your mind: there is **always** an afterwards in the chastening of God, and He is always, in all things, in total control of what we go through. Once we realise this and understand that the 'afterwards' will be infinitely better than what was *before*, we shall be able to endure it. If we don't know about the 'afterwards', then we will be discouraged and may give up.

> *the sorrow that is according to the will of God produces a repentance without regret, leading to salvation, but the sorrow of the world produces death.*
>
> 2 Cor 7.10

---

2. Galatians 2.20
3. 2 Corinthians 4.12

CHAPTER THIRTEEN

Paul's second letter to Corinth has much to say about the subject of enduring through suffering. It is interesting that Corinth, as a Greek city, was very much under the spirit that mixed humanist philosophy with the occult. This is becoming more active in our day too. We will truly be sifted in the coming days through godly sorrow, and it is vital we accept this heavenly training with joy and faith, as we see the end from the beginning. You can start right now by praising God for any adversity in your life. This is a decision that should flow from our spirit. The mature Christian is Spirit-led: the Holy Spirit speaks to our spirit, and our spirit tells our minds what to think, our bodies what to do and our appetites what they can and can't have. To be an end-time survivor, an overcomer, we need to grow up fast, and cannot make decisions based on feelings alone. When we are *Spirit-led*, faith grows, discernment increases and heavenly strength flows through us to do God's will.

Consider it all joy, my brethren, when you encounter various trials, knowing that the testing of your faith produces endurance

James 1.2-3

Jesus said that:

If anyone wishes to come after Me, he must deny himself, and take up his cross and follow Me. For whoever wishes to save his life will lose it; but whoever loses his life for My sake will find it. For what will it profit a man if he gains the whole world and forfeits his soul? Or what will a man give in exchange for his soul? For the Son of Man is going to come in the glory of His Father with His angels, and will then repay every man according to his deeds

Matthew 16.24-27

The principle of dying to self is not taught much today but is something we need to relearn. Your present sufferings, trials, issues and problems have been permitted by the Lord to train you now for the things to come. This daily exercising of our faith will build it up, as we endure, pray and overcome. The only faith that is worth anything is *tested* faith, heated in the fire and refined as pure gold. The Lord loves you enough to discipline you *now*, so that you will not fail *then*.

For consider Him who has endured such hostility by sinners against Himself, so that you will not grow weary and lose heart. You have not yet resisted to the point of shedding blood in your

CHAPTER THIRTEEN

striving against sin; and you have forgotten the exhortation which is addressed to you as sons:

'My son, do not regard lightly the discipline of the Lord, nor faint when you are reproved by Him. For those whom the Lord loves He disciplines, and He scourges every son whom He receives.'

Hebrews 12.3-6

For Bible-believing people extreme times will result in amazing provision. Moses brought over a million people out of Egypt through the wilderness, yet God provided water from the rock and manna from Heaven for every single person. Elijah was fed by a raven. The times we are facing will be harder than those of the Israelites, so we can expect miracles of provision. Just as Jesus warned the Christians to flee before Titus razed Jerusalem, we can expect the voice of God to speak into our lives when needed. We will need the faith of Abraham, and the courage of Joshua for the coming days. For many, faith is suddenly going to become the reality of *things hoped for, the conviction of things not seen,*[4] whether food or health. In every area, we will find our God absolutely faithful. He cannot deny His own nature, and must provide.

How will faith come unless we first understand the promises of God? Are you one who just does 'your daily chapter', or do you really *study*[5] your Bible to show yourself approved of God?

If you are a church leader, I want to challenge you: have you taken any practical steps to prepare your people for the days ahead? The days are short and I suspect that the days of persecution will come very quickly once they start. It is therefore imperative to ground ourselves in the word of God. If your Bible were to be taken off you, how much could you remember? Again, it is important to memorise key verses for the coming days. You could start right now with a verse from this chapter.

I hope that you are beginning to get excited about the privilege of being chosen to live and possibly die, in these days.

As a final thought in this introduction, won't it be good that as you see the prophetic checklist unfold to know that very soon...

---

4. Hebrews 11.1
5. 2 Timothy 2.15

- your Saviour is coming back for you
- you will be living in a Kingdom based on righteousness and justice
- you will be reunited with loved ones who have died in Christ
- you will get to meet the people you have been reading about in your Bible
- you will have eternity in the presence of God

Yes, we must endure hardship, but what a salvation!

We will now proceed to explore how we can prepare as end-time survivors, starting with Jesus' specific advice. We will also consider the Lord's Prayer and the subject of martyrdom. Finally, we'll look at some practicalities.

Part 2 – Jesus' End-Time Parables & Instructions

In Chapter 2 we considered in detail the events of the Spine of prophecy. Jesus closed this discourse with a combined package of parables, advice and instruction. Let's take a look at what He said, and see how we should respond.

Referring back to the parallel presentation of the Spine in Chapter 1, Jesus gave nine pieces of advice:

- **The Fig Tree** – this concerned the rebirth of Israel, and was examined in Chapter 2
- **The Sheep and Goat Nations** – concerning how Christ will judge the nations in regard to their treatment of the Jews, and was discussed in Chapter 9
- a group of **Seven parables and instructions**, insights specifically for those living in the end-times, who are faced with the events that Jesus described in the Spine. (You may want to quickly turn to the presentation of the Spine on the table in chapter 2):

Chapter Thirteen

Seven End-Time parables and instructions

	Parable	Instruction / advice	From Luke (given earlier in the Temple's Court of Women to 'some' of the disciples)	From Matthew / Mark (given later on the Mount of Olives to Peter, James, John & Andrew)
1		guard your heart	✓	
2		days of Noah		✓
3	thief in the night			✓
4	faithful & wise servant			✓
5	ten virgins			✓
6	talents			✓
7	man going to a far country			✓

In scripture, seven is the number of divine blessing and rest, and it is interesting that the Lord gives us this package of seven instructions / parables. Let us consider each in turn. The first instruction was given to the wider group of Jesus' followers (whilst in the Court of Women) two days before Jesus was crucified.

- A general warning to **guard your heart** by not allowing it to be overcome or distracted by hangovers (!), intoxication or anxiety. Instead they were commanded to 'watch and pray'. There will no doubt be some Christians who fail to heed this. Keep an eye on your brothers and sisters and pray for them systematically.

The remaining six instructions were shared later on the Mount of Olives only with Jesus' inner circle of disciples. These would be amongst His final words of advice to them before the Cross. We should note that these instructions and warnings were not meant for unbelievers, but for His followers.

- The **days of Noah** were evil times when we know that God judged the earth through a flood that inundated the known world at that time. One of the causes of iniquity in those days was sexual interaction between humans and angelic beings. It is interesting that many today in the Church do not believe that Noah lived, or even that there was a flood. Jesus believed it though, and so should we. Noah's family responded practically by preparing the Ark that would deliver them from the waters, and one can imagine the opinions of those who passed by on those hot, sunny days as they saw Noah and his sons hard at work on the Ark. Are you prepared to obey God's instructions now, though the world (and some in the church) might consider you foolish? He will be speaking, advising, counselling and guiding. Are you listening? It seems too that life went on as normal with people eating, drinking, and marrying. The world carried on as though everything was normal, but God's chosen were working to a different programme. Jesus says that His return will be so sudden that men working in the field, or women grinding at the mill will be suddenly separated. The advice again is to *'watch therefore'*, and the context is one of careful preparation whilst ignoring the criticism and scorn of bystanders.

- The ***thief in the night*** is able to break into the house of the unprepared, so we are advised to *'be ready'*. Again the implication is to be awake in the night, watchful and guarding.

- The ***faithful and wise servant*** provided sustenance at the right time for his household and was blessed when his master arrived. This speaks not only of a state of watchful preparedness, but also of a thoughtful and effective provision for those for whom we are responsible. It is both 'spiritual' and highly practical. The evil servant however ate and got intoxicated with drunkards whilst his master's arrival was delayed. It seems that for some believers, pressure and complacency will be too much and they will succumb to the ways of the world.

- The kingdom of heaven is likened to ***5 wise virgins*** who kept their lamps topped-up with oil and trimmed to provide maximum illumination. This would require diligence and regular attention 'little and often' to keep those lamps working at maximum efficiency, providing a steady and bright light. The foolish virgins were complacent and inattentive and consequently, shut out. The advice yet again is to *'watch therefore'* because we don't know the day nor hour when the Son of Man will come.

- The kingdom of heaven is again likened to a man who entrusted ***talents*** to his servants. A Jewish talent[6] was 3,000 shekels 'of the

---
6. The English word 'talent' meaning a gift or ability is derived from this term

Chapter Thirteen

Sanctuary', or 6,000 Roman denarii, either way a considerable sum. We explored this parable in Chapter 12, and should be careful to provide our Master with a return on His major investment in us. We can 'invest' our testimony, help those in need, give money, pray, use our spiritual gifts, or encourage others. We may also have a specific role as elder, prophet, pastor or teacher. Have you asked the Lord what talent He has invested in you? We also have family responsibilities, so being a father, mother, husband or wife is a worthy service too. Whatever we do should be done to the glory of God, whether driving your taxi or washing the dishes. All are of value to Him if approached prayerfully. The key is to discern and know what God has entrusted to you, and provide Him with a return on His investment. Whatever you do, do it with all your heart.[7] I heard a wonderful story of a Chinese lady Christian who was a surgeon. The communists imprisoned her for her beliefs. She took real joy in cleaning the toilets at the prison, and shone as a witness in that place. If we are faithful in the small things when no-one is watching, we will be given stewardship over much.

- The final instruction is from Mark's Gospel, and relates to the man who went to **the far country**. Note here again how the Master gives *authority* to His servants, a specific *'work'* to each, and the commandment to *watch*. We are warned three times in this brief story to 'watch', but what does this mean?

Watching

This advice was given by Jesus in special reference to the end-times, and at His final opportunity to counsel His disciples before the Cross. In the above accounts, the word to *'watch'* is used five times, whilst to *'pray'* is used twice. It seems then that watching is vital at the time of the end.

Two Greek words are used to describe the activity of watching:

- ***Gregoreo***, (as in Matthew 24.42) means to keep oneself awake in the night, to keep vigilant and to be spiritually alert

- ***Agrupneo*** (as in Mark 13.33 or Luke 21.36) is a sleepless state, when we are

---

7. Colossians 3.23-24

CHAPTER THIRTEEN

watchfully intent upon a thing

It seems that *gregoreo* is a personal decision made by the individual, whereas *agrupneo* is a condition imposed from outside. Either way, once we find ourselves in this nocturnal state of sleeplessness we have a choice on what to do with our mind and spirit. We can, for example, spend the time in anxious thoughts, or can take the opportunity to direct our thinking towards God. In this state we may receive revelation from Him, be restored, pray, or meditate on scripture. This recharges us for the day ahead and renews our strength.[8] As an aside I can testify that I received a good deal of the content of this book either late at night or early in the morning. Furthermore, on occasions I was awoken by the Holy Spirit with specific content that needed to be written down. Once I did this, I slept peacefully. Obedience to this prompting *trains* our spirit to listen to God and greatly sharpens our discernment, like any skill, through practice. Next time we use that discernment, it will be more finely tuned.

Like all revelation however, it must be tested against the word of God.[9] Just because something is received in a dream, a night watch, or apparent 'prophecy' does not guarantee it is of God. We must learn to discern the spirit of truth from the spirit of error. If it is not Biblical – bin it.

Watching has to do with attentive, active listening, awaiting some event or instruction that must be acted upon. There are differing types of prayer and these are about making our requests known to God. It is interesting that the ratio of watching to listening is 5:2 in the accounts given by Jesus. How does this compare with your experience? When you pray do you just talk *at* God? In the last 24 hours, how much opportunity did you really give Him to speak into your life?

We can 'watch' wherever we are, whether free or imprisoned, even when we are tired. Rather than worry about sleeplessness and the day ahead, we should be excited by the opportunity to be a watchman, 'staying up' with the Lord.

During the 2012 Olympics, I listened to a five-time Olympic Gold champion who was being questioned about the subject of how sleeplessness the night before a

---

8. Isaiah 40.31
9. 1 John 4.1-6

big event affects the performance of athletes. He said it had no effect at all, because your body 'gets the sleep it needs', and that some of his best performances followed a sleepless night. I have learned from personal experience that often my mind needs to process things through, and once this is done I am able to sleep. The key in 'watching' is to place one's focus on God: meditate on scripture, pray, reflect, listen, test, and see what God shows you.

Psalm 1 says:

> *Blessed is the man who does not walk in the counsel of the wicked, Nor stand in the path of sinners, nor sit in the seat of scoffers! But his delight is in the law of the Lord, and in His law he meditates day and night. He will be like a tree firmly planted by streams of water, which yields its fruit in its season, and its leaf does not wither, and in whatever he does, he prospers*

It is very clear that this meditative watching is vital to our welfare in the last days. Start tonight.

The soldier on watch duty doesn't just work at night though. He is vigilant at all times, takes nothing for granted, and continually checks for anything amiss. In the armed forces your life and the lives of those around you might depend on it. The watchman is vigilant and focused when others are distracted, dismayed, depressed, or just weary. He or she is ever watchful, looking for things that are different from normal, such that he may take the appropriate action for the wellbeing of those in his responsibility.

Specific Do's and Don'ts

As well as the parables provided above, Jesus also wove through the Spine certain advice about how to respond to specific end-time events. Again, it is no coincidence that there are seven instructions.

Chapter Thirteen

End-Time – Specific responses

	Signs	Advice
False Christs	Many will claim to be Jesus Christ, and will mislead many. They will say that *the time is at hand, follow me*	**Don't follow them**
National Turmoil	When you see wars, disturbances, and reports/rumours of wars	**Don't be afraid** (the end does not follow immediately)
Persecution & Interrogation	Believers will be delivered up to the courts, flogged in synagogues, brought before Kings and Governors for Jesus' name sake, and arrested	**Don't worry** about what to say: the Lord will give the wisdom to speak
Abomination of Desolation	The Abomination of desolation	Those in Judea (the region around Jerusalem) must **flee immediately** (don't even go back to get your coat, or go back into the house) **Pray** that your flight will not be in winter, or on a Sabbath
Counterfeit signs & wonders	False Christs and false prophets will arise, showing signs and wonders such that even the elect could be led astray. When they say look here, look there!	**Ignore them.** Don't go to the wilderness or the inner rooms, because the coming of the son of man will be like lightning, flashing from the eastern sky to the western sky
Signs in Heaven & earth	The sun will be darkened, the moon will not give its light, the stars will fall from the heavens. Nations dismayed, perplexity at the roaring of the sea and the waves, and men fainting from fear in expectation of what is coming on the earth. The angelic powers in the heavens will be shaken	When *these things* begin to take place, straighten up, and **lift up your heads**, because your redemption is drawing near!
Israel	The fig tree	**Watch the fig tree** (Israel) and all the trees (the nations): as soon as they put forth leaves you will know that summer is near

Chapter Thirteen

Summing these up we have:
- don't follow falsehood
- don't be afraid
- don't worry about what to say
- flee / pray concerning the abomination of desolation
- ignore counterfeits
- look up!
- watch Israel

Each of these is tied to a specific need and is linked to the appearance of certain conditions. Yet more reason to watch and pray.

Part 3 – The Kingdom Prayer

In preparing His disciples for the coming Kingdom, Jesus provided them with specific advice on how to pray:

> *When you pray, you are not to be like the hypocrites; for they love to stand and pray in the synagogues and on the street corners so that they may be seen by men. Truly I say to you, they have their reward in full. But you, when you pray, go into your inner room, close your door and pray to your Father who is in secret, and your Father who sees what is done in secret will reward you. And when you are praying, do not use meaningless repetition as the Gentiles do, for they suppose that they will be heard for their many words. So do not be like them; for your Father knows what you need before you ask Him. Pray, then, in this way:*

Our Father who is in heaven,
Hallowed be Your name.
'Your kingdom come.
Your will be done,
On earth as it is in heaven.
'Give us this day our daily bread.
'And forgive us our debts, as we also have forgiven our debtors.
'And do not lead us into temptation, but deliver us from evil.
For Yours is the kingdom and the power and the glory forever. Amen.

Matthew 6.5-13

It comprises ten clauses:

10 Clauses of the Lord's Prayer

Our Father in heaven	1st: A statement of God's sovereignty
Holy is Your name	2nd: Jehovah's Name.
May Your kingdom come	3rd: An affirmation that God's kingdom is coming
May Your will be done on earth as it is being done in heaven	4th: This looks forward to the Millennium
Give us today our daily bread	5th: A request for food and sustenance
Forgive us our debts as we forgive those we owe	6th: This includes debts, offences and sin, and our attitude to others
Do not lead us into temptation	7th: A request for spiritual guidance in times of extreme testing
But deliver us from the evil one	8th: Protection and escape from Antichrist
For Yours is the kingdom and the power and the glory	9th: An acknowledgment of the Lord's Divine Glory, and the coming of the Millennium
Forever. Amen	10th: The eternal completion, looking towards the New heavens and New earth to come

Its first three clauses acknowledge who God is. The golden rule when we pray should always be to first declare some quality of the Lord. We should enter His gates with thanksgiving, and His courts with praise.[10] Don't rush in with your requests first! The next four clauses allow and encourage us to make known our needs, in this case bread, forgiveness, guidance and deliverance. We are coming into days when those who do not have the mark of the Beast will not be able to buy bread, so it must be provided. We will also need to be delivered from the 'evil one', the Beast. In finishing, again the prayer focuses on the Lord and the coming Kingdom. Through these times, we should always be looking ahead to the coming Kingdom. The Lord's Prayer, as it is also known, is our key to prayer in the times to come. Memorise it.

Part 4 – Dealing with practicalities

The events we have described in the preceding chapters will have a tangible impact on us all. How should we respond on a practical level? Here are some thoughts:

---
10. Psalm 100.4

Chapter Thirteen

Employment

As we near the end, we will experience a relentless criminalising of Christian practice. It follows that we will have to adapt accordingly. Even now we see Christians whose livelihoods have been impacted or removed by legislation, for example those in public bodies such as schools, social services, or those who run small hotels. There are still currently plenty of professions where a Christian may work without compromise or fear, but time is short. Don't be caught by surprise, but take measures now to prayerfully consider your options. The Lord will provide our needs, but I suggest that we may need to be flexible, adapting our lifestyle and career to the situations encountered.

The Authorities

There will no doubt come a time where we are brought in front of the legal authorities to explain our Christian behaviour. Jesus demonstrated that there is time to speak and a time to remain silent. He spoke to Pilate but ignored Herod. He didn't go out of His way to antagonise or provoke them. We know from the study above that we will be given the words at that time, so need not prepare any long speeches. Paul and Silas praised God in prison – start your training now by praising him for the little problems in your life.

Subsistence

I know there are some who have already taken to the hills to escape the Tribulation. I can understand their motivation, but would suggest they may be a little premature. There is no doubt that society is beginning to break down, with increasing problems in civil government, weather, the economy, lawlessness and the moral inversion of national laws.

We could go on, but have covered the majority of these factors earlier in the book. These issues will give rise to problems such as personal security, energy supply and provision of food. Whilst I am not yet off to the woods to build my shelter, I do believe in taking practical, sensible precautions to safeguard my livelihood. We know the 'system' is going to break, so simple planning such as growing some of our own food, keeping a small stock of basic provisions, having fallback plans for energy (heat and light) and being security conscious is common sense.

Ask God what he wants you to do, then put it into operation, asking Him to bless your plan.

Salt and Light

As we have seen in our studies, things aren't just going to get harder for believers, but for the world too. We will have many opportunities to share our faith and provisions with those around us. Revival often occurs in times of adversity, so we must be bold in letting our light shine out by telling them about Jesus, sharing our testimonies and giving a helping hand. They will know we are Christians by our selfless love.

The purpose of salt is to forestall decay, and we should take every opportunity to push back at the world. This might involve lobbying members of your government, holding the media to account, or getting involved in local issues. As it has been said, evil triumphs when good men do nothing. We know that eventually a time is coming for those in the west when we will not be tolerated, but that is not yet come. Men like Lord Shaftesbury and William Wilberforce were prepared to get their hands dirty and get involved, and changed the course of history.

Part 5 – Martyrdom

For to me, to live is Christ and to die is gain. But if I am to live on in the flesh, this will mean fruitful labor for me; and I do not know which to choose. But I am hard-pressed from both directions, having the desire to depart and be with Christ, for that is very much better
Philippians 1.21-23

We all have to die – it is one of life's certainties, and its timing is in the Lord's hands. I have recounted earlier how my own father died in faith. I can honestly say that I did not grieve at his death, but was filled with an overwhelming and heaven-sent peace and joy. The death of the Christian is not something to be mourned but celebrated. Death is merely a separation, when as Paul describes above, our spirit goes to be with the Lord.

The act of martyrdom, being killed for one's faith in Christ, merely accelerates the progression of the believer into the glorious presence of Christ. In days gone by, martyrs were able to rejoice at their deaths and were given grace to endure them. Many, like Stephen, were able to forgive their persecutors at the end. The faith-filled believer will have no fear of death, nor should we fear the loss of our brothers or sisters in Christ. I believe this is the ultimate sign of Christian faith. Jesus said there was no greater love than a man lay down his life for his brother.

> *O death (Sheol), where is your victory? O death (Hades), where is your sting?*
>
> 1 Corinthians 15.55

We need faith to live by, and faith maybe one day to die by. Jesus told us:

> *Be faithful until death, and I will give you the crown of life*
>
> Revelation 2.10

You should read again the wonderful promise to the martyrs killed in the Great Tribulation,[11] which concludes:

> *the Lamb in the center of the throne will be their shepherd, and will guide them to springs of the water of life; and God will wipe every tear from their eyes*
>
> Revelation 7.17

It is clear then that there are special rewards for those who die in the faith. Who knows what the days ahead will bring, but the Lord. Trust Him and He will provide us with the grace to endure it.

Part 6 – Conclusion

When I began this book, I was in trepidation about what the future would hold. I am now excited about the way ahead, for one simple reason: **the Kingdom is coming; the King will soon be with us.**

---

11. Revelation 7.9-17

CHAPTER THIRTEEN

Faith Story

Jesus is the author and perfecter of our faith,[12] and we should be looking to Him. He writes every chapter, every paragraph, every sentence and every word of your personal faith story. He even provides the punctuation, the fine day to day details that make sense of the bigger picture. Your story has been designed to glorify Him, and is written and individually tailored for you. That means every event, every problem, every crisis, every issue in your life today exists to train you for Kingdom service. He permits, allows, causes and controls everything[13] that comes your way. He chastens and trains every son who He receives.[14]

Faith is the currency of His kingdom, and how you respond to these events, and what you believe now will determine your eternal wealth and status. How much have you got in that Kingdom bank account, that heavenly pension plan? Has this faith stood the test, so that you have demonstrated your ability to endure?[15] The road ahead will not be easy, but was never intended to be so. During the Last Supper, and a few hours after Jesus had shared the end-time prophecies from the temple and Olivet, He told His disciples:

> ***If the world hates you, you know that it has hated Me before it hated you.*** *If you were of the world, the world would love its own; but because you are not of the world, but I chose you out of the world, because of this the world hates you. Remember the word that I said to you, 'A slave is not greater than his master.'*
>
> ***If they persecuted Me, they will also persecute you;*** *if they kept My word, they will keep yours also*
>
> John 15.18-20

We must constantly remember that He is in control, He is our Boss, and His decisions about our lives and prayers are final. He was Pilate's Boss too and, as Jesus told him at His trial, the world would have had no authority over Him (or us) unless His Father had allowed it. We need to learn to endure patiently. As my wife so succinctly pointed out, we need to accept 'that *whatever* He decides is fine'. We cannot tell Him what to do, then become resentful when the answer doesn't

---

12. Hebrews 12.2
13. Romans 11.36
14. Hebrews 12.6
15. James 1.3

immediately materialise to our satisfaction. It is through faith and *patience* that we inherit the Kingdom. This will test us in the extreme, particularly as we see our loved ones suffering. But the wisdom of God sees the end from the beginning, and peace will flood your spirit as you learn to abide in Him, see the situation through His eyes, and come into the 'afterwards' of Hebrews 12.11. This momentary and light affliction[16] will bring an eternal weight of glory as we learn to look beyond the visible into the unseen realm of heaven.

The darker it becomes, the brighter you will shine. He will never let you down, but you must realise that He seeks your *eternal* wellbeing, not your *immediate* satisfaction.

> *But the path of the righteous is like the light of dawn that shines brighter and brighter until the full (perfect) day*
>
> Proverbs 4.18

This perfect day described here is the day of Christ's return.

We started our journey on the Mount of Olives in chapter one. We end this chapter at that same place.

> *After He had said these things, He was lifted up while they were looking on, and a cloud received Him out of their sight.*
>
> *And as they were gazing intently into the sky while He was going, behold, two men in white clothing stood beside them. They also said, Men of Galilee, why do you stand looking into the sky? This Jesus, who has been taken up from you into heaven, will come in just the same way as you have watched Him go into heaven.*
>
> Acts 1.9-11

---

16. 2 Corinthians 4.17-18

Chapter 14   The Millennium and after

Great is the LORD, and greatly to be praised, in the city of our God, His holy mountain. Beautifully elevated, and the joy of the whole earth, is Mount Zion on the slopes of the north, the city of the great King. God, who is in her palaces, has made Himself known as a stronghold

Psalm 48.1-3 (paraphrased)

Figure 46. Looking towards Mount Zion.

Part 1 – Introduction

Picture the scene a few minutes after Armageddon has finished. Look out over the destruction, the countless dead on the blood-soaked Plain of Jezreel in northern Israel. The smoke rises from the wrecked military hardware of the Beast's vanquished forces. The city of Jerusalem, like every other city around the world, has been devastated by the biggest earthquake the world has ever experienced. The saints who endured the Tribulation are mingling with the people of Israel who survived the battle and those who returned with Christ, both Jew and Christian. The Jews finally 'looked *upon the One that they pierced*' and found their salvation. There is a real sense of triumphal joy, a new beginning, and much hard work ahead to restore the earth. We are in our new bodies too – completely restored and with some amazing new abilities.

There are many questions: How shall we worship now? What is happening around the rest of the planet? When will the Marriage Supper take place? There seems so much to do, so much to learn. We will see that many (but not all) of these questions were answered by the prophets five hundred years before Christ came to visit us.

Understanding the Millennium is not a priority for most Christians. This is a mistake, because I would estimate that as much as 5%, one verse in every twenty, of your Bible is given to describing it.[1] Woven in between prophecy and poetry is a remarkably detailed picture of Christ's thousand year reign on earth.

Our blindness in this area stems in part from the Church's habit of helping itself to the promises that God made to Israel. How many times, for example, have you listened to a sermon on the *'dry bones'*? You were almost certainly told that this was a picture of restoration in the Church. Wrong! Read it again - the prophecy is directed *specifically* at Israel. I wonder how many have actually heard some preaching where this passage *has* been applied to Israel? I would guess not many. I am not saying that the Lord doesn't restore, but there are better references for that topic. Most Christians have been programmed over the years to replace '*Israel*' with '*church*', and if we are honest, the habit is deeply ingrained. So, having recognised this error, we need to allow the Holy Spirit to 'renew our minds' and begin to read prophecy as it was meant to be read. I know from personal experience that it takes time and practice to unlearn this deeply ingrained habit. The Millennium will then take on a quite different and

---

1. Whilst not a comprehensive list, the reader may look at Isaiah 49-66; Jeremiah 23 & 30-33; Ezekiel 36-37 & 40-48; and Zechariah 10-14. There are many other Millennial sources to be found throughout the Bible, including for example well over 200 verses from the Psalms. These are often interwoven with Messianic prophecies of Jesus visit during Roman times, and other prophecy that foretells Israel reclaiming her land. In the New Testament much of the teaching concerning the coming Kingdom of God is Millennial

literal meaning and a whole new area of doctrine will be opened up. Learn this lesson and truth will start to drop into its rightful place and you will never read your Bible in the same way again. You need not worry that the Church will be left out, because we do find Gentile involvement in these passages. We saw in chapter 7 how we may legitimately apply these truths by analogy and example to the church, so these passages are relevant to Christians too. The focus and primary meaning though is Israel. The golden rule in the Kingdom of God is: *first the Jew, then the Gentile*.[2]

There is no doubt that much is presently hidden from our view, but a great deal has been disclosed to us, if only we care to look for it. We can thus build a strong understanding not just of the Millennium, but also get a glimpse of what is to follow. If the Lord would not have us muse on this topic then it would have remained completely hidden. The fact that He has chosen to share it means we should study it.

So why did He choose to reveal it? You may have already guessed the answer. We have seen that we must endure a lot of trouble to get to the Kingdom of God, our destination. We therefore need hope *now*, something to look forward to *now* and something to keep us going through the dark times, like a distant lamp on the darkest of nights. Paul said that he was pressing on towards his goal, the upward call from God in Christ Jesus.[3]

Ultimately, what our journey is all about is defined by

Thy kingdom come, Thy will be done on earth as it is in heaven

The Millennium, simply stated, is when the Kingdom of God comes to earth. Many Christians use the Lord's Prayer every day and utter this truth without any understanding of what it is saying to them. It is no accident that two out of the ten clauses (again 20%) of the Lord's Prayer concern the Millennium. The doctrine has been right under our noses all the time but we failed to see it. Believers certainly experience wonderful and miraculous aspects of the kingdom right now (such as healing, provision and deliverance) but there is no doubt that the best is yet to come.

---

2. Romans 1.16; 2.9-10
3. Philippians 3.14

Chapter Fourteen

In chapter 12 we looked at spiritual geography. As a Christian, if you were to die right now you would go to Heaven / Paradise. Praise God! But when Christ returns, He will establish His earthly kingdom and, as we saw in chapter 11, will bring you back with Him. Our ultimate destination therefore is not heaven, but earth. If you receive this fact with faith and understand the promises that go with it, then the brief years of tribulation will be more tolerable.

> *Now faith is the assurance (substance) of things hoped for, the conviction (evidence) of things not seen*
>
> Hebrews 11.1

With this wonderful end in mind, even this often-quoted verse takes on new meaning, and helps us to visualise Christ's earthly kingdom with the eye of faith. Some of this *evidence of things not seen* relates to unfulfilled or partially fulfilled prophetic promises. For example, Israel has returned to the Promised Land, but most Jews don't yet acknowledge their God, and the peace they yearn for is a distant dream. A time is coming though when the prophecies relating to them will have been fulfilled.

Our approach in chapter 14 will be to delve into Millennial prophecy to see what has been revealed. I hope you are excited by this. If not, you should be! What we will discover is a story of restoration in four areas:

- restoration of the land
- restoration of the city
- restoration of worship
- restoration of the people

Most of what we are about to describe is certain, but we will also allow ourselves a little speculation as we build up the picture. Please progress prayerfully and check for yourselves what the Bible says!

Part 2 – Restoration of the Land

In chapters 10 and 11 we took a detailed look at Armageddon. The battle is over

CHAPTER FOURTEEN

and it is time to clean up. Ezekiel is our guide:

> *Then those who inhabit the cities of Israel will go out and make fires with the weapons and burn them, both shields and bucklers, bows and arrows, war clubs and spears, and for seven years they will make fires of them. They will not take wood from the field or gather firewood from the forests, for they will make fires with the weapons; and they will take the spoil of those who despoiled them and seize the plunder of those who plundered them, declares the Lord God.*[4]
>
> *On that day I will give Gog a burial ground there in Israel, the valley of those who pass by east of the sea, and it will block off those who would pass by. So they will bury Gog there with all his horde, and they will call it the valley of Hamon-gog. For seven months the house of Israel will be burying them in order to cleanse the land. Even all the people of the land will bury them; and it will be to their renown on the day that I glorify Myself,*[5] *declares the Lord God. They will set apart men who will constantly pass through the land, burying those who were passing through, even those left on the surface of the ground, in order to cleanse it. At the end of seven months they will make a search. As those who pass through the land pass through and anyone sees a man's bone, then he will set up a marker by it until the buriers have buried it in the valley of Hamon-gog. And even the name of the city will be Hamonah. So they will cleanse the land.'*
>
> *As for you, son of man, thus says the Lord God,*[6] *'Speak to every kind of bird and to every beast of the field, assemble and come, gather from every side to My sacrifice which I am going to sacrifice for you, as a great sacrifice on the mountains of Israel, that you may eat flesh and drink blood. You will eat the flesh of mighty men and drink the blood of the princes of the earth, as though they were rams, lambs, goats and bulls, all of them fatlings of Bashan. So you will eat fat until you are glutted, and drink blood until you are drunk, from My sacrifice which I have sacrificed for you. You will be glutted at My table with horses and charioteers, with mighty men and all the men of war, declares the Lord God.*
>
> *And I will set My glory among the nations; and all the nations will see My judgment which I have executed and My hand which I have laid on them. And the house of Israel will know that I am the Lord their God from that day onward*
>
> Ezekiel 39.9-22

The first seven months of the Millennium will be spent clearing away the dead from

---

4. This possibly describes a future weapons technology, whose material is flammable – maybe a development of today's carbon fibre
5. This suggests that the day of the Lord's glory does not take place until Israel has been cleansed, at least seven months after the great battle and Jesus' return. This day may identify the timing of the Marriage Supper of the Lamb
6. Is the Father speaking here to the Son?

CHAPTER FOURTEEN

Israel, a task in which every Israelite will participate. Most people will be familiar with the scenes of devastation following the Japanese earthquake and tsunami of March 2011. Emergency workers waded through the carnage, placing little flags to mark the location of the 19,000 bodies they found. Approximately 23 million tons of debris had to be removed and thousands of people were homeless. We cannot imagine the scenes after Armageddon, the greatest battle the world will ever see, nor estimate the damage that will have occurred leading up to it. However, if we take the more probable size of the army of Gog (see chapter 10) then there will be 1.2 million dead. Ezekiel's account reads like a newspaper article.

The chaotic scenes aren't just due to the battle though. We also know that the events of the Phobetron that led up to the Tribulation will have scorched, bruised and shattered the earth on a global scale. As we saw in chapter 11, Zechariah[7] foretells that when Jesus' feet touch the Mount of Olives, it will split in two, making a large valley that will stretch from Jerusalem down to the Dead Sea. A new river of fresh life-giving and healing water will flow out of Jerusalem both east to west.

---

7. Zechariah 14.4 & 8

Chapter Fourteen

Figure 47. Speculative location of the new Zion River valley and the Great Plain.

Ezekiel adds further detail to our picture:

the mountains also will be thrown down, the steep pathways will collapse and every wall will fall to the ground.[8] *Zechariah further declares All the land will be changed into a plain from Geba to Rimmon south of Jerusalem.*[9]

The area described, stretching about 40 miles north to south, is currently hill country. The God of Israel will morph the land surface to meet His requirements.

Let us enlarge our picture still further.

On that day the Lord made a covenant with Abram, saying, To your descendants I have given this land, from the river of Egypt as far as the great river, the river Euphrates

Gen 15.18

This promise was never fulfilled for Abraham. Even King David's kingdom did not extend this far. In the Millennium though, the borders of Israel will stretch

---
8. Ezekiel 38.20
9. Zechariah 14.10: As with many sites in ancient Israel, there are two possible locations for Rimmon. The picture above has assumed Rimmon is south of Jerusalem / Zion

Chapter Fourteen

from the Brook of Egypt in the south and west to the Euphrates in the north and east. Ezekiel[10] provides us with the western border on the Mediterranean, and also (possibly) the eastern border where the Euphrates meets the Persian Gulf. It may even extend south east throughout modern Arabia, but that would be pure speculation.

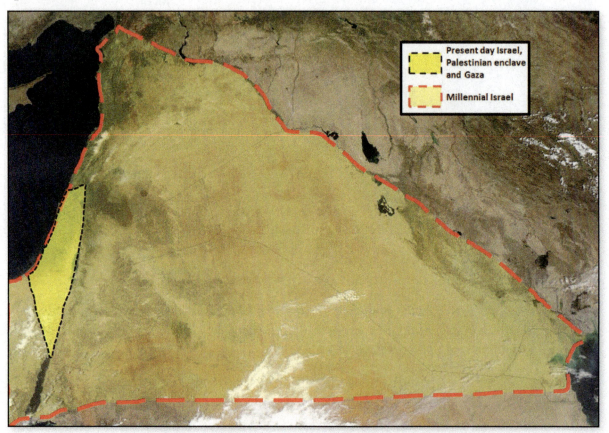

Figure 48. Speculative borders of Millennial Israel.

The work of restoration, reconstruction, repair and re-organisation will be the largest project ever performed by man. What better leader could we have than the God-man, Jesus Christ, our creator. This was the one who spent 18 years as a carpenter in Joseph's shop and looked out from Nazareth over the plain of Jezreel, the site of the then future battle.

We will now consider other aspects of the restoration. The table below presents

---

10. Ezekiel 47.18 & 20

a selected summary of what is to come. It describes how the ruined cities will be rebuilt and the desolated land will be ploughed to allow crops to be grown.

Produce of the Land

Those who study prophecy concerning modern Israel will know that many of these verses have already been partially fulfilled by Israel's return to the land. They have for example already rebuilt and repopulated many cities, and Israel is one of the world's largest producers of fruit. It is clear though that there is far more to come, and that what we presently see in Israel is a mere shadow of the good times ahead. If we take these verses together, then what emerges is an agricultural economy of arable farms, livestock and fisheries. These will produce grain, wine, oil, milk, medicines and honey. This is not an exhaustive list, but serves to illustrate how the Lord will restore the land to fruitfulness and blessing.

Millennial Produce of the Land

Reference	Blessing
Isaiah 51.3	Indeed, the LORD will comfort Zion. He will comfort all her waste places, and her wilderness He will make like Eden, and her desert like the garden of the LORD
Isaiah 55.13	Instead of the thorn* bush the cypress will come up, and instead of the nettle the myrtle will come up. (* Thorns and thistles are the marks of the cursed ground in Genesis 3.18. This has now been revoked. Gardeners everywhere will rejoice!)
Jeremiah 11.5	In order to confirm the oath which I swore to your forefathers, to give them a land flowing with milk and honey, as *it is* this day.' Then I said, Amen, O LORD
Jeremiah 31.12	They will come and shout for joy on the height of Zion, and they will be radiant over the bounty of the LORD—Over the grain and the new wine and the oil, and over the young of the flock and the herd. And their life will be like a watered garden, And they will never languish again
Jeremiah 31.28	As I have watched over them to pluck up, to break down, to overthrow, to destroy and to bring disaster, so I will watch over them to build and to plant, declares the LORD
Jeremiah 32.15	For thus says the LORD of hosts, the God of Israel, Houses and fields and vineyards will again be bought in this land
Ezekiel 36.8-9	But you, O mountains of Israel, you will put forth your branches and bear your fruit for My people Israel; for they will soon come. or, behold, I am for you, and I will turn to you, and you will be cultivated and sown

Reference	Blessing
Ezekiel 36.29	I will call for the grain and multiply it, and I will not bring a famine on you. I will multiply the fruit of the tree and the produce of the field, so that you will not receive again the disgrace of famine among the nations
Ezekiel 36.33-34	'Thus says the Lord GOD, On the day that I cleanse you from all your iniquities*, I will cause the cities to be inhabited, and the waste places will be rebuilt. The desolate land will be cultivated instead of being a desolation in the sight of everyone who passes by. (* The fruitfulness is related to the cleansing i.e. this prophecy is Millennial, although we have seen a partial fulfilment since 1948)
Ezekiel 47.9-10 (This describes the river that will flow out of Jerusalem, and infers that the Dead Sea will teem with sea fish)	It will come about that every living creature which swarms in every place where the river goes, will live. And there will be very many fish, for these waters go there and *the others* become fresh; so everything will live where the river goes. And it will come about that fishermen will stand beside it; from Engedi to Eneglaim* there will be a place for the spreading of nets. Their fish will be according to their kinds, like the fish of the Great Sea, very many (* En-Gedi lies on the western shore of the Dead Sea. The site of En Eglaim is uncertain)
Ezekiel 47.12	By the river on its bank, on one side and on the other, will grow all *kinds of* trees for food. Their leaves will not wither and their fruit will not fail. They will bear every month because their water flows from the sanctuary, and their fruit will be for food and their leaves for healing
Zechariah 10.1	The LORD who makes the storm clouds, and He will give them showers of rain, vegetation in the field to *each* man
Zechariah 14.20	In that day there will *be inscribed* on the bells of the horses, HOLY TO THE LORD.

Part 3 – Restoration of the City

The city of Jerusalem will have been largely destroyed. We know that every wall will have fallen due to the large earthquakes, and also that the city has been attacked and ravaged by Antichrist's army of Gog.

> *Thus says the LORD, 'Behold, I will restore the fortunes of the tents of Jacob, and have compassion on his dwelling places. And the city will be rebuilt on its ruin, and the palace will stand on its rightful place*
>
> Jeremiah 30.18

The ruin (or mound) that Jeremiah describes is the rubble created by the conflict. Jeremiah goes on:

> *Behold, days are coming, declares the Lord, when the city will be rebuilt for the Lord from the Tower of Hananel to the Corner Gate. The measuring line will go out farther straight ahead*

to the hill Gareb;[11] then it will turn to Goah. And the whole valley of the dead bodies and of the ashes, and all the fields as far as the brook Kidron, to the corner of the Horse Gate toward the east, shall be holy to the Lord; it will not be plucked up or overthrown anymore forever

Jeremiah 31.38-40

The area described encapsulates the current Old City of Jerusalem. This verse links the construction of the new city to the clearance of the slain and is clearly Millennial. We now turn to Isaiah

Foreigners will build up your walls, and their kings will minister to you. For in My wrath I struck you, and in My favor I have had compassion on you.

Your gates will be open continually. They will not be closed day or night, so that men may bring to you the wealth of the nations, with their kings led in procession

Isaiah 60.10-11

Jerusalem will be rebuilt by foreigners and paid for by Gentile wealth.

For Zion's sake I will not keep silent, and for Jerusalem's sake I will not keep quiet, until her righteousness goes forth like brightness, and her salvation like a torch that is burning. The nations will see your righteousness, and all kings your glory; And you will be called by a new name which the mouth of the LORD will designate. You will also be a crown of beauty in the hand of the LORD, and a royal diadem in the hand of your God. It will no longer be said to you, Forsaken, nor to your land will it any longer be said, Desolate. But you will be called, My delight is in her, and your land, Married, for the LORD delights in you, and to Him your land will be married. For as a young man marries a virgin, so your sons will marry you, and as the bridegroom rejoices over the bride, so your God will rejoice over you.

On your walls, O Jerusalem, I have appointed watchmen.[12] All day and all night they will never keep silent. You who remind the LORD, take no rest for yourselves, and give Him no rest until He establishes and makes Jerusalem a praise in the earth.

The LORD has sworn by His right hand and by His strong arm, I will never again give your grain as food for your enemies, nor will foreigners drink your new wine for which you have labored. But those who garner it will eat it and praise the LORD, and those who gather it will drink it in the courts of My sanctuary.

Go through, go through the gates, clear the way for the people. Build up, build up the highway. Remove the stones, lift up a standard over the peoples. Behold, the Lord has proclaimed to the

---

11. The hill Gareb has been associated with Betheza to the north east of the city. The location of Goath is uncertain
12. The role of the watchman was explored in chapter 13. Here we see the job description

Chapter Fourteen

end of the earth, say to the daughter of Zion, Lo, your salvation comes, behold His reward is with Him, and His recompense before Him.

And they will call them, The holy people, the redeemed of the LORD, and you will be called, Sought out, a city not forsaken.

Isaiah 62.1-12

A New Name

Isaiah declares that Jerusalem is to be called by a new name. He is not alone in this assertion.

New Names of Millennial Jerusalem

Reference	Name
Isaiah 62.2	And you will be called by a new name, which the mouth of the LORD will designate
Isaiah 62.4	It will no longer be said to you, Forsaken, nor to your land will it any longer be said, Desolate. But you will be called, My delight is in her, (*Hephzibah*), and your land, Married (*Beulah*). For the LORD delights in you. (*Hephzibah* is Probably a reference to marriage. *Beuhlah* means married)
Isaiah 62.12	And you will be called, 'Sought out'
	A city not forsaken
Isaiah 66.1	Heaven is My throne and the earth is My footstool. Where then is a house you could build for Me? And where is a place that I may rest?
Isaiah 66.20	My holy mountain Jerusalem
Jeremiah 3.17	At that time they will call Jerusalem 'The Throne of the LORD,'
Jeremiah 33.16	In those days Judah will be saved and Jerusalem will dwell in safety; and this is *the name* by which she will be called: the LORD is our righteousness.' (Jehovah Tsidkenu)
Ezekiel 48.35	the name of the city from *that* day *shall be*, 'The LORD is there' (Jehovah Shammah. It is interesting to compare this name with Isaiah 62.4, using the Hebrew word *shamamah* for 'desolate'. In what seems like a Hebrew play on words, Jerusalem changes from *desolation*, to the 'Lord is there'. This is a wonderful picture of our own salvation and restoration)
Zechariah 8.3	Zion
	The City of Truth
	The Mountain of the Lord of Hosts
	The Holy Mountain

Scriptural names reveal nature. When a name is changed, it infers a new status or role. Abram ('exalted father') became Abraham ('father of a multitude') to signify how El Shaddai had changed and blessed him.[13] Jacob became Israel. Saul of Tarsus became Paul. Jerusalem's new names reveal her new status as the permanent earthly residence of the Lord and the seat of His government. One day, you too will receive a new name, written on a white stone and presented to you by Jesus Himself.[14]

The Natural Realm

It is not just the land that is healed, but the animal kingdom will change too.

And the

- *wolf will dwell with the lamb, and the*
- *leopard will lie down with the young goat, and the*
- *calf and the young lion and the fatling together. And a little boy will lead them. Also the*
- *cow and the bear will graze, their young will lie down together, and the*
- *lion will eat straw like the ox. The nursing child will play by the hole of the*
- *cobra, and the weaned child will put his hand on the*
- *viper's den.*

They will not hurt or destroy in all My holy mountain, for the earth will be full of the knowledge of the Lord as the waters cover the sea

Isaiah 11.6-9

The view from the top

Our final glimpse of the new city is from the top of a high mountain, sitting alongside Ezekiel.

In the visions of God He brought me into the land of Israel and set me on a very high mountain,

---

13. The changing of Abram's name required the addition of the 5th letter of the Hebrew alphabet '*heh*'. Hebrew letters are also used as numbers, and 5 is the number of grace. If one speaks the word '*heh*' it sounds like breathing, which is what the Lord did when he breathed his new name and identity into Abraham
14. Revelation 2.17

Chapter Fourteen

> *and on it to the south there was a structure like a city*
>
> Ezekiel 40.2

> *This is the law of the house: its entire area on the top of the mountain all around shall be most holy. Behold, this is the law of the house*
>
> Ezekiel 43.12

It seems then that the city rests on the southern slopes of the mountain, and that the summit has been reserved as a sacred area for the new Sanctuary.

Part 4 – Restoration of worship

In chapter 8 we considered the progression of Temples that the children of Israel have used to worship God. The Temples of Solomon and Herod were impressive, but nothing to compare with what is to come. Around 592BC, whilst Ezekiel was exiled in Babylon, he received a vision. We have just read how he was taken to a high mountain to enjoy the view of the new city. Let us see what followed:

> *So He brought me there; and behold, there was a man whose appearance was like the appearance of bronze, with a line of flax and a measuring rod in his hand; and he was standing in the gateway. The man said to me, Son of man, see with your eyes, hear with your ears, and give attention to all that I am going to show you; for you have been brought here in order to show it to you. Declare to the house of Israel all that you see.*
>
> Ezekiel 40.3-4

The last 8 chapters of Ezekiel describe the new city and new Sanctuary in Israel. Before we proceed we need to confirm which period Ezekiel is describing; the context of the prophecy; the location and geography; and the purpose of the Temple.

Ezekiel 40-48 – Prophetic Context

In the preceding Chapters 36-37, we hear Ezekiel describe the regathering of Israel into its own land, out of the context of the valley of dry bones, the Nazi death camps. We have already seen how from the mid-1940's, the Jews poured into their promised land. Chapters 38-39 then describe how Gog and Magog[15] will descend upon Israel to destroy her, but are themselves destroyed by the Lord. These mirror the events

---

15. Gog and Magog will feature again at the end of the Millennium (Revelation 20.8).

described in both Revelation and Zechariah. We can therefore be confident that the structures described in chapters 40-48 are to follow the return of Christ, and take place in Israel during the Millennium.

Geographical Context

Ezekiel presents us with a highly detailed plan and dimensions. The key to appreciating these structures described is to understand their size and scale. As was common in the ancient near-east, the measurement was given in 'reeds' and 'great cubits'. The 19th century theologian EW Bullinger advises us that:

- A great cubit[16] is 25.025" or 0.63M
- a measuring rod or reed[17] is 12' 6" or 3.8M

Applying these measurements to Ezekiel's vision allows us to establish the size and scale of the Sanctuary.

---

16. There are differing interpretations of the length of a cubit, and this is complicated by the fact that there was more than one standard in place in Bible times (see 2 Chronicles 3.3). The 'Royal' or 'Temple' or 'great' cubit used here by Ezekiel (because it concerned the Royal Sanctuary) was equivalent to seven handbreadths, on which Bullinger's calculations are based. Modern archaeology has also identified a shorter cubit of 20-21" based on six handbreadths
17. The 'measuring reed' is defined as '6 cubits and a handbreadth' (Ezekiel 40.5)

Chapter Fourteen

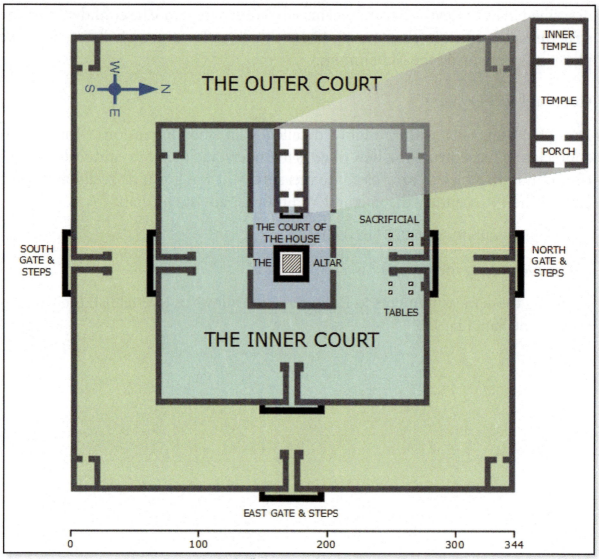

Figure 49. Ezekiel's Sanctuary according to Bullinger.

Study of Psalm 48 now takes on a completely different meaning, and jumps off the page as it tells us to walk around Zion, wander all about her, number her towers, look well at her bulwarks, and think about her palaces. One day soon, we will. According to Isaiah, you will also eat a picnic[18] and enjoy some very fine wine in the courts of the Sanctuary. As you gaze around from your mountain-top vista, you

---

18. Isaiah 62.8-9

Chapter Fourteen

will be able to consider how Israel has been restored.

The Sanctuary is located within a larger 'holy' district, set apart for the Lord, and known as the Oblation.[19] Again, based on Ezekiel's plans and measurements, we are able to construct the zones or "Holy District" in which the Sanctuary is located.

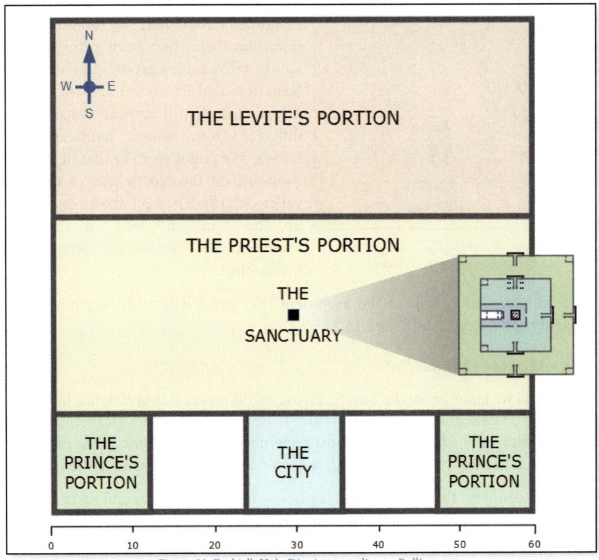

Figure 50. Ezekiel's Holy District according to Bullinger.

---

19. An oblation is an offering. See Ezekiel 48.20

CHAPTER FOURTEEN

Having established the scope of the greater district, it will be fascinating to speculate how this fits into the local geography around Jerusalem. If we overlay the plan of the Holy District over present-day Israel we can appreciate the scale of the redevelopment. In letting our imagination loose here, we should remind ourselves that when Jesus returns there will be tremendous geological changes to Jerusalem and its surrounds. There is no doubt that it will appear considerably different from today's landscape and layout. We might surmise that the City of Zion sits on the North side of the new valley described in Zechariah 14, which is on the southern slope of the holy Mountain. The Sanctuary is located upon the summit.

Figure 51. Approximate scope of the Millennial Holy District of Israel.

This adds further weight to the argument that Israel will push way beyond its present borders in the Millennium.

Purpose of the Temple

So what do we know about the Sanctuary, the '4th Temple'? It is Millennial, located in an enlarged Israel, and concerns the twelve tribes of Israel,[20] although there are clues that Gentiles will be involved. We must remember that at the time of the prophecy, the Church had not yet been revealed, so would not be explicitly mentioned here.

Jeremiah confirms that the temple has priests, an altar, offerings and sacrifices:

> *For thus says the LORD, 'David shall never lack a man to sit on the throne of the house of Israel; and the Levitical priests shall never lack a man before Me to offer burnt offerings, to burn grain offerings and to prepare sacrifices continually'*
>
> Jeremiah 33.17-18

---

20. Ezekiel 47.13

Ezekiel 45.13 – 46.24 describes the rituals in detail, including Sabbaths, sacrifices, burnt offerings, trespass and sin offerings, preparation of sacrifices, and appointed feast days. The Feasts of Tabernacles and Passover are to be celebrated, so it is clear that we will be remembering how the Lord delivered His people out of bondage.

This system seems at odds with our view that the Dispensation of Law had finished at the Cross, so how can this be? Surely, Christ's sacrificial death was a once-for-all offering to take away the sins of the world, and therefore there is no further need for a temple? We are provided with clues however, and there are suggestions of certain differences between what Ezekiel saw and the Mosaic Law:

Mosaic Law v 4th Temple ritual

Mosaic Law	4th Temple
Priest had to be consecrated (Lev 8.1-10)	Priest was already consecrated i.e. in a state of permanent holiness (Ezekiel 43.25)
Altar anointed with oil to symbolise the Holy Spirit (Lev 8.11)	No anointing – the Holy Spirit does not need to be represented as He is already present
Offerings are personal i.e. for the atonement and forgiveness of individuals	Offerings are national i.e. as an act of worship on behalf of the Nation of Israel, rather than for forgiveness

It seems therefore that there will be a new system of worship and sacrifice in the Millennium. This will not be to earn salvation, for that has already been freely given by the Lord and received by the saints. We will all be in a permanent state of holiness: redeemed, cleansed; sanctified; justified and set apart to God. We also know that the Lord will be present in person in His Sanctuary to receive our worship.

Thus says the LORD of hosts,

Behold, a man whose name is (the) Branch, for He will branch out from where He is; and He will build the temple of the LORD. Yes, it is He who will build the temple of the LORD, and He who will bear the honor and sit and rule on His throne. Thus, He will be a priest on His throne, and the counsel of peace will be between the two offices

Zechariah 6.12-13

It seems then that the Law was a mere foreshadowing of what is yet to come in the Millennium. It was only ever intended as a temporary and interim measure.

Chapter Fourteen

It has been described as a teacher or 'governess', whose purpose was to train Israel in the difference between right and wrong, the holy and the profane. It would be a mistake to consider that the method of worship in the Millennium will just be a 'carry over' or residue from the Age of Law. Instead, it points to something better, a new covenant in the future. Clearly, there is much that we do not understand, as we presently *'see through a glass darkly'*, but there is coming a time when we will see *'face to face'*. It is a mystery yet to be revealed.

Under the Law, only Moses saw the Lord face to face. Here, we will all see Him. Ezekiel declares that the name of the new city will be 'the Lord is there' or Jehovah Shammah. It will therefore be His residence, where He dwells amongst His people.

It will not just be the children of Israel who come up to worship here.

> *Then it will come about that any who are left of all the nations that went against Jerusalem will go up from year to year to worship the King, the LORD of hosts, and to celebrate the Feast of Booths. And it will be that whichever of the families of the earth does not go up to Jerusalem to worship the King, the LORD of hosts, there will be no rain on them. If the family of Egypt does not go up or enter, then no rain will fall on them; it will be the plague with which the LORD smites the nations who do not go up to celebrate the Feast of Booths. This will be the punishment of Egypt, and the punishment of all the nations who do not go up to celebrate the Feast of Booths*
>
> Zechariah 14.16-19

The families of the earth (that is Christians) are invited too. Hallelujah!

The 4th Temple or Sanctuary is confused by some with the 3rd Temple. We have already shown that the 4th cannot exist until the Millennium, and the 3rd will have been desecrated by Antichrist during the Great Tribulation, and will probably be destroyed by the great earthquake that occurs on Christ's return.

One final thought: at the end of the Millennium the earth and heavens, including this 4th Temple, will pass away. The new heavens and new earth will then be created by the Lord and the New Jerusalem will descend out of Heaven.

The Apostle John describes this day at the end of time:

> *I heard a loud voice from the throne, saying, Behold, the tabernacle (dwelling) of God is among men, and He will dwell among them, and they shall be His people, and God Himself will be among them*
>
> Revelation 21.3

Chapter Fourteen

I saw no temple in it, for the Lord God the Almighty and the Lamb are its temple
Revelation 21.22

It seems then that the ultimate purpose of Tabernacle, Temples and the Millennial Sanctuary is to prepare the redeemed for the time when they would no longer be needed.

Part 5 – Restoration of the People

So far, we have looked at the restoration of places: the land, the city and the place of worship. It is now time to consider how the peoples are to be restored. In earlier chapters we saw how when the Lord comes we will be caught up into the air, and our bodies changed in the twinkling of an eye. Those who returned with Christ from heaven will receive their resurrection bodies then too. No more sickness, infirmities, disease, old age or death! What can we discern about life in the Millennium?

Rewards and Recompense

We considered eternal judgment in chapter 12, but will briefly summarise them again here. These included

- the dragnet, and separation of wheat and tares – to separate true from false believers
- The Throne of Christ's Glory – a judgment based on gentile treatment of the Jews
- The Bema / Judgment Seat of Christ – an assessment for reward, based on the Christian believers quality of service

It is reasonable to assume that the first two judgments take place immediately after Christ's return, with the Bema following. Daniel 12.12 tells us that those who attain to the 1,335 days are blessed. We might presume that this indicates those who have come through the above.

Your status here depends upon your previous conduct. The last will be first.

Chapter Fourteen

The first will be last.[21] Servant and slave will be the greatest.[22] Those who invested their minas well will govern cities.[23] Those who invested talents wisely will receive more. Those who left their homes, families, land, and were persecuted will receive a hundredfold increase, as well as eternal life.[24] Selflessness, servanthood and honest satisfying endeavour will be the norm in this 'new age' society.

Marriage Supper

We saw in Isaiah 62.4 that the new names of Jerusalem speak of one who was forsaken, now being married. This is consistent with the promised invitation of the Saints to the Marriage Supper of the Lamb: Jesus is the Bridegroom and Israel and His Church the Bride.

Righteous Government

On a practical level, the world will need to be organised and governed. How will this work?

> *For a child will be born to us, a son will be given to us, and the government will rest on His shoulders. And His name will be called Wonderful Counsellor, Mighty God, Eternal Father, Prince of Peace. There will be no end to the increase of His government or of peace, on the throne of David and over his kingdom, to establish it and to uphold it with justice and righteousness from then on and forevermore.*
>
> Isaiah 9.6-7

No more democracy. No more dictatorship. No more corrupt, self-serving politicians. No more injustice. No more crime. Instead, we will have an ever-increasing righteous theocratic government and ever increasing peace. There can be no peace without righteousness and justice, and in the Millennium we will have them all. The King is here and His Kingdom has come.

The Father will decide who sits at Jesus' right and left hand.[25]

---

21. Matthew 20.16
22. Matthew 20.25-27
23. Luke 19.11-27
24. Mark 10.29-31
25. Matthew 20.23

CHAPTER FOURTEEN

David raised up

The reference to David's throne is intriguing:

> *Then I will set over them one shepherd, My servant David, and he will feed them; he will feed them himself and be their shepherd*
>
> Ezekiel 34.23

> *My servant David will be king over them, and they will all have one shepherd; and they will walk in My ordinances and keep My statutes and observe them. They will live on the land that I gave to Jacob My servant, in which your fathers lived; and they will live on it, they, and their sons and their sons' sons, forever; and David My servant will be their prince forever*
>
> Ezekiel 37.24-25

> *Incline your ear and come to Me. Listen, that you may live, and I will make an everlasting covenant with you, according to the faithful mercies shown to David.*
>
> *Behold, I have made him a witness to the peoples, a leader and commander for the peoples. Behold, you will call a nation you do not know, and a nation which knows you not will run to you, because of the LORD your God, even the Holy One of Israel. For He has glorified you*
>
> Isaiah 55.3-5

> *But they shall serve the Lord their God and David their king, whom I will raise up for them*
>
> Jeremiah 30.9

If we take these verses literally, as we should, then the message is that David, Israel's greatest-ever king, will have a position of leadership and command in Christ's government, enacting statutes and judgments on behalf of the Lord. If this is so, it is a remarkable demonstration of the grace and mercy of God. David, due to his murder of Uriah, was not allowed to build the Temple. Yet in the future Kingdom of God, it seems that he will inhabit the Lord's Palace as His executive.

We are also told that nations unknown to them will run to Israel. I would suggest that this can only be the Church. This is also suggested by Zechariah:

> *So many peoples and mighty nations will come to seek the LORD of hosts in Jerusalem and to entreat the favor of the LORD.' Thus says the LORD of hosts, 'In those days ten men from all the nations will grasp the garment of a Jew, saying, Let us go with you, for we have heard that God is with you.*
>
> Zech 8.22-23

Chapter Fourteen

O Jacob My servant, do not fear, declares the LORD, For I am with you. For I will make a full end of all the nations where I have driven you, yet I will not make a full end of you

Jeremiah 46.8

The Lord will make an end to all the nations to which the Jews were driven. There are very few nations today that do not have some Jewish exiles amongst their populations. It looks like there will be many new nations in the Millennium!

Resurrection bodies

The Sadducees asked Jesus about marriage relationships in the resurrection. Here is His response:

The sons of this age marry and are given in marriage, but those who are considered worthy to attain to that age and the resurrection from the dead, neither marry nor are given in marriage; for they cannot even die anymore, because they are like angels, and are sons of God, being sons of the resurrection

Luke 20.34-36

Our resurrection bodies will be like those of the angels. This means we will have new powers and abilities that we could only dream of when we were human. When Jesus was in His resurrected body He was able to walk through walls, and suddenly appear or disappear. This should be a lot of fun, and I can't wait to try it. Jesus' body was solid flesh though, as Thomas was able to put his finger into His wounds, and Jesus was able to eat a piece of broiled fish after His resurrection.

The principal chapter in the New Testament describing resurrection is 1 Corinthians 15.[26] Here, Paul describes:

So also is the resurrection of the dead. It is
- *sown a perishable body, it is raised an imperishable body; it is*
- *sown in dishonor, it is raised in glory; it is*
- *sown in weakness, it is raised in power; it is*
- *sown a natural body, it is raised a spiritual body.*

If there is a natural body, there is also a spiritual body

(vv42-44)

At present, our 'natural' bodies are severely limited by the influence of our carnal

---
26. Note the eight elements in the verse. Eight, being 7+1 is the number of resurrection, and signifies a new beginning.

mind and the aging process. In the Millennium, your spiritual body will be spirit-led and will never age. This is the body which will be our new vehicle to serve God and enjoy eternal life.

> *For our citizenship is in heaven, from which also we eagerly wait for a Savior, the Lord Jesus Christ; who will transform the body of our humble state into conformity with the body of His glory, by the exertion of the power that He has even to subject all things to Himself*
>
> Philippians 3.20-21

It will be transformed and conformed to the likeness of Jesus' body. This is further attested by John[27]: *we know that when He appears,* **we will be like Him**, *because we will see Him just as He is.*

The bodies of some will shine with glory:

> *Those who have insight will shine brightly like the brightness of the expanse of heaven, and those who lead the many to righteousness, like the stars forever and ever*
>
> Daniel 12.3

There are mysteries yet to be revealed in the Millennium:

> *I will multiply men on you, all the house of Israel, all of it; and the cities will be inhabited and the waste places will be rebuilt. I will multiply on you man and beast; and they will increase and be fruitful; and I will cause you to be inhabited as you were formerly and will treat you better than at the first. Thus you will know that I am the LORD*
>
> Ezekiel 36.10-11

Where does the multiplication of the house of Israel come from? There are many references to children in the Millennial prophecies, yet Jesus said we would not marry. We don't know, so will just have to wait and see.

There are many other things of which we can be certain of though:

- Ezekiel 36.12: there will be no more bereavement
- Ezekiel 36.26: the children of Israel will receive a new heart and new spirit (Christians already have this)
- Jeremiah 31.13-14: there will be a lot of dancing, rejoicing and satisfaction
- Jeremiah 33.11: we will hear the voice of joy

---

27. 1John 3.2

CHAPTER FOURTEEN

So the ransomed of the LORD will return, and come with joyful shouting to Zion, and everlasting joy will be on their heads. They will obtain gladness and joy, and sorrow and sighing will flee away

Isaiah 51.11

What about the Church?

If the above seems rather Israel-centric, that is because it is. The centre of the world is now not Washington, Beijing or London but the newly-named Jerusalem. World government flows not through the UN, but from Israel. The good news though is that as Christians we are joint heirs with the remnant of Israel, the Jews.

*For **as many as are the promises of God, in Him they are yes;** therefore also through Him is our Amen to the glory of God through us. Now He who establishes us with you in Christ and anointed us is God, who also **sealed us and gave us the Spirit in our hearts as a pledge***

2 Corinthians 1.20-22

The Holy Spirit in you is your personal guarantee that each and every promise He made to Israel is yours, now and then. And just to provide further confirmation

*For **you are all sons of God through faith in Christ Jesus.** For all of you who were baptized into Christ have clothed yourselves with Christ. There is **neither Jew nor Greek,** there is neither slave nor free man, there is neither male nor female; for you are **all one in Christ Jesus.** And **if you belong to Christ, then you are Abraham's descendants, heirs according to promise***

Galatians 3.26-29

As joint heirs you stand to inherit **all** that Israel was promised with your new Jewish brothers and sisters in Christ.

Praise the Lord!

Part 6 – Final Judgment

We now reach the end of the Millennium. We have enjoyed a thousand years of peace and tranquillity. We have received further healing and restoration of mind and emotions. We have forgotten past hurts and disappointment. We have been trained and prepared for eternity. But first, the Lord has some final business to attend to:

> *When the thousand years are completed, Satan will be released from his prison, and will come out to deceive the nations which are in the four corners of the earth, Gog and Magog, to gather them together for the war; the number of them is like the sand of the seashore. And they came up on the broad plain of the earth and surrounded the camp of the saints and the beloved city, and fire came down from heaven and devoured them. And the devil who deceived them was thrown into the lake of fire and brimstone, where the beast and the false prophet are also; and they will be tormented day and night forever and ever.*
>
> Revelation 20.7-10

Satan's ability to deceive the nations results in rebellion and a very short conflict. Who these nations are, and how they came to allow themselves to be deceived is another mystery. The name of Gog and Magog (as we saw previously with Armageddon) represent a confederation of Godless and rebellious nations under Satanic leadership. We do know though why the Lord has allowed this to happen. In the great resurrection chapter, Paul explains:

> *But each in his own order: Christ the first fruits, after that those who are Christ's at His coming, then comes the end, when He hands over the kingdom to the God and Father, when He has abolished all rule and all authority and power.* ***For He must reign until He has put all His enemies under His feet.*** *The last enemy that will be abolished is death. For* ***He has put all things in subjection under His feet.*** *But when He says, All things are put in subjection, it is evident that He is excepted who put all things in subjection to Him.*
>
> *When all things are subjected to Him, then the Son Himself also will be subjected to the One who subjected all things to Him, so* ***that God may be all in all***
>
> 1 Corinthians 15.23-28

This passage summarises God's overall plan for Christ to deliver the Kingdom to His Father, now at the great culmination of the ages, or *fullness of the times*:

> *He made known to us the mystery of His will, according to His kind intention which He purposed in Him with a view to an administration suitable to the fullness of the times, that is, the summing up of all things in Christ, things in the heavens and things on the earth*
>
> Ephesians 1.9-10

Following the destruction of Gog and Magog, and Satan's consignment to the Lake of Fire, it is time for the final resurrection of the dead and Great White Throne judgment (see chapter 12). This will take place in the valley of Jehoshaphat, to the east of Jerusalem where the Kidron brook used to flow. The earthquakes at Christ's return will have reshaped and possibly enlarged this area into a giant arena to allow the congregation of the dead to be gathered there. The dead, both great and small, are now reunited with their physical bodies to receive their final verdict. Everyone will bow their knee and confess that Jesus Christ is Lord.

> *For behold, in those days and at that time, when I restore the fortunes of Judah and Jerusalem, I will gather all the nations and bring them down to the valley of Jehoshaphat. Then I will enter into judgment with them there on behalf of My people and My inheritance, Israel, whom they have scattered among the nations*
>
> *Let the nations be aroused and come up to the valley of Jehoshaphat, for there I will sit to judge all the surrounding nations. Put in the sickle, for the harvest is ripe. Come, tread, for the wine press is full. The vats overflow, for their wickedness is great. Multitudes, multitudes in the valley of decision!*
>
> *For the day of the LORD is near in the valley of decision*
>
> Joel 3.1-2 & 12-14
>
> *Then I saw a great white throne and Him who sat upon it, from whose presence earth and heaven fled away, and no place was found for them. And I saw the dead, the great and the small, standing before the throne, and books were opened; and another book was opened, which is the book of life; and the dead were judged from the things which were written in the books, according to their deeds. And the sea gave up the dead which were in it, and death and Hades gave up the dead which were in them; and they were judged, every one of them according to their deeds. Then death and Hades were thrown into the lake of fire. This is the second death, the lake of fire. And if anyone's name was not found written in the book of life, he was thrown into the lake of fire*
>
> Revelation 20.11-15

All the enemies of God have now been brought under Christ's feet, the Kingdom has been established and the last enemy, death, has been cast into the Lake of Fire.

Part 7 – All things new - New heavens and new earth

We now witness another 'day of the Lord', that will exceed everything that has gone before:

> *But the day of the Lord will come like a thief, in which the heavens will pass away with a roar and the elements will be destroyed with intense heat, and the earth and its works will be*

burned up.

Since all these things are to be destroyed in this way, what sort of people ought you to be in holy conduct and godliness, looking for and hastening the coming of the day of God, because of which the heavens will be destroyed by burning, and the elements will melt with intense heat! But according to His promise we are looking for new heavens and a new earth, in which righteousness dwells

2 Peter 3.10-12

We cannot confuse this day with the day of Jesus' return, as here we have 'all things dissolved' to make way for the new heavens and new earth. So the heavens and earth are consumed by fire, and elements are reconstituted back to the atomic level and then remade. Turn back to chapter 3 and read the final passages of Revelation. This is a whole new beginning. The New Jerusalem, a 1,500 mile-wide cube and filled with the glory of God, now descends out of the new heaven to the new earth. There is no need for the sun or moon, because the Lamb is its light. There is no need for a temple, because the Lord God Almighty and Lamb are its temple. There is no longer any sea. There are no more tears, death, mourning, crying, or pain, as the former things have passed away. There is no longer any night, nor any curse. The dwelling of God is with men. Forever.

The only way to gain entrance here is if your name has been written in the Lamb's Book of Life.

He who testifies to these things says, Yes, I am coming quickly. Amen. Come, Lord Jesus.

The grace of the Lord Jesus be with all. Amen

Revelation 22.20-21

CHAPTER FOURTEEN

The Sinner's Prayer – an open invitation

If whilst reading this book you have been convicted of your personal sin, and a realisation that you do not have the assurance of salvation, and have never committed your life to the Lord, then the invitation is 'come'.

Jesus Christ came into the world to save sinners. He died once, for all of us, at the Cross. The grave couldn't hold Him and He rose again on the third day. He is now seated at His Father's right hand.

*if you **confess with your mouth** Jesus as Lord, and **believe in your heart** that God raised Him from the dead, you will be saved*

Romans 10.9

"Lord Jesus Christ / Yeshua Messiach,

I know that I am a sinner and have fallen short of Your standards. I recognise that You came to earth and lived a perfect, sinless life. You took every one of my sins upon Yourself on the cross, so that I could be reconciled with your Father. Your shed blood cleanses me from all sin. I know that You have risen from the dead, and now sit at your Father's right hand where You intercede for me. Right now I decide to repent of my sin and acknowledge and confess You as my Lord, my Saviour and my God.

Amen"

If you have prayed this prayer, you now need to seek out a local Christian or Messianic fellowship for further teaching.

Well done, good and faithful servant.

You have been faithful over a few things, so I will make you ruler over much

Enter now into the joy of thy Lord

Bibliography

Title	Author
The Carta Bible Atlas	Aheroni, Yohanon. Avi-Yonah, Michael. Rainey, Anson F.. Safrai, Ze'ev. Notley, R.Stephen
The Carta Jerusalem Atlas	Bahat, Dan
A Historical Atlas of the Jewish People	Barnavi, Eli
The Jerusalem Temple	Backhouse, Robert Rev
How to enjoy the Bible	Bullinger, E.W.
Number in Scripture	Bullinger, E.W.
The Companion Bible	Bullinger, E.W.
Witness of the Stars	Bullinger, E.W.
A Guide to Biblical Sites in Greece and Turkey	Fant & Reddish
Rome and Jerusalem	Goodman, Martin
Josephus – The essential works	Maier, Paul. L
Evidence that demands a verdict	McDowell, Josh
Fields of Fire	Notholt, Stuart
The world turned upside down	Phillips, Melanie
Foundation Series	Prince, Derek
The Destiny of Israel and the Church	Prince, Derek
The Quest	Ritmeyer, Leen
A Test of Time	Rohl, David
The Lost Testament	Rohl, David
Jerusalem – The Biography	Sebag Montefiore, Simon
Satellite Bible Atlas	Schlegel, William
After America	Steyn, Mark
Vines Expository Dictionary of New Testament Words	Vine, W.E.
God's Plan to protect His people in the coming depression	Wilkerson, David

Picture References and Credits

Figure	Reference / Credit
1	Worshippers at the Western retaining wall of Herod's Temple Credit: Israeli Ministry of Tourism www.goisrael.com
2	Judaean Prutah from the time of Herod Archelaus. The lowest denomination coin in circulation at the time of Christ. Credit: Neil Turner
3	Herod's temple looking west (HolyLand Hotel Model). The Court of Women, the location of the first prophecy, is the open area in front of and below the Sanctuary. The shofarim were located in the porticoes around its sides. Credit: Hadar Sela ©2013
4	View from Mount of Olives looking south-west towards the Temple Mount. This position was Jesus' probable perspective for the second prophecy. Credit: Public Domain. Library of Congress http://lcweb2.loc.gov/service/pnp/ppmsca/02700/02705v.jpg
5	Jesus' final prophecies - Word cloud Credit: Neil Turner
6	The Siege and Destruction of Jerusalem by the Romans under the Command of Titus. Credit: David Roberts 1796-1864. Public domain.
7	VESPASIAN. 69-79 AD. Æ Sestertius. Minted to celebrate Rome's victory over Judaea Credit: Classical Numismatic Group, Inc. http://www.cngcoins.com GNU 1.2
8	Destruction of the Jewish Temple. Credit: Nicolas Poussin 1594-1665. Public domain.
9	The Destruction of the Temple of Jerusalem. Credit: Francesco Hayez. Public domain.
10	Broken pavement at the SW corner of the Temple Mount. Here the Roman soldiers threw down massive building blocks of the Temple's Royal Portico to shatter the pavement of the street below. Credit: www.anneinpt.wordpress.com
11	Titus's Arch in Rome shows the 'triumph' that followed the destruction of Jerusalem. Credit: Public Domain.
12	The Dome of the Rock Credit: Israeli Ministry of Tourism. www.goisrael.com
13	Unripe Figs from Israel Credit Hadar Sela ©2013
14	John on Patmos. Credit: Abigail Joy Bowen ©2013
15	The Valleys of Jerusalem and the Name of God. Credit: Artwork by Dr. Leen Ritmeyer ©2013
16	The Sun Credit: NASA
17	Revelation: Word Cloud. Credit: Neil Turner.
18	The 7 Seals. Credit: Abigail Joy Bowen ©2013
19	The 7 Trumpets Credit: Abigail Joy Bowen © 2013

Figure	Reference / Credit
20	The 7 Bowls Credit: Abigail Joy Bowen © 2013
21	The ash plume of Eyjafjallajokull, Iceland Credit: NASA
22	Earthrise. Credit: NASA
23	Lion with Eagles wings Credit: Abigail Joy Bowen © 2013
24	The Balfour Declaration Credit: Public Domain.
25	The Bear. Credit: Abigail Joy Bowen © 2013
26	The Leopard. Credit: Abigail Joy Bowen © 2013
27	Storm Clouds Credit: NOAA
28	Asteroid DA14. Credit: NASA
29	Significant earthquakes Based on USGS database.
30	The Western Wall Plaza at night. The ashlar stones that formed the retaining wall of Herod's temple are the larger blocks that extend two-thirds of the way up the wall. Credit: Hadar Sela ©2013
31	Wild Olives trees in Israel Credit: Hadar Sela ©2013
32	The 3rd Temple – showing speculative location between the Dome of the Rock and Mosque of Omar. Developed from an original image by Hadar Sela.
33	Model of the Tabernacle, as seen in Israel, Timna Park. Credit: Credit Ruk7. Licensed under the Creative Commons Attribution-Share Alike 2.5 Generic licence from https://en.wikipedia.org/wiki/File:Stiftshuette_Modell_Timnapark.jpg
34	Altar to Zeus in the Pergamonmuseum, Berlin. Credit: Jan Mehlich. Licensed under the Creative Commons Attribution-Share Alike 2.5 Generic licence from http://commons.wikimedia.org/wiki/File:Berlin_-_Pergamonmuseum_-_Altar_01.jpg
35	The Beast. Credit: Abigail Joy Bowen © 2013
36	Lightning. Credit: NOAA
37	The Phobetron: lightning, fire and smoke. Credit: Abigail Joy Bowen © 2013
38	Bar Code. Credit: Public Domain.
39	The Jezreel Valley and Lower Galilee. Credit: © Schlegel Satellite Bible Atlas. Used by Permission.

Figure	Reference / Credit
40	Looking north-east from Har Megiddo across Highway 66 and over the plain of Jezreel. Nazareth, Jesus' home is ten miles away on the left horizon. The Hill of Moreh is right of centre, with Tabor to its left. This vast plain will be the battlefield for Armageddon. Credit: Hadar Sela ©2013
41	The route to Armageddon Credit: Neil Turner.
42	Sun through the trees at Galilee. Credit: Tal Glick Israeli Ministry of Tourism. www.goisrael.com
43	The Plain of Jezreel from the mountains of Gilboa. Credit: Hadar Sela ©2013
44	Michelangelo – extract from the Last Judgment Public Domain.
45	End Time Survivor. Credit: Abigail Joy Bowen © 2013
46	Looking towards Mount Zion. Credit: Abigail Joy Bowen © 2013
47	Speculative location of the new Zion River valley and the Great Plain. Credit: Modified from NASA image.
48	Speculative borders of Millennial Israel Credit: Modified from NASA image.
49	Ezekiel's Sanctuary according to Bullinger. Credit: Ruth Turner ©2013
50	Ezekiel's Holy District according to Bullinger. Credit: Ruth Turner ©2013
51	Approximate scope of the Millennial Holy District of Israel. Credit: Original image from NASA modified by Ruth Turner.

CPSIA information can be obtained at www.ICGtesting.com
Printed in the USA
LVOW02*1457061015

457157LV00005B/9/P